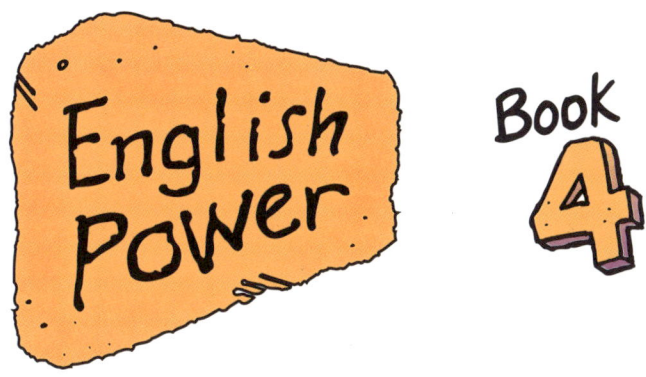

English Power

Book 4

Eshuys, Guest & Phelan

Eshuys, Guest & Phelan

JACARANDA

First published 1994 by
John Wiley & Sons Australia, Ltd
33 Park Road, Milton, Qld 4064

Offices also in Sydney and Melbourne

Typeset in 11 pt on 13 pt Plantin

National Library of Australia
Cataloguing-in-Publication data

Eshuys, Jo.
  English power. Book 4.

  Includes index.
  ISBN 0 7016 3102 3.

  1. English language — Rhetoric — Juvenile literature.
  2. English language — Usage — Juvenile literature.
  3. English language — Problems, exercises, etc. —
  Juvenile literature. I. Guest, Vic. II. Phelan, Peter.
  III. Title.

808.042

Illustrations: David Cox (pp. 85, 93, 99, 131, 132,
133); Craig Jackson (pp. 1, 30, 32, 38, 41, 44, 46,
49, 54, 56, 60, 65, 73, 76, 84, 105 (left), 108, 110,
117, 128, 134, 139, 156, 157, 158, 162, 165, 167,
177, 179, 185, 193, 199, 206, 226, 228, 229, 255,
266, 292); Paul Lennon (pp. 127, 129, 130, 147,
285, 302); Caroline Magerl (pp. 78 (top), 81, 82,
124, 126, 143); Mieke den Otter (pp. 10, 11, 16, 19,
75, 78/79, 90, 102, 105 (right), 257, 260, 276, 280);
Fiona Whipp (pp. 200, 202, 203, 271); and the
Wiley Art and Cartography Departments.

Cover illustration: Caroline Magerl

Printed in Singapore
10 9 8 7 6

CONTENTS

ACKNOWLEDGEMENTS

The author would like to give particular thanks to Donna Eshuys and Gerry Guest for research, typing and general consultancy. They also warmly thank Ronna Butler for her work as language consultant, and Cathy Costello for her assistance in research and selection of literature.

The authors and publisher gratefully acknowledge permission to reproduce copyright material in this book.

Text extracts

(p. 2) "Let go" by Jack Davis (copyright owner not traced); (p. 4) extract from *Power to Choose* by Haydn Sargent, Boolarong Publications; (pp. 6–7) "'Lost' generation fights its own war" by Shane Rodgers, reprinted courtesy the *Courier-Mail*; (pp. 8–23) extracts from *Looking for Alibrandi* by Melina Marchetta, Penguin Australia; (p. 13) "At seventeen" by Janis Ian, reproduced by kind permission of Festival Music Pty Ltd; (p. 24) "Sixteening" by Mayanti Wijeyaratne (copyright owner not traced); (p. 25) "On growing up" by Diane Paquin (copyright owner not traced); (p. 26) "Ambition" by Steven Herrick (copyright owner not traced); (p. 27) "Doctor to patient" from *Towards Sunrise Poems* by Bruce Dawe, Longman Cheshire Pty Ltd; (p. 28) extract from *Six Thinking Hats for Schools, Book 3*, by Edward de Bono, © 1992, the Perfection Learning Corporation, Des Moines, Iowa, reprinted with permission of the publisher; (p. 29) "Conformity" by Andrew Bolt, and *The Death of Henry Ellis* by Annette Lawson (copyright owners not traced); (pp. 37–66) extracts from *To Kill a Mockingbird* by Harper Lee, William Heinemann; (p. 74) "Let me make this perfectly clear" by Gwendolyn MacEwen, permission granted by the author's family; (p. 76) "The door" from *Selected Poems* by Miroslav Holub, translated by Ian Milner and George Theiner (Penguin Books, 1967) © Miroslav Holub 1967, translation © Penguin Books Ltd 1967; (p. 77) "Down the drain" by Geoff Goodfellow; (p. 78) "The child who walks backwards" from *The Garden Going On Without Us* by Lorna Crozier, used by permission of the Canadian Publishers, McClelland & Stewart, Toronto; (p. 78) "Hero" from *So Far So Good* by Mick Gowar, HarperCollins Publishers Ltd; (p. 80) "Cousin Nell", "Cousin Daisy" and "Jennifer Chubb-Challoner" by Roger McGough, reprinted by permission of the Peters Fraser & Dunlop Group Ltd; (p. 81) "Headache" by Michael Rosen, Scholastic Publications 1988; (p. 82) "Cut" by Sylvia Plath, Faber & Faber Ltd; (p. 83) "Picture of childhood" by Yevgeny Yevtushenko, from *The City of Yes and the City of No and Other Poems*, translated by T. Tupikina-Glaessner, I. Mezhakoff-Korjakin and Goeffrey Dutton, Sun Books; (p. 85) "Be specific" from *When the Teacher Says "Write a Poem"* by Mauree Applegate Copyright © 1965 by Mauree Applegate. Copyright Renewed. Reprinted by permission of HarperCollins Publishers, Inc. (p. 86) "Noise" by Jessie Pope, reproduced by permission of *Punch*; (p. 87) "Friendships" by Erica Fryberg; (p. 90) "Sea fever" by John Masefield, reproduced by permission of the Society of Authors as the literary representative of the Estate of John Masefield; "Streemin" by Roger McGough, reprinted by permission of the Peters Fraser & Dunlop Group Ltd; (p. 92) "Colour bar" by Oodgeroo of the tribe Noonuccal (formerly known as Kath Walker) in *My People*, Third Edition 1990, published by John Wiley & Sons Australia; (p. 93) "To my son Joe" by Steven Herrick (copyright owner not traced); (p. 94) "Mrs Swipe speaks out" by Bruce Dawe from *Sometimes Gladness — Collected Poems 1954–1987*, Third Edition, Longman Cheshire Pty Ltd; (p. 96) "Vincent" by Don McLean, reproduced by kind permission of MCA Music Australia Pty Ltd; (p. 98) "Two haiku" by Roger McGough, reprinted by permission of the Peters Fraser & Dunlop Group Ltd; (p. 98) "My brother" by Bruce Dawe from *Sometimes Gladness — Collected Poems 1954–1987*, Third Edition, Longman Cheshire Pty Ltd; (p. 99) "Magpies" by Judith Wright from *Collected Poems*, Angus & Robertson, reproduced with permission; (p. 100) "Mid-term break" by Seamus Heaney from *Death of a Naturalist*, Faber & Faber; (p. 105) "Integration as a process" by Liam O'Connor (copyright owner not traced); (p. 105) "The old prison" by Judith Wright from *Collected Poems*, Angus & Robertson,

"To know and not to do is not yet to know."

Chapter 1 LOOKING FORWARD

Content

- Making decisions
- Influences
- Generation gap
- Relationships
- Respect
- Freedom
- Responsibility
- Self-discovery
- Independence
- Work
- Conformity

Skills

- Making decisions
- Identifying influences
- Setting goals
- Using the writing process
- Interpreting tables
- Analysing relationships
- Discussing issues

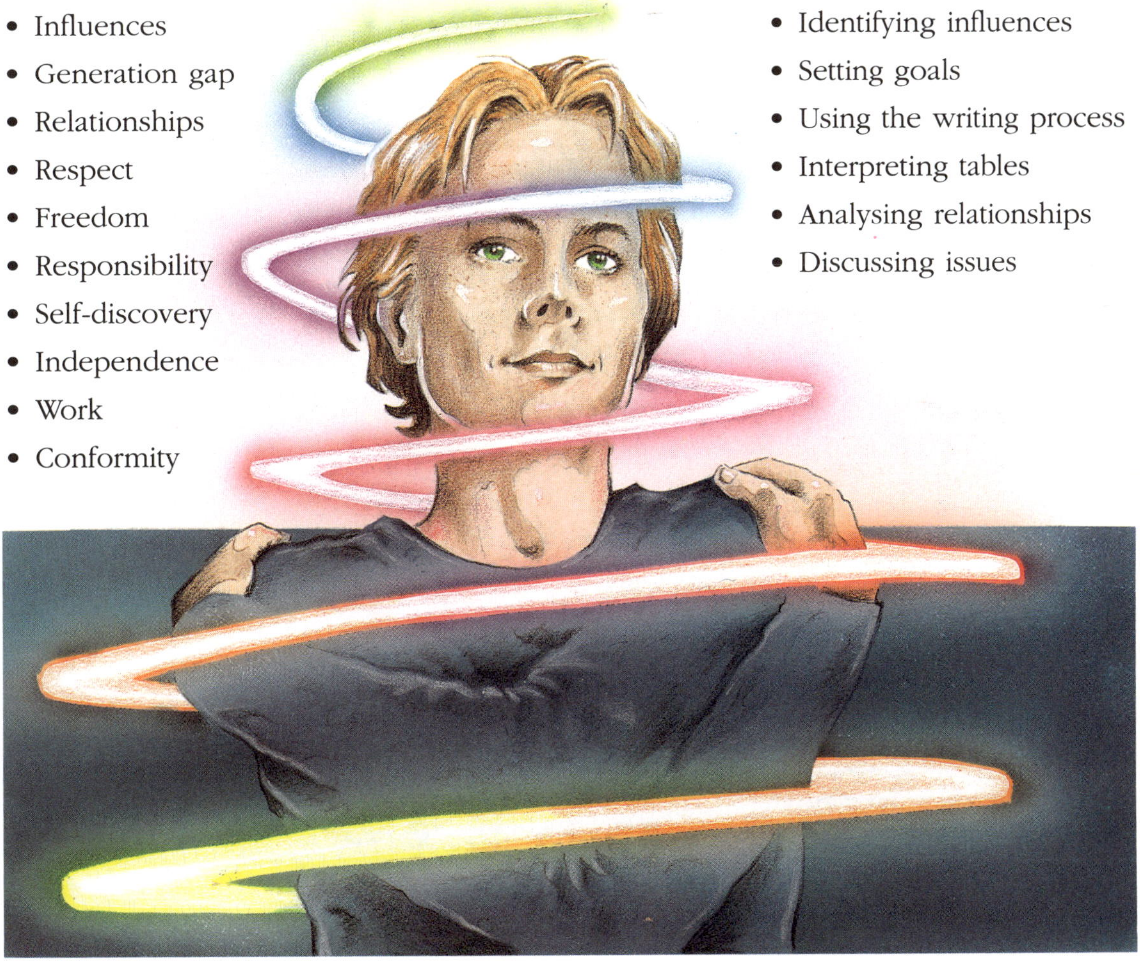

Let go

Let go of my hand
let me be what I want to be
Let go of my hand
the sands of time
are trickling before me
I have not yet
achieved what I want to be
let go of my hand
I want to stand alone
in a sea of words
pluck out the phrases
soar like a bird
I want to stand on a mountain
wait for the dawn
yet be aware of
the approach of a storm
I want to fashion a rainbow
that arcs through the sky
and iron out the dilemmas
between you and I

Jack Davis

 # Decisions! Decisions!

When you were five years old, who decided on the clothes you wore, the food you ate, the places you visited, the time you went to bed? Who makes these decisions now? What influenced these decisions? Look at the chart below and complete the questionnaire on page 3.

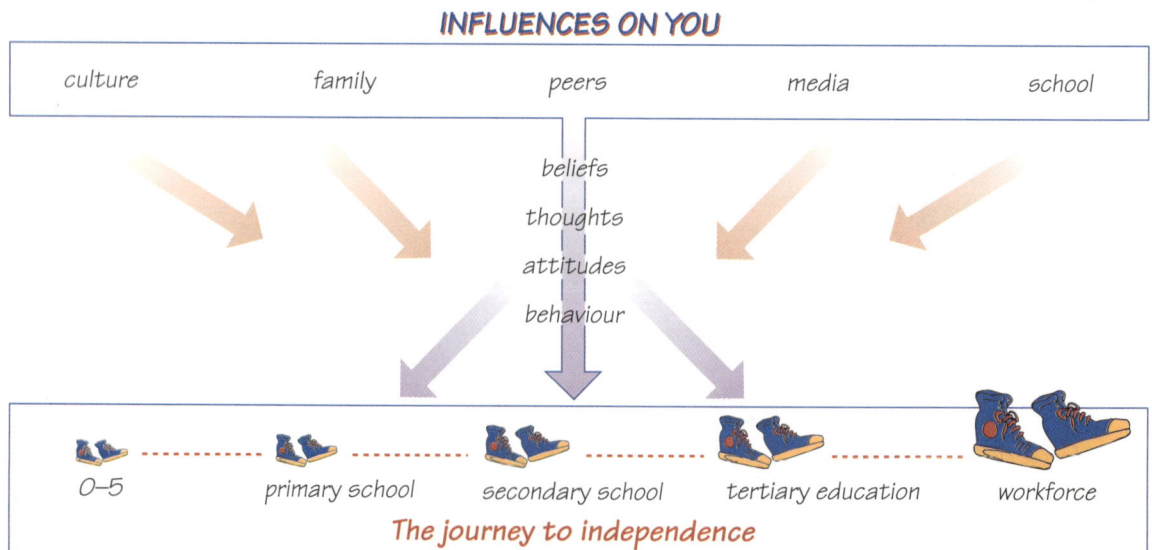

INFLUENCES ON YOU

| culture | family | peers | media | school |

beliefs
thoughts
attitudes
behaviour

0–5   primary school   secondary school   tertiary education   workforce

The journey to independence

The older we get, the more independent we become, and the more decisions we have to make.

Influences

1. Indicate what influences you most in each of the following areas of your life.

Area of your life	Influences:				
	Culture	Family	Peer	Media	School
1. The food you eat	☐	☐	☐	☐	☐
2. The clothes you wear	☐	☐	☐	☐	☐
3. Your hairstyle	☐	☐	☐	☐	☐
4. Sport you play	☐	☐	☐	☐	☐
5. Attitude to environment	☐	☐	☐	☐	☐
6. Your choice of friends	☐	☐	☐	☐	☐
7. Your hobbies	☐	☐	☐	☐	☐
8. The subjects you choose to study	☐	☐	☐	☐	☐
9. Your future career	☐	☐	☐	☐	☐
10. Attitude to politics	☐	☐	☐	☐	☐

2. In groups add five more things to the questionnaire.

3. What seems to be the biggest influence in your life at the moment?

4. (a) What do you feel will be the five major decisions you have to make over the next five years?
   (b) What do you think will be the major influence in each of your decisions?

Ambitions and dreams

When making important decisions make sure they are consistent with your overall goals. Read what Haydn Sargent has to say.

What is a goal? A goal is an ambition, a dream, a desire you can define.

When American motivator and businessman James Rohn was in my studio, he offered this sensible bit of advice: '**Don't leave the development of your potential to chance.**' Yet, for some peculiar reason, many of us do. We just wander through life with no plan, no goals, no idea of what we really want out of life, out of our relationships, out of our marriages, out of our jobs. Occasionally a wonderful but rather vague idea comes into our heads about something we want to own or would like to achieve. We never get around to actually planning to do it. We never sit down and put anything on paper. We expect it to stay in our minds, forgetting that our minds are being bombarded with all the other daily demands of living. In many cases we just bounce from one crisis to another, lurching from one disaster to another. Is that your experience? I call that 'the pinball philosophy of life'.

You can easily identify the people who are into the pinball philosophy. They're the ones who are always talking about 'One day I'm gunna' or 'If only I'd'. An honest man by the name of James Albury once wrote the following epitaph for himself, to be placed on his gravestone:

'He slept beneath the moon,
he baked beneath the sun;
He lived a life of going to do,
and died with nothing done.'

I believe you've got to be able to put your goals on paper. As a matter of fact, I think it's essential to put your goals on paper. You need to be able to define and explain each one in a simple sentence and they have to be worthwhile to command your respect. In doing this you set a pattern, you know where you are and what you are doing with your unique, one shot at life.

Haydn Sargent

5. What do you think is the benefit of setting goals?

6. (a) What is "the pinball philosophy of life"?
   (b) What problems can arise for a person with that outlook?

7. Why is it a good idea to put your goals on paper?

8. Goal-setting in life is important, but so are the qualities of:
   • self-esteem
   • having a positive attitude
   • being self-motivated
   • having the courage to act on your decisions.
   In small groups discuss the importance of these and rank them in order of importance to your group.

9. Identify your goal for each of the following areas:
   (a) career
   (b) school
   (c) finances
   (d) relationships
   (e) family
   (f) mental well-being
   (g) physical well-being.

10. Think about your career choice. What subjects would best suit your career choice? Refer to a Job Guide for information.

11. Imagine yourself ten years from now. Use your imagination to complete the following form.

   1. Address: ....
   2. Qualification: ....
   3. Occupation: ....
   4. Salary: $ .... per week
   5. Marital status: ....
   6. Children: ....
   7. After-work activities: ....

The generation gap

"A lost generation" or "the nation's hope for the future" — these provide the topics for many articles. Read the article on pages 6 and 7 and see how you respond to its conclusions. Then answer questions 12–17 below.

12. What has been the general view on youth, especially since the 1960s?

13. What are the popular perceptions about today's youth?

14. Look at the eight subjects that teenagers and parents argue about.
    (a) Can you make any generalisations about differences between the male and female responses?
    (b) What is the overall difference between the responses of teenagers and of parents?
    (c) Comment on any surprises for you in this table.

15. In groups, look at the table on youth myths. In each case, why do you think there is such a difference between what most people think and the reality? Report to the class.

16. What "war" is the youth of today fighting?

17. (a) According to Marcus Ganley, why does the generation gap exist?
    (b) Do you agree or disagree with his view? Explain.

'Lost' generation fights its own war

WHAT TEENAGERS AND PARENTS ARGUE ABOUT

Subject	What teenagers say %						What parents say %		
	Rarely		Sometimes		Often		Rarely	Sometimes	Often
	M	F	M	F	M	F			
Friends	78	78	16	19	6	2	72	22	5
General behaviour	44	53	40	31	16	16	45	45	10
Sexual behaviour	93	96	3	2	3	1	97	3	0
Going out	76	71	15	13	10	16	77	18	4
Drugs or alcohol	97	93	0	5	3	2	93	3	3
Housework cleaning room	46	36	24	28	30	36	28	42	31
Loud music	66	65	17	18	17	17	61	23	15
Independence	65	77	20	12	15	11	69	23	8

Source: Australian Institute of Family Studies

YOUTH MYTHS

Description	What most people think	The reality
Being happy	62%	90%
Teenage parent	32.4%	3.7%
Heroin addict	16.5%	N/A
Street kid	21.6%	Less than 3%

Source: Noller Callan, Burdekin Homeless Report

TOP table shows the percentage of teenagers who argue with their parents and what they argue about. Youth Myths table shows the percentage of teenagers most people think are happy or in trouble, compared with the reality. Most people underestimate the happiness of teenagers and overestimate their problems.

SHANE RODGERS REPORTS:

YOUNG people are described as anything from a lost generation to the great hope for Australia's future.

Over the decades, and most notably in the '60s, youth has been synonymous with rebellion and challenging the values and priorities of a society dominated by older decision-makers.

In the 1990s younger members of the community are facing the same sorts of image problems — usually associated with the elderly.

If you believe some of the popular perceptions you might well think Australia's under-25s are mostly lazy, binge-drinking, roller-blading, school-skipping, disrespectful, street kids.

In reality, the vast majority of them go to school, want to get a job, get on well with their parents and elders and live comfortably and happily at home.

They do, of course, have their problems.

Thousands of them are struggling to find work, they suicide more often than any other group on the planet and a number of them are homeless and addicted to drugs.

Their world is different from the one their parents grew up in.

They are more likely to come from a broken family, have both their parents in the workforce and be instantly exposed, via television, to all the harsh realities of the world.

They also are the first generation not to be part of a major war. But they are fighting their own war as they bear the brunt of the worst economic downturn in 60 years.

Research by Patricia Noller and Victor Callan, of the University of Queensland, suggests most people have an over-pessimistic view of the problems facing young people.

A survey involving 512 respondents found, on average, that only 62 percent of people thought teenagers were reasonably happy with their lives.

Research on the topic suggests the real figure is about 90 percent.

People thought 32.4 percent of teenage girls were likely to become pregnant (reality 3.7 percent).

There was an expectation that one in five teenagers would become a street kid. Based on the Burdekin report on homeless children, the reality was probably closer to 2 or 3 per cent.

According to Australian Institute of Family Studies research fellow Robyn Hartley, employment is the key difference between modern teenagers and their parents.

Today young people spend more time in education but still have a reduced chance of joining the work force.

Aside from that, they retain many of the traditional values held by their parents.

Ms Hartley interviewed a group of young people at age 16 and again at age 23 and found that 80 percent of them planned to marry one day.

They might leave it longer than their parents and perhaps live in a de facto relationship, but they retained a willingness to find a partner and make a commitment.

Ms Hartley said the problem of finding employment affected some young people's outlook on a range of issues because they were uncertain about their future.

There was a tendency for the older age groups (20- to 24-year-olds) to be still living with their parents, she said.

"Some leave and then return. Some are forced back because there is nowhere to go."

Ms Hartley said even though homelessness affected only a small percentage of teenagers, it was a growing problem and could not be ignored.

"It's not as if a lot of these kids are leaving home for the hell of it," she said.

"There's a lot of younger kids who are in real dire straits because they are having hassles or they've had to handle a degree of violence or sexual abuse at home."

Another institute study, involving more than 400 families in Victoria, found a strong degree of harmony between high school students and their parents.

The only significant source of frequent fights was housework and cleaning.

Most families never or rarely fought over such issues as sexual behaviour, drugs and alcohol, friends or going out.

Youth Futures Council spokesman Marcus Ganley said there remained a degree of "intergenerational stress" because some older people still had the misconception that only lazy people could not get a job.

He said the council regarded giving young people a say in major decisions as a key priority.

"The big problem with all the decisions being made is that the people making them aren't the ones who will feel the full impact of them," Mr Ganley said.

"We are seeking an input into any decisions which will have a greater impact on the adults of tomorrow than the adults of today."

This included decisions in such areas as the environment, the economy and Australia's role in the world.

The council is run by a 13-member executive and has more than 1000 members from around the state.

Mr Ganley said the group had held talks with large businesses suggesting a greater role for youth in company decision-making.

"People tend to recognise that it's a good idea but it's hard to convince them to take that next real step," he said.

"There seems to be a perception that to get into positions of power you have to be fairly old.

"If that perception is strong enough it then becomes a real barrier."

Courier-Mail, 9 October 1993

18. In small groups write an article to your local newspaper on the challenges you think young people will face when they leave school. Use the writing process below.

The writing process

Brainstorm — get your thoughts down in any order.

Plan — organise your thoughts.

Draft — write a first draft without worrying too much about spelling or sentence construction.

Conference — share ideas with other groups and your teacher to get advice and ideas.

Edit — correct errors and make changes.

Publish — present your article in its final form.

Looking for Alibrandi

a novel by Melina Marchetta

Josephine Alibrandi is seventeen, and in her final year at St Martha's, an exclusive school for girls. This is a year when she falls in love, meets her father for the first time and gains a deeper understanding of life.

Josephine feels her greatest problem is attending a school dominated by rich people. Josephine came from a primary school where the students were predominantly Greek and Italian and where she had felt comfortable. She came to St Martha's on a six-year scholarship in Year 7. Now, in Year 12, she has been voted as vice-captain of the school and is determined to settle down and do well.

Panic was my first reaction to the multiple choice options which lay on my desk in front of me. I glanced at the students around me before turning back to question three. I hated multiple choice. Yet I didn't want to get question three wrong. I didn't want to get any of them wrong. The outcome would be too devastating for my sense of being.

So I began with elimination. 'D' was completely out of the question, as was 'A', so that left 'B' and 'C'. I pondered both for quite a while and just as I was about to make my final decision I heard my name being called.

'Josephine?'

'Huh?'

'I think you mean "I beg your pardon" don't you, dear?'

'What are you doing? You're reading, aren't you, young lady?'

'Um ... yeah.'

'Um, yeah? Excellent, Josephine. I can see you walking away with the English prize this year. *Now stand up.*'

So my final school year began. I had promised myself that I would be a saint for this year alone. I would make the greatest impression on my teachers and become the model student. I knew it would all fail. But just not on the first day.

Sister Gregory walked towards me and when she was so close that I could see her moustache, she held out her hand.

'Show me what you're reading.'

I handed it to her and watched her mouth purse itself together and her nostrils flare in triumph because she knew she was going to get me.

She skimmed it and then handed it back to me. I could feel my heart beating fast.

'Read from where you were up to.'

I picked up the magazine and cleared my throat.

'"What kind of friend are you?"' I read from *Hot Pants* magazine.

She looked at me pointedly.

'"You are at a party",' I began with a sigh, '"and your best friend's good-looking, wealthy and successful boy-friend tries to make a pass. Do you: A — Smile obligingly and steal away into the night via the back door; B — Throw your cocktail all over his Country Road suit; C — Quietly explain the loyalty you have towards your friend; D — Tell your friend instantly, knowing that she will make a scene".'

You can understand, now, why I found it hard to pick between 'B' and 'C'.

'May I ask what this magazine has to do with my religion class, Miss?'

'Religion?'

'Yes, dear,' she continued in her sickeningly sarcastic tone. 'The one we are in now.'

'Well ... quite a lot, Sister.'

Early in the story we are introduced to Josephine's close friends.

There are four of us who hang out together and we make the most unlikely group. Most of the other students in the school are in clone groups. They all look similar. Either blond yuppies or European trendies. Either intellectuals or 'the beautiful people'.

Our group represents all types, yet we hadn't fitted into any of them in Year 7.

Anna Selicic is your typical Slavic-looking girl. Long blonde hair and blue eyes and that healthy red-cheek look. She's the most nervous person I have ever known. She puts her hand up in class and whispers the answer with dread. It's as if she thinks that if she whispers the wrong answer a blade will come hurtling across the room and decapitate her. She stands like a stunned mullet if guys approach us and still hasn't been kissed, despite her good looks.

Then there's Seraphina. It's pretty difficult describing her. She has to be the most brazen person I've ever met. She can look a person straight in the eye and lie her heart out. She can bitch about a person for three hours straight and then turn around and crawl to them. Winning them over with what they see as sincerity. The three of us tend to look on in disgusted fascination. She has black roots and blonde hair teased from here to eternity. She's skinny yet voluptuous and tends to dress in whatever the latest rock or pop star is wearing. Since she was fourteen she has never been without a boyfriend for more than a week and she's the only one of us who's slept with a guy. Her father, like most Italian fathers, thinks she's the Virgin Mary and like most Italian fathers is dead-set wrong.

I have a funny relationship with Sera. As the only two of Italian ancestry in the group we have a thin bond and I find that when I'm in her home I crawl more to her parents than to anyone in the world. I'm charming and kiss them on both cheeks, knowing deep down as they kiss me back that they'd think nothing of tearing my family or myself to shreds. I'm not sure why I put up with it. Maybe for acceptance, because I think that if you're an outcast with your own kind you'll never be accepted by anyone.

Sometimes I really don't like her. But other times she makes me laugh more than anyone I know. Those times are mostly in church or class or places where you have to control yourself but can't. I envy her, I think. People really bitch about her at St Martha's. She's a yuppie's nightmare. Her father's a fruit grocer. She's the stereotype of a wog yet she doesn't give a damn. She just gives the finger.

And last, but never least, is Lee Taylor, whose main objective in life is to hang out with wax-heads down at the southern beaches and who thinks it's cool to come to school with a hangover.

God knows why, because her father is an alcoholic. That's why she's with us and not 'them'. Because she went to primary school with 'them' and her father came to pick her up from a birthday party once, blind drunk. Nobody was allowed to go to her place after that.

Lee and I have a weird relationship. We pretend we have nothing in common, yet we can talk for hours on any subject. We pretend we come from two different parts of society, yet both of us are middle-class scholarship students. We pretend that our families have nothing in common because people in her family use words like 'wog' and mine happen to be 'wogs'. Yet I respect her more than any of my friends, although I couldn't tell her that because we both pretend we don't know the meaning of the word.

She's one of those people you think is quite plain until you're sitting in front of her and realise just how attractive she is. Straight brown hair streaked with gold by the sun, freckles on her nose and hazel eyes which never look directly at you when she speaks. Yet you can't call her a coward. I think she has so much emotion she doesn't want to show, she makes sure nobody sees it.

We grew up in the midst of the snobs of St Martha's and discovered that somehow brains didn't count that much. Money, prestige and what your father did for a living counted. If your hair wasn't in a bob or if your mother didn't drive a Volvo you were a nobody.

That's where the problem lies between myself and our school captain, Ivy Lloyd, who we call Poison Ivy. I was awarded the insulting task of being her deputy. We hate each other's guts, probably because we've been competitive all our lives. She's one of those girls with perfect white skin and not one split end in her strawberry-blonde hair. She's a bore though. She's obsessed with school-work and whenever we get assignments back she looks over to me to try to find out how well I went. Sometimes when she's looking and I know that I've probably received the highest mark, I shake my head in a sorrowful way as if I'm devastated. Then as we're walking out of the classroom and she has an ecstatic grin on her face, I'll show Sera my mark and she'll scream it out hysterically.

Yes, I know. I'm immature and vain about my brains, but you can't imagine how wonderful it is to beat Poison Ivy. It doesn't happen very often. I remember the first day of school in Year 7. She walked up to me in a really snotty way and said 'I hear you're the recipient of the English scholarship'. I remember thinking that she wanted to be my friend. I was so thrilled, imagining the slumber parties and holidays we'd be spending together. But I was only given ten seconds to dream, because she looked me up and down and then walked away. The look kind of said it all.

We are also introduced to the male friends in Josephine's life. There is John Barton:

Picture this. School captain of St Anthony's. Son of a member of parliament. Greatest debater who ever lived. Good-looking. Popular. Tell me, what more could I want out of life?

For him to be equally in love with me, that's what.

. . . and Jacob Coote, school captain of Cook High.

My friends think he's gorgeous. His hair is brown, shoulder-length, not cut into any particular style and his eyes are green and they always seem to be laughing at you.

19. When you read the first extract, at what stage did you realise Josephine was not sitting for a test? What do you think about this opening?

20. What impression do you get of Josephine from these extracts? Use evidence to support your answer. You can do this by lifting short quotes from the extracts. For example:
    Josephine feels something of an outcast among "the snobs of St Martha's".

We are given snapshots of each of Josephine's friends. Anna is beautiful but is "... like a stunned mullet" with boys. We see Anna's shyness, Sera's brassiness and Lee's depth. Each physical description is accompanied by an insight into each girl's personality; her strengths and weaknesses. In this way the characters come alive.

We are made to feel a certain way towards Anna, Sera and Lee by the words the author uses to describe them. For example, consider Anna.

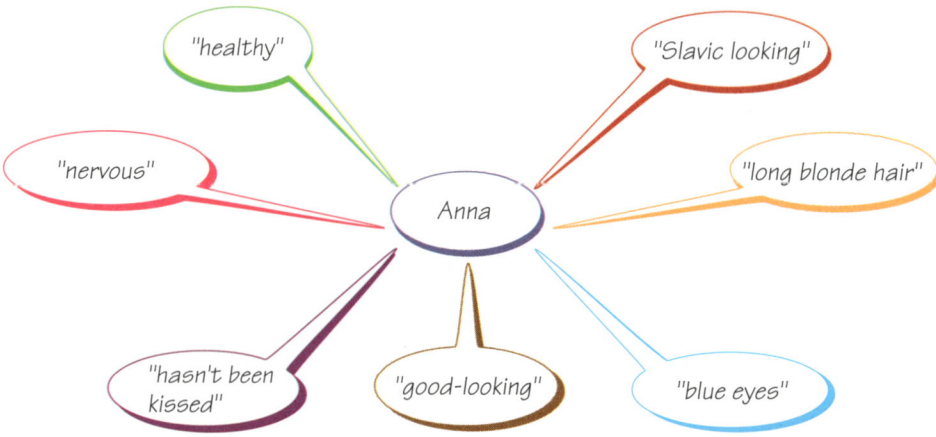

21. (a) How do these words tend to make you feel about Anna?
    (b) Make character webs for Sera and Lee.
    (c) How do you feel about them?
    (d) Which of the girls would you be most interested in getting to know? Why?

22. How do you think the author wants you to feel about Ivy Lloyd? Use words from the story to support your answer.

Although Josephine dislikes Ivy she realises:

No matter how much I hate Poison Ivy, I want to belong to her world. The world of sleek haircuts and upper-class privileges. People who know famous people and lead educated lives. A world where I can be accepted.

Please, God, let me be accepted by someone other than the underdog.

23. (a) What did she mean by underdog?
    (b) What do you think she meant by the whole statement?

Early in the story Josephine describes herself:

I have a few blemishes. (I hate using the word 'pimple'.) I'm average height and probably will never be able to get away with wearing a bikini in this lifetime, and my hair is a legacy from my father. It's curly and needs restraining at all times.

She refers to the song At Seventeen *by Janis Ian; here are the words.*

At seventeen

I learned the truth at seventeen
that love was meant for beauty queens
And high school girls
With clear-skinned smiles
who married young and then retired.
The Valentines I never knew,
the Friday night charades of youth
Were spent on one more beautiful,
At seventeen I learned the truth
And those of us with ravaged faces,
Lacking in the social graces,
Desp'rately remained at home
Inventing lovers on the phone
Who called to say, 'Come dance with me',
and murmured vague obscenities.
It isn't all it seems
at seventeen.
A brown eyed girl in hand-me-downs —
whose name I never could pronounce,
Said 'Pity please, the ones who serve,
They only get what they deserve.' The
rich relationed home town queens
Marries into what she needs:
A guarantee of company
And haven for the elderly.
Remember those who win the game
Lose the love they sought to gain
In debentures of quality and dubious integrity.
Their small town eyes will gape at you
in dull surprise when payment due
Exceeds amounts received
At seventeen.

To those of us who know the pain
of Valentines that never come,
and those whose names were never called
when choosing sides for basketball.
It was long ago and far away,
the world was younger than today,
And dreams were all they gave for free
to ugly duckling girls like me.

We all play the game and when we dare
to cheat ourselves at solitaire
Inventing lovers on the phone,
repenting other lives unknown.
That call and say, 'Come dance with me',
and murmur vague obscenities
at ugly girls like me
at seventeen.

Janis Ian

Expectations

"So what are you going to do next year?" is a common question for those in their final year of school. Josephine speaks to John Barton and finds that coming from a rich and powerful family can have its drawbacks.

'What about you?' I asked.

He looked at me in mock horror.

'Could you imagine me not going into law and then politics?'

'Yeah. I reckon you'd make a good teacher. I watched the little debaters come up to you. You're very patient with them.'

'My father would have a stroke.'

'You're a snob.'

He shook his head. 'No, I'm a realist. My father is a politician, my grandfather was a politician and my great grandfather was a backer of the first Liberal prime minister. My father believes that we have the breeding to one day give this country the best prime minister it has ever had. It was something his father told him and something his father's father told him. On my birthday, every year, he stands on a soap box.'

John stood on the chair and pulled his fringe back, imitating his father's receding hair-line.

'One of my sons,' he began in a droning voice, 'will one day lead this country back into the path of glory and I feel it can easily be John ...

'I've slightly exaggerated the case, but how can you escape his type of thinking and tradition? ... I don't want a lot of responsibility in life. Does that sound weak and unambitious? Well, that must mean that I am weak and unambitious. I don't want to climb to the top, Josephine. I'm comfortable enough where I'm standing. But when you have a father who is a minister in parliament, you are expected to have ambition. And when you can't work out your ambition, good old Dad does.'

Dialogue is a powerful tool in translating John Barton's deep sense of despair. John's imitation of his father is more powerful than if he had simply told Josephine about his father's expectations. In this way we hear his father's "droning voice" without even meeting him. Although Mr Barton isn't described, our imagination creates an image of a man who is demanding and overbearing.

John's tone changes when he explains his "lack" of ambition. Note the repetition of "I don't", and the words "unambitious" and "weak". These words make him seem helpless.

28. What expectation does John Barton's father have of him?

29. What do you think John means by "... how can you escape his type of thinking and tradition?"

30. Imagine that John conveys his feelings to his father. Describe the conversation that takes place.

31. What expectations does your family have of you to perform? In what ways is that helpful?

At one stage of the book John's father goes through his son's mail and finds out that John hasn't won the maths competition. Josephine asks John about his father's reaction.

'It's not the words that come out of his mouth. It's the looks, Josie. The disappointment.'

'I'm sure your father loves you, John.'

'Oh, he does,' he said nodding. '... When I win a debate. When I win a football game. When I get elected school captain. When I win, win, win,' he gritted. 'And when I lose he hates me.'

32. (a) What feelings is John expressing?
    (b) Describe the looks you think John's father gives him.
    (c) What do you think will happen to John Barton? Why? Compare your answer with a partner.

John's helplessness and bitterness is in contrast to the girls' attitudes as they discuss their future over a cappuccino at Harley's, their local hangout.

'I'm going to be a fashion designer,' Sera suggested after we sat in a booth which had just been vacated.

'I know so many people doing fashion designing,' Anna said, flicking the page. 'You end up working as a sales assistant in Katie's or Sussan's.'

'Make-up artist?'

'Sera, admit it, you're not artistic,' I told her bluntly.

'Are you saying my make-up doesn't look good?'

'I knew this would happen,' Lee said, slamming the book shut.

'If I wasn't thinking of doing law, I'd be a translator for the Italian consulate in some mysterious country,' I told them, dreaming of how exciting it would be. 'But I know that the proper Italians would pick out my Sicilian accent. The northerners are snobs just because they're blonde.'

'I'm blonde and my parents aren't from the north,' Sera said, using my glasses again for a mirror.

Lee, Anna and I exchanged glances.

'Should I tell her, girls?' I asked, feigning pity.

'Go ahead, Josie,' Lee said, adopting a sad voice.

I took hold of Sera's hand gently.

'Sera, my poor sweet disillusioned Sera. You were not born with that colour hair,'

'No?' Anna said, horrified, before we all burst out laughing.

Sera grabbed the careers book from Lee's hands and flicked through it again.

'How about teaching?'

'How about the public service? You'd be happy there, Sera.'

Sera looked at me suspiciously, wondering if I was teasing her.

'I'm going to be doing teaching,' Anna said definitely. 'The Catholic Campus at Strathfield.'

'I can see you as a teacher,' Lee agreed.

'No way,' I laughed. 'Anna will always be a McDonalds worker to me.'

After leaving Harley's Josephine and Lee continue to discuss their futures. Lee is dejected. She is uncertain of her future and feels she could end up like her ineffectual parents. Josephine disagrees.

'. . . We're masters of our own destiny.'

'That's rubbish. If your father's a dustman, you're going to be a dustman and if your father's filthy rich, you're going to be filthy rich because he'll introduce you to his rich friend's son. People breed with their own kind. Rest assured that John Barton will marry one of the Poison Ivys of the world, just like his brothers have married daughters of the well-known. The rich marry the rich, Josie, and the poor marry the poor. The dags marry the dags and the wogs marry the wogs. The western suburbs marry the western suburbs and the north shore marry the north shore. Sometimes they cross-breed, though, and marry into the eastern suburbs.'

She sighed sadly, shivering from the cold breeze that was coming from the water. 'And we all end up where we started.'

'That's not true. My future has nothing to do with what my family did.'

'Josie, whether you want to admit it or not, you are going to be a barrister because of your father. Without being there he's still managed to be the greatest influence of your life.'

Josephine and Jacob Coote become close friends. Her relationship with him causes her to reconsider her beliefs and values. Josephine tries to explain to him what it's like to be Italian.

'... There are rules.'

'Bloody hell, you're all weird. What would you do?'

'Me? I'd like to be a rebel Italian. I'd like to shock everyone and tell them to stick their rules and regulations. If anyone ever died, I'd wear bright colours to the funeral and laugh the loudest. But I can't.'

'Why not?'

I looked at him and wondered if he understood.

'Because I have no father. Because if I did all those things hypocrites would shake their heads smugly and say "See, I told you she couldn't amount to anything." They're waiting for me to make an error so they can compare me and my mother.'

'But what's the big deal? Everyone has babies without being married these days. Everyone lives together and gets remarried,' he said, turning on his side.

I shook my head. 'I can't explain it to you. I can't even explain it to myself. We live in the same country, but we're different. What's taboo for Italians isn't taboo for Australians. People just talk and if it doesn't hurt you it hurts your mother or your grandmother or someone you care about.'

'I'd hate them all. I'd hate to be Italian.'

'No,' I smiled, looking at him. 'You can't hate what you're part of. What you are. I resent it most of the time, curse it always, but it'll be part of me till the day I die. I used to wish when I was young that my mother had made a mistake and that my father wasn't the son of an Italian, but an Australian. So I could be part of the "in crowd" you know. So if you said "Let's go away for the weekend" I could say "Hey, sure thing". But there is this spot inside of me that will always be Italian. I can't explain it in any other way.'

Another time Jacob is angry with Josephine because she won't introduce him to her grandmother.

'I knew it,' I shouted angrily. 'This is why it'll never work between us, Jacob. We live two different lives and you can't understand that. Why can't you understand my life? Things aren't as easy for me as they are for you. You can do whatever you please but I can't because there are some things that could offend people I love. You live with such freedom, Jacob. You live without religion and culture. All you have to do is abide by the law.'

Later, Jacob introduces her to his father. In contrast to Josephine who grew up without knowing her father, Jacob had grown up without a mother.
Things develop and Jacob makes sexual advances to Josephine.

'Welcome to the nineties, Josephine. Women don't have to be virgins any more.'

'*No*, you welcome to the nineties, Jacob! Women don't have to be pushed into things any more.'

'What is it? A prize or something?' he scorned.

'No. It's not a prize and I'm not a prize. But it's mine. It belongs to me and I can only give it away once and I want to be so sure when it happens, Jacob. I don't want to say that the first time for me was bad or it didn't mean a thing or that it was done in my school uniform.'

'But you're almost eighteen. You're old enough. Everyone else is doing it.'

'And next year someone is going to say to someone else "but you're only sixteen, everyone else is doing it". Or one day someone will tell your daughter that she's only thirteen and everyone else is doing it. I don't want to do it, Jacob, because everyone else is doing it.'

'How about let's do it because we want to. I want to anyway,' he said grabbing my hands together.

'But I don't know if I love you enough and I don't even know if you love me enough. We don't even love each other, Jacob.'

We lay there in silence until he nudged me.

'I do a bit, you know,' he said gruffly.

'You do what a bit?'

'You know. Like you ... whatever ... love you a bit.'

He seemed a bit flustered and I hugged him.

'I think I kind of love you too, Jacob.'

38. In these extracts, strong words capture Josephine's emotions. They give an edge to the intensity of her feelings. You can hear her shouting and visualise her aggressive stance. Write out the key descriptive words that capture these emotions.

39. Why would Josephine like to shock the Italian community?

40. Another time Josephine remarks, "... like religion, culture is nailed into you so deep you can't escape it. No matter how far you run." What do you think she meant by this statement? Do you feel it's true? Explain.

41. What cultural forces influence you most in life?

42. What do you think Josephine meant by, "You live without religion and culture. All you have to do is abide by the law."?

In the bedroom scene note the clever repetition of "welcome to the nineties" and how Josephine stands Jacob's argument on its head. Again we can almost hear the conversation and visualise the body language. "he scorned" … "grabbing my hands together". This fast-moving animated part of the scene is in contrast to the last part of the scene where the emotional momentum is suddenly slowed: "We lay there in silence."

43. Why do you think Josephine resists Jacob's advances?

44. Imagine you are being pressured into one of the following situations. What would you say and do to resist the pressure? Role-play the scene in pairs or small groups.
    • smoking
    • drinking
    • wagging school
    • taking drugs

At the annual walk-a-thon, instead of looking after the Year 7s who were her responsibility, Josephine wags it with her friends. Afterwards they go to Sera's to watch a video and eat pizza. Although her friends are relaxed Josephine is tense. Next day her worst fears are realised when she is called to the principal's office.

'How responsible were you yesterday, Josephine? I want you to tell me how responsible you were. There were twelve-year-old girls in that last lot, Josephine. Darlinghurst is a dangerous area. You were there to make sure nothing could happen to them. You were responsible.'

I swallowed and shrugged.

'I wasn't responsible yesterday.'

'Do you know what responsibility is, Josephine? If you don't, try following Ivy Lloyd around one day. That is responsibility.'

My blood boiled at the mention of Ivy's name.

'I'm just as responsible as Ivy, Sister. Yesterday was a one-off.'

'Ivy doesn't have "one-offs". She's responsible from the moment she walks into this school till the moment she walks out.'

Good for Ivy, I wanted to say.

'I made a decision late last year which I've regretted during this year, Josie, but now I know it was the right one,' she said. 'You were voted school captain but I gave the job to Ivy because I knew she'd do a better job.'

'What?' I shouted. 'Why?'

'Need you ask me that after yesterday?'

'I wouldn't have done what I did yesterday if I was school captain,' I said.

'Yes you would, Josephine, and that's what I was afraid of. You and your friends are trendsetters. The girls look up to you. They copy what you do. They'll probably slap you on the back to congratulate you when you get back into class. I couldn't afford to have my school captain set such a bad example.'

'You're wrong. We're not trendsetters and they don't look up to us. They think they're more superior than us.'

'Believe that, if that's what you want to believe, but I can't have you being a leader, Josie. I'm thinking seriously of choosing another vice captain.'

'You can't do that,' I said standing up. 'It's the only thing I have going for me in this school.'

I was embarrassed because I was crying, but I didn't realise until then how much it meant to me to be a prefect.

'Things would have been so different for me if I was school captain,' I told her. 'I would have felt different. What did I do for you to take that away from me?'

'A lot, Josephine. There was that time you walked like an Egyptian up to communion in front of the bishop.'

A Sera dare.

'And the time you stood up at the Catholic Association's seminar and said the church stank with its rules on the IVF issue.'

'I said it sucked.'

'Yes, and you said it in front of the bishop.'

'I have the right to an opinion.'

'Yes, you do, but you're not the first person who ever had one, Josephine. You seem to think you are. You have to learn that sometimes you have to keep your mouth shut, because what you do reflects on this school and on me and others. They don't make you principal of a school because you're middle-aged and wear a habit. You have to stop believing that your actions are always right and you have to remember that you aren't a leader because you're given a title. You're a leader because of what is inside of you. Because of how you feel about yourself. Having a badge saying you're school captain shouldn't have stopped you doing what you did yesterday. You should be able to do that on your own. Now go back to class and think about that.'

I walked out, crying all the way down the corridor and it wasn't until I got to the end that I stopped.

Trendsetters. Examples. School captain. Leaders. The words kept on running through my head and I began to see that maybe Sister wasn't lying.

Everyone loved Anna and everyone wanted to be Lee's friend and although Sera got on everyone's nerves she still managed to make people do the most incredible things and nobody ever called her a wog because she didn't give a damn.

And me? I was voted school captain. Socially we weren't as shitty as we thought we were. So I turned around and walked back into her room without knocking.

'I'm really sorry, Sister. Don't call me a liar because I do mean it.'

She looked up, no forgiveness in her eyes. 'I'm not here to make you feel good, Josie.'

'You're supposed to forgive me. You're a nun.'

'Priests have the authority to forgive, Josephine. Nuns don't.'

'So I go around with this sin on my soul for the rest of my life?'

'No, only until I think you mean it. Until I can trust you again. You have great potential, Josephine, but so do many others. It's up to you to use that potential.'

'I'm not a sheep,' I whispered.

'You were yesterday, Josephine.'

When I walked back into the classroom I did get pats on the back.

'Better than going on the dumb walk-a-thon,' everyone said.

'What I did was wrong,' I told them quietly.

'What's the big deal?' someone asked. 'Don't let her make you feel guilty.'

'One of the Year 7 kids could have been grabbed by a mad man. I was responsible for them. That's what the big deal was. I was wrong in what I did yesterday.'

I was wrong, I thought to myself. I honestly believed it. Not because Sister Louise told me or because she made me believe I was. I knew deep down that I was wrong and I think that my emancipation began at that moment.

---

45. (a) What was Josephine's task on the walk-a-thon?
    (b) Do you feel she acted responsibly or irresponsibly? Explain.

46. (a) What reasons did the principal put forward for not allowing Josephine to be school captain?
    (b) Do you think this was a responsible decision or do you feel she didn't have the right to alter a democratic vote? Give reasons for your answer.

47. Do you feel that students in the junior school look to the seniors as role models? Explain.

48. "Things would have been so different for me if I was school captain ..." What do you think Josephine meant by this? Do you agree with her?

49. If you had been the principal how would you have handled Josephine in this situation?

50. "... I think that my emancipation began at that moment." What do you think Josephine meant by this?

RESPECT

Respect is a recurring theme throughout the story.

Respect for friends

We sat alongside each other without speaking for a while. He's the type of person you can do that with. It wasn't an embarrassing silence, just a comfortable one. As if we both respected each other's private thoughts.

Lee and I have a weird relationship. We pretend we have nothing in common, yet we can talk for hours on any subject. We pretend we come from two different parts of society, yet both of us are middle-class scholarship students. We pretend that our families have nothing in common because people in her family use words like 'wog' and mine happen to be 'wogs'. Yet I respect her more than any of my friends, although I couldn't tell her that because we both pretend we don't know the meaning of the word.

Cultural heritage

There's always something that shouldn't be said or done. There are always jobs I have to learn because all good Italian girls know how to do them and one day I'll need to look after my chauvinistic husband. There's always someone I have to respect.

I hate the word 'respect'. It makes me sick to my stomach.

Respect for family

Sometimes I feel that no matter how smart or how beautiful I could be they would still remember me for the wrong things.

That's why I want to be rich and influential. I want to flaunt my status in front of those people and say 'See, look who I can become'.

Mama says that satisfaction isn't what I should search for. Respect is. Respect?

I detest that word. Probably because in this world you have to respect the wrong people for the wrong reasons.

Sometimes he's a tough guy and I can imagine him bashing someone's head in and other times he's this real nice sensitive guy who smiles at babies and helps old women across the street. He smokes dope, drinks and I think he sleeps with a lot of girls, but on the other hand he really loves his family and has respect for people.

'You misintrepid everything, Jozzie.'

'It's "mis-interpret everything",' I corrected, rolling my eyes.

'You are without respect, Jozzie. Just like your mother. Always wit no respect.'

'Mama is good to you, Nonna,' I shouted angrily. 'If she is ever rude to you it's because you pester her about every single thing possible.'

'Don't you talk to me like that, Jozzie.'

'Why? You sit there and pick a fight deliberately and then you wonder why I argue back?'

'I did not pick a fight, Jozzie. I just said that you and Christina are rude and should treat me better. I am an old woman now and I deserve respect.'

'Yes, Nonna,' I muttered, bored.

51. When is respect something Josephine can accept and like and when does she reject the idea of respect? Support your answer with evidence from the extracts.

52. Of all the types of respect described in these extracts which is most important to you? Why?

53. Do you feel her mother was right when she advised Josephine to search for respect rather than satisfaction? Explain.

54. Why do you think Josephine respected Lee more than any of her friends?

55. What do you respect most in a friend?

56. What would you like people to respect in you?

Inner journeys

It's good to look back, to consider where you came from, to understand where you are now in life before choosing your future path. Other people's feelings, released in poetry, can prompt us to make our own inner journeys and to reflect on the various paths we will take in life.

> 57. Read the following poem on being sixteen and then write your own poem on how you feel about being your age.

Sixteening

It's
Never been easy
Sixteening:
Reading Lawson,
Groping for meaning;
Performing on a stage unset,
Yearning for all the applause
You can get.

Feeling guilty
For deeds undone:
Trying to connect
With anyone:
Searching for words
With crystal meaning:
Never been easy
Sixteening.

Head full
Of new whims every week,
Like treetops that trap
Morning mist off a creek:
Pushing out feelers
And pulling them in:
Trying to leave off
Where others begin:
Standing tall
When your heart's leaning:
Never been easy
Sixteening.

Mayanti Wijeyaratne (16)

For Better or For Worse

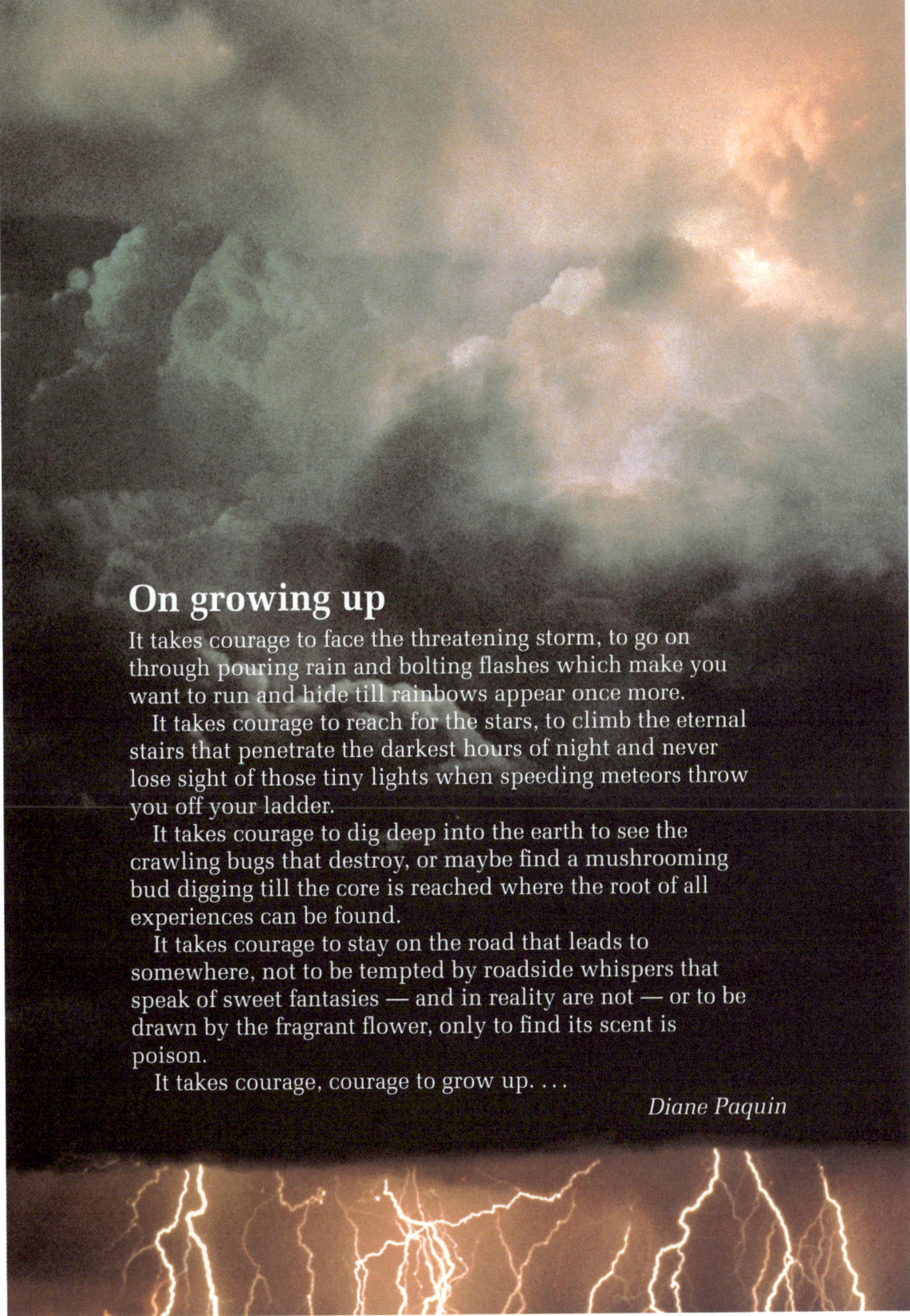

On growing up

It takes courage to face the threatening storm, to go on through pouring rain and bolting flashes which make you want to run and hide till rainbows appear once more.

It takes courage to reach for the stars, to climb the eternal stairs that penetrate the darkest hours of night and never lose sight of those tiny lights when speeding meteors throw you off your ladder.

It takes courage to dig deep into the earth to see the crawling bugs that destroy, or maybe find a mushrooming bud digging till the core is reached where the root of all experiences can be found.

It takes courage to stay on the road that leads to somewhere, not to be tempted by roadside whispers that speak of sweet fantasies — and in reality are not — or to be drawn by the fragrant flower, only to find its scent is poison.

It takes courage, courage to grow up. . . .

Diane Paquin

58. What is Diane Paquin (page 25) saying about growing up?

59. (a) Make a list of the challenges you feel young people face in today's world.
    (b) Write down your feelings about each challenge.
    (c) Use your notes from (a) and (b) to write a poem.
    (d) Give your poem a title.

Ambition

to Joe

for a start
don't sell things
don't wear a smile for people
you think are richer than you.
know your hands.
throw a ball against a wall until
you can hit the white dot and know
why you drew that dot there in the first place.
ambition is a word people link
with money, or fame.
think of the first time you
hit that white dot and
how much it meant to you.
you were the only one who knew.
become strong with your hands
with your head.
when people ask you what you want to be
say what you think.
don't answer if you wish.
or say
I want to be able to hit the white dot every throw.

Steven Herrick

60. What did you enjoy about this poem? Why?

61. In your own words describe the advice the poet is giving his son, Joe.

62. What do you feel is the significance of "the white dot"?

63. What is your "white dot"?

64. Why do you think he has called the poem "Ambition"?

Doctor to patient

Please sit down. I'm afraid I have some
rather bad news for you: you are now seventeen
and you have contracted an occupational disease called
unemployment. Like others similarly afflicted
you will experience feelings of
shock, disbelief, injustice, guilt, apathy, and aggression
(although not necessarily in that order)
and you'll no doubt be urged to try the various
recommended anodynes: editorials in newspapers,
voluntary unpaid work for local charities, booze,
other compulsive mind-destroyers, prayer, comforting
talks with increasingly less-interested friends.
It is small comfort to know that the disease
is universal and can accommodate
the middle-aged and thirtyish and strikes down
those in camps in Kompong Sam and Warsaw.
However, you will discover, as time passes,
that your presence in itself will make others
obviously uncomfortable. Try not to let
your shadow, at this stage,
fall across your neighbour's plate; eat
with the right hand only; do not touch
others in public (this can be easily
misconstrued); keep always
down-wind, if possible. Please remember
you have now become our common vulnerability
personified. Oh yes, and, by the way,
you will be relieved to know the disease
is only in a minority of cases terminal.

Most, that is, survive. Next, please.

Bruce Dawe

65. According to Bruce Dawe, what feelings does an unemployed person experience? What feelings do you think *you* would experience?

66. What do you think the word "anodynes" means? Compare your answer with a partner before checking your dictionary.

67. "...you will discover, as time passes, that your presence in itself will make others obviously uncomfortable". Do you think this would be the case? Explain.

68. Bruce Dawe likens unemployment to a medical condition. Find words in the poem that support this concept.

69. Often a poem can express feelings more powerfully than an article. Do you feel this is the case with this poem? Explain.

70. Do you think the overall message is one of hope or despair? Explain.

Employment in the future

What do you think employment will be like in the future? Perhaps we will:

- work only three days a week
- take a year's leave every five years to retrain
- share a job
- work from home rather than go to a central place
- retire much earlier
- work one year on, one year off.

Can you suggest what employment will be like?

One way of discussing this issue is by using the "six thinking hats" method, first suggested by the famous thinker Edward De Bono. The aim of "six thinking hats" is to improve the way thinking takes place. The method is simple. There are six imaginary hats, each a different colour. Each of the hats indicates a different type of thinking.

 **Red hat**. Emotions. Intuition, feelings and hunches. No need to justify the feelings. How do I feel about this right now?

 **Yellow hat**. Good points. Why is this worth doing? How will it help us? Why can it be done? Why will it work?

 **Black hat**. Bad points. Caution. Judgement. Assessment. Is this true? Will it work? What are the weaknesses? What is wrong with it?

 **Green hat**. Creativity. Different ideas. New ideas. Suggestions and proposals. What are some possible ways to work this out? What are some other ways to solve the problem?

 **White hat**. Information. Questions. What information do we have? What information do we need to get?

 **Blue hat**. Organisation of thinking. Thinking about thinking. What have we done so far? What do we do next?

Keep these thoughts in mind.

- Six thinking hats can be used by an individual or a group.
- All six hats don't have to be used every time.
- You can choose the order in which they are to be used.
- The black hat is often overused and the green hat is the most underused.
- If used in a group one colour can be used one at a time by the whole group *or* each member of the group can wear a different coloured hat.

> 71. In groups, use the "six thinking hats" method to write a report on "Employment in the future". To get organised, begin with everyone wearing a blue hat. Present your report to the class.

Conformity

Adolescent society:
Earnest voices,
Confident gestures.
The subjects, trivia;
The poses, forced.
An awkward subject arises;
The murmurs check —
Then, gathering,
Flow around,
Back into well-worn channels
Where navigation is sure,
Destination obvious.
No wish to founder
On the rocks of uncertainty.
Adolescent society.
　　— Uneasy voyage.

Andrew Bolt (16)

72. According to Andrew, how do adolescents behave? Do you agree? Explain.

73. (a) What does Andrew feel is most difficult about adolescence?
　　(b) Do you agree with him? Why/why not?

74. What part of the poem best reflects the title "Conformity"?

The Death of Henry Ellis

The little man had been charged with murder. To be accosted by a complete stranger was not a pleasant experience, but to have that same stranger thrust a murder charge in his face was an indignity. He objected. The stranger merely looked grim.

'I charge you,' he said, 'with the murder of Henry Ellis.'

The little man stared. 'May we sit down?' he asked. And they sat down on the nearest doorstep.

'Now,' said the stranger, 'I have some questions.'

'Wait!' cried the little man. 'Henry Ellis is alive!'

'Henry Ellis is dead,' said the stranger.

'But I am he. He is me, Henry Ellis, and I am very much alive.'

'Henry Ellis is dead,' said the stranger, 'and now we will proceed. When I apprehended you, you were returning home from a job you have held for thirty years, and during that time you have never advanced, never moved either up or down.'

'I don't see ...'

'Were you or were you not?' snapped the stranger.

'I was,' answered the little man.

'In the past thirty years you have read the same newspaper, eaten the same meals, said the same things, forgotten your wife's birthday six years running ...'

'This is entirely irrelevant,' cried the little man, who by this time was feeling very naked.

The stranger peered at him through horn-rimmed spectacles.

'You are charged,' he said, 'with having strangled Henry Ellis by conformity and habit and, on finding him dead, disposing of him in a meat-mincer.'

'*Meat-mincer*?' gasped the little man.

'The meat-mincer of society,' said the stranger. 'Furthermore, you are charged with ignorance in the first degree. Our records show that you have never picked a flower, never walked along a beach, never heard music in the wind, never laughed, never hated, never even loved. In fact, Henry Ellis, you are dead.'

'I don't understand,' said the little man.

'That also is on our records. And now I have but one thing left to say. Because of your crime, Henry Ellis is dead. It was a careless crime, but you still have a chance. You may join Henry Ellis in oblivion, or you may begin to live. The choice is yours.'

Slowly the little man walked down to the beach. He stood in the sand and listened to the waves. He took off his shoes and tie and walked in the water. He looked at the polished platforms of rock like sleeping sunsets and laughed with the wind.

Bowing to the sea, he gave it his briefcase, his hat and his evening paper. Then, with his shoes in one hand and a piece of driftwood in the other, he ran through the golden evening on his way to the railway station, stopping only once to put a dandelion in his buttonhole.

Annette Lawson (16)

75. What is the message of the story? Do you agree with it? Explain.

76. What job do you think the little man did?

77. Who do you think the stranger was? Explain.

78. What were the three charges laid against the little man?

79. Do you think this is a positive or negative story? Explain.

80. Write your own creative short story called *Looking Forward*.

S E L F

ASSESSMENT

Name: ....

1. Can I?

Write "yes" or "no" in the box. If you write "no", go back over your work until you can write "yes".

- Identify the various influences on me .... ☐
- Set my future goals .... ☐
- Interpret tables of figures .... ☐
- Be assertive .... ☐
- Use the "six thinking hats" method .... ☐

2. Your reaction

(a) Which extract did you like best? Say why.
(b) Which activity did you like best? Say why.
(c) Which skill do you need to work on most? What can you do to improve it?

3. For your folio

From the work you have done in this chapter, choose the pieces you want to include in your folio. Each piece of work in your folio should include a cover sheet which shows the date it was completed, the title, the purpose and the audience.

4. Ongoing skills

Complete the table below by:
- placing a tick at the point at which you feel you usually achieve in each skill
- shading in the range of your achievement in each skill.

When you have completed the table place it in your folio.

Am I improving in these skills?	Level of achievement		
	Same as before	Improving	Much better
Example: Oral work		✓	
Cooperating in group work			
Explaining my answers			
Discussing issues			
Writing poetry			
Empathising with others			
Oral work			
Using the writing process			
Identifying language techniques			

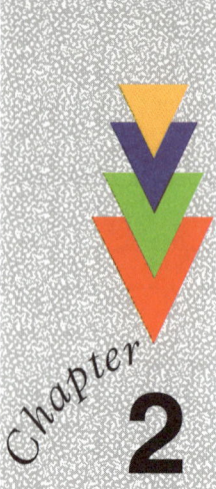

Chapter 2 THE NOVEL

Content

- *To Kill a Mockingbird* — the background
- Elements of the novel
- The town of Maycomb
- Characters
- Chapter-by-chapter breakdown, including commentary, issues and language features
- Interpreting the issues
- Text response — the analytical essay

Skills

- Identifying the elements of the novel
- Analysing the novelist's style
- Interpreting the issues
- Writing an analytical essay

To Kill a Mockingbird

a novel by Harper Lee

Novelists usually have a tremendous creative urge, a desire to explore relationships and experiences, and to pass on to the world what they feel. The writer's message or central idea is what makes up the underlying theme and lies at the very heart of a novel

Novelist Harper Lee grew up in a small town in Alabama and therefore has a deep knowledge of the people, their background and social habits. She has also experienced the prejudices and narrow-mindedness of such a town.

Her story *To Kill a Mockingbird* is a reflection of some of the problems of American society: the hell of racial prejudice, of an unloving family life, of class distinction, of religious intolerance and of sexist attitudes.

On the other hand, the story has a message of tolerance, of understanding another person's point of view and of being able to stand in another person's shoes.

 A background of hate

The American Civil War

Between 1861 and 1865 a bitter conflict raged between the northern and southern states of America. The South was largely agricultural and in 1850 had nearly four million black slaves working on plantations. One of the issues in the civil war was slavery. The North won and the slaves were freed. However, this did not change the way most whites in the South treated the blacks. Blacks were segregated from whites and were denied jobs and education. Many whites despised and feared the blacks who were often lynched or had their houses burnt to the ground. This terror continued through to the 1930s when the situation was made even worse by the Great Depression.

The 1930s — the Great Depression

In the 1930s the world suffered a devastating depression in which millions went without jobs, food, housing or hope. The southern states of America were hit hard as the region depended on agriculture and demand for these goods fell rapidly. The poverty of the 1930s added to the bitterness and resentment of the poorer whites who were ready to blame anyone for their situation.

Ku Klux Klan

The Ku Klux Klan formed in the South in 1865. The name comes from the Greek word *kyklos*, meaning circle. Circles or organisations of white men sprang up across the South. Their aim was to stop the blacks from gaining the rights of white people. In 1871, one hundred and sixty-three blacks were lynched or shot in just one county. Between 1865 and the 1930s thousands of blacks were murdered or tortured and their homes burned. The blacks continued to live under this threat until the civil rights movement began to gain strength in the 1960s.

To Kill a Mockingbird – elements of the novel

Setting
Maycomb, Alabama in the 1930s. There was a background of slavery, racism and poverty.

Plot
The first part of the story centres on Boo Radley and the attempts of the children to meet him. The second part centres around Tom Robinson who is on trial for rape.

Themes
• The problems of growing up
• Justice and injustice
• Courage
• Respect for the individual
• Prejudice:
  –legal
  –racial
  –educational
  –religious
  –sexual

Characters
The main characters are Atticus, his daughter Scout and his son Jem.

Style
The story is told through the eyes of Scout, recalling her childhood. It includes:
• Southern dialogue
• humour
• powerful imagery
• detailed observation
• use of symbolism.

Maycomb

The layout of the town is important to the story. Harper Lee gives us a clear idea of the streets, the houses and the people who live in them. She also describes the shops, the churches, the school, the courthouse and the rubbish dump. The map below shows a student's impression of the town after reading the novel. How does it compare with the way you visualise it?

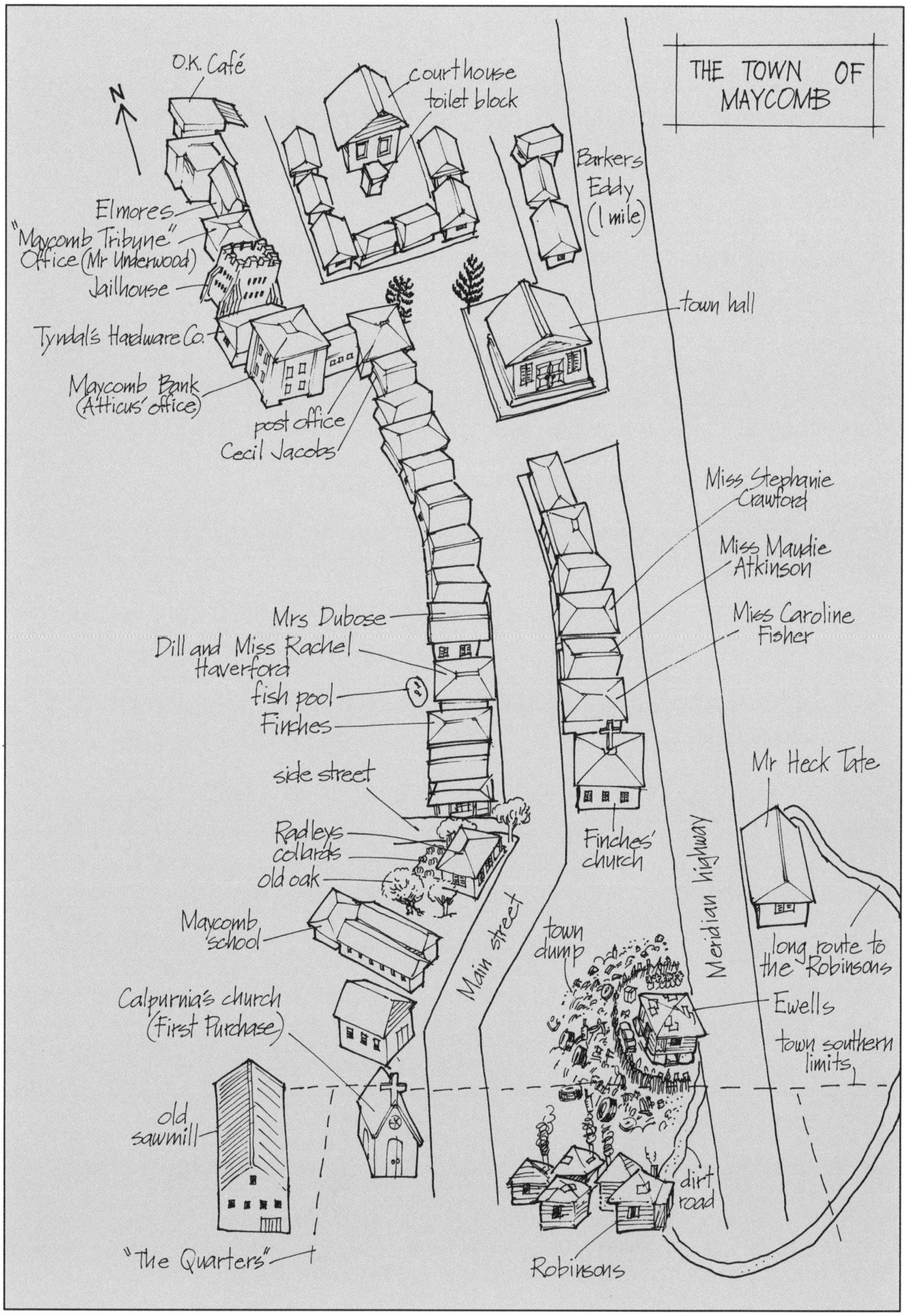

THE TOWN OF MAYCOMB

O.K. Café

courthouse toilet block

Barkers Eddy (1 mile)

Elmores
"Maycomb Tribune" Office (Mr Underwood)
Jailhouse

town hall

Tyndal's Hardware Co.

Maycomb Bank (Atticus' office)

post office
Cecil Jacobs

Miss Stephanie Crawford

Miss Maudie Atkinson

Miss Caroline Fisher

Mrs Dubose
Dill and Miss Rachel Haverford
fish pool
Finches

side street

Radleys
collards
old oak

Mr Heck Tate

Maycomb school

Finches' church

Calpurnia's church (First Purchase)

Main street

town dump

Meridian highway

long route to the Robinsons

Ewells

town southern limits

old sawmill

dirt road

"The Quarters"

Robinsons

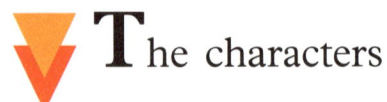

The characters

Atticus Finch: a lawyer who defends Tom Robinson. Father of Scout and Jem.

Scout (Jean Louise) **Finch**: Atticus' young daughter who is the narrator of the story.

Jem Finch: Scout's older brother.

Calpurnia: the Negro housekeeper who has raised Jem and Scout.

Aunt Alexandra: the children's aunt who comes to care for them during Tom Robinson's trial.

Francis: Aunt Alexandra's grandson.

Uncle Jack Finch: the bachelor uncle who visits every Christmas.

Dill (Charles Baker Harris): Jem and Scout's friend who lives in Mississippi but comes every summer to Maycomb to stay with his aunt Rachel.

Miss Rachel: Dill's aunt who lives next-door to the Finches.

Miss Maudie: a neighbour and friend of the Finch family.

Mrs Dubose: a very old lady who shouts abuse at the children as they pass her house.

Boo (Mr Arthur) **Radley**: the phantom neighbour the children have never seen.

Mr Nathan Radley: Boo's brother who seldom speaks even though he is seen every day.

Heck Tate: the sheriff, who is a good friend of the Finches.

Judge John Taylor: the judge at the trial of Tom Robinson.

Mr Gilmer: the prosecuting lawyer at the trial.

Tom Robinson: a young Negro who is accused of raping Mayella Ewell.

Bob Ewell: the irresponsible father of several children, who lives on the dole and drinks heavily.

Mayella Violet Ewell: his daughter, who accuses Tom Robinson of raping her.

Mr Walter Cunningham: a poor but proud farmer who refuses charity.

Reverend Sykes: a friendly and respected Negro minister.

Miss Stephanie Crawford: a neighbour who is the local gossip.

Miss Caroline Fisher: one of Scout's teachers.

Mrs Merriweather: a local lady who writes the Halloween pageant.

Dolphus Raymond: a white man who prefers to live with the Negroes.

Mr B. B. Underwood: owner of the town's newspaper.

Mr Link Deas: Tom Robinson's boss.

1. As you read the novel you will come across all of these characters. Create a file on the main characters using the headings below. The file will help you make a character and relationships web of the people in the novel.

Character	Personality	Key relationship

 Getting inside the novel

CHAPTER 1

The story is told by Scout, who looks back to the time when her brother Jem broke his arm and the events that led up to this incident. She recalls that it happened when she was six and Charles Baker Harris, known as Dill, came to stay in Maycomb for the summer. We are introduced to members of Scout's family and to the setting, the "tired old town" of Maycomb in the southern state of Alabama. Her father, Atticus Finch, is a lawyer, a man of position in the town who has a good relationship with his children. We are also introduced to the Radley house which is the focus of interest for the first part of the story.

The Radley Place jutted into a sharp curve beyond our house. Walking south, one faced its porch; the sidewalk turned and ran beside the lot. The house was low, was once white with a deep front porch and green shutters, but had long ago darkened to the colour of the slate-grey yard around it. Rain-rotten shingles drooped over the eaves of the veranda; oak trees kept the sun away. The remains of a picket drunkenly guarded the front yard — a 'swept' yard that was never swept — where johnson grass and rabbit-tobacco grew in abundance.

Inside the house lived a malevolent phantom. People said he existed but Jem and I had never seen him. People said he went out at night when the moon was high, and peeped in windows. When people's azaleas froze in a cold snap, it was because he had breathed on them. Any stealthy crimes committed in Maycomb were his work. Once the town was terrorized by a series of morbid nocturnal events: people's chickens and household pets were found mutilated; although the culprit was Crazy Addie, who eventually drowned himself in Barker's Eddy, people still looked at the Radley Place, unwilling to discard their initial suspicions. A Negro would not pass the Radley Place at night, he would cut across to the sidewalk opposite and whistle as he walked. The Maycomb school grounds adjoined the back of the Radley lot; from the Radley chicken-yard tall pecan trees shook their fruit into the school yard, but the nuts lay untouched by the children: Radley pecans would kill you. A baseball hit into the Radley yard was a lost ball and no questions asked.

2. What does this passage from the novel lead you to expect of Boo Radley?

3. Why is it that people who are different are often treated with suspicion and even fear?

The language of Harper Lee

The story is told from a child's point of view, which creates a sense of innocence and humour. Scout is too young to realise the full significance of some of her experiences even though you, the reader, may.

Although the story is told from the child's point of view it is not told in a child's language. Harper Lee uses dialogue which often includes colloquialisms from the southern United States. For example:

collard — a type of cabbage
stumphole whisky — illegal whisky
flivver — a cheap Ford car
Hoover cart — a simple two-wheeled cart named after President Hoover.

Her language also creates an atmosphere of mystery, as in the description of the Radley place. Note the use of imagery created by strong verbs, adverbs and adjectives: "shingles drooped over the eaves", "a picket drunkenly guarded the front yard" and "morbid nocturnal events".

She also uses repetition, for example, "people" in the second paragraph of the extract, giving her language rhythm and flow. She draws on our senses, using alliteration to help bring to life her descriptions, such as this one of the town.

> Somehow, it was hotter then; a black dog suffered on a summer's day; bony mules hitched to Hoover carts flicked flies in the sweltering shade of the live oaks on the square. Men's stiff collars wilted by nine in the morning. Ladies bathed before noon, after their three o'clock naps, and by nightfall were like soft tea-cakes with frostings of sweat and sweet talcum.

4. Which of the five senses does Harper Lee draw upon in this extract? Give examples to support your answer.

5. A major character in the story is Atticus. What do you learn about him from the first chapter? Begin a character web of Atticus like the one below and add to it as you read the novel.

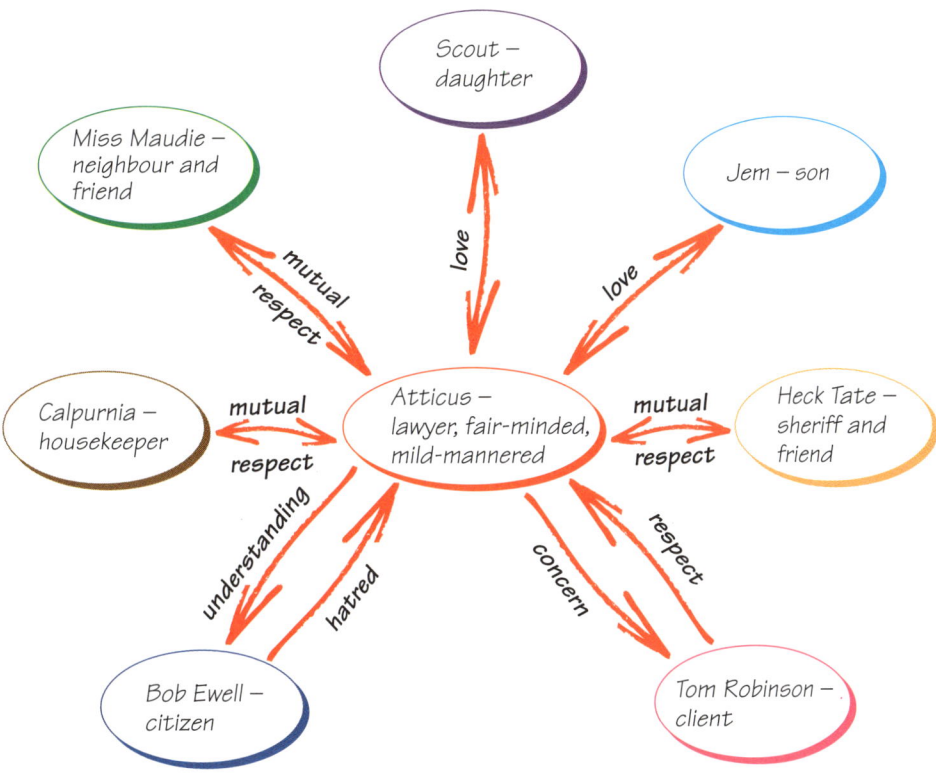

6. Scout describes Boo Radley as a "malevolent phantom". What does this mean? Compare what you have written with a partner before checking your dictionary.

7. There are other character descriptions in this chapter, for example of Calpurnia. Select the two lines you found most powerful in the description of Calpurnia.

8. We are not told how Jem broke his arm until late in the story. As you read the novel, find out who else has an injured arm. What is the connection?

9. The Radley house is described in detail in this chapter.
   (a) What atmosphere does Harper Lee create about this house?
   (b) What words are used to give you the strongest images?
   (c) In what way does the illustration capture the description?

10. Think back to your early childhood. Was there some house, person or place you thought was mysterious or menacing? Describe your early experience and fears.

11. What impression do you get of Maycomb?

12. The detailed description of the town gives the feeling that the town was hot and tired and the people had little motivation.
    (a) Select the words and phrases that reflect this feeling.
    (b) Identify two examples of alliteration in the extract.

CHAPTERS 2 & 3

After the summer holidays Scout has her first experiences of school. Her first day is disappointing and she is confused when her teacher Miss Caroline, who is new to the school and to the town, tells her that her father was wrong to have taught her to read.

I suppose she chose me because she knew my name; as I read the alphabet a faint line appeared between her eyebrows, and after making me read most of *My First Reader* and the stock-market quotations from *The Mobile Register* aloud, she discovered that I was literate and looked at me with more than faint distaste. Miss Caroline told me to tell my father not to teach me any more, it would interfere with my reading.

'Teach me?' I said in surprise. 'He hasn't taught me anything, Miss Caroline. Atticus ain't got time to teach me anything,' I added, when Miss Caroline smiled and shook her head. 'Why, he's so tired at night he just sits in the living-room and reads.'

'If he didn't teach you, who did?' Miss Caroline asked good-naturedly. 'Somebody did. You weren't born reading *The Mobile Register*.'

'Jem says I was. He read in a book where I was a Bullfinch instead of a Finch. Jem says my name's really Jean Louise Bullfinch, that I got swapped when I was born and I'm really a —'

Miss Caroline apparently thought I was lying. 'Let's not let our imaginations run away with us, dear,' she said. 'Now you tell your father not to teach you any more. It's best to begin reading with a fresh mind. You tell him I'll take over from here and try to undo the damage —'

'Ma'am?'

'Your father does not know how to teach. You can have a seat now.'

13. (a) Why is Scout confused?
    (b) What is your reaction to the teacher's judgement?
    (c) What gives the extract a touch of humour?

Scout makes several mistakes during her first day and is punished by her teacher.

Miss Caroline stood stock still, then grabbed me by the collar and hauled me back to her desk. 'Jean Louise, I've had about enough of you this morning,' she said. 'You're starting off on the wrong foot in every way, my dear. Hold out your hand.'

I thought she was going to spit in it, which was the only reason anybody in Maycomb held out his hand: it was a time-honoured method of sealing oral contracts. Wondering what bargain we had made, I turned to the class for an answer, but the class looked back at me in puzzlement. Miss Caroline picked up her ruler, gave me half a dozen quick little pats, then told me to stand in the corner. A storm of laughter broke loose when it finally occurred to the class that Miss Caroline had whipped me.

Disappointed in her experiences at school she complains to her father, Atticus, who explains:

'First of all,' he said, 'if you can learn a simple trick, Scout, you'll get along better with all kinds of folks. You never really understand a person until you consider things from his point of view —'

'Sir?'

'— until you climb into his skin and walk around in it.'

Atticus said I had learned many things today, and Miss Caroline had learned several things herself. She had learned not to hand something to a Cunningham, for one thing, but if Walter and I had put ourselves in her shoes we'd have seen it was an honest mistake on her part. We could not expect her to learn all Maycomb's ways in one day, and we could not hold her responsible when she knew no better.

Commentary and issues

In these chapters we are introduced to characters whose families will be important later in the story, and we become aware of their backgrounds and attitudes. We also discover some of Atticus' wisdom.

Harper Lee's portrayal of the school education system is far from complimentary. She contrasts Scout's sterile experiences at school with the rich learning experiences she has in the world outside the classroom.

14. What do you think makes an education system meaningful and worthwhile?

The language of Harper Lee

Harper Lee's use of dialogue makes the characters seem real. Some colloquialisms used in these chapters include:

Yeb'm — Yes, ma'am.

quarter — 25c (a quarter of a dollar)

nickel — 5c

dime — 10c

scrip stamps — charity stamps exchanged for goods.

Scout's reaction to school, especially the reading scene, is dealt with using humour, as is the scene where Scout thinks Miss Caroline is going to spit in her hand. Harper Lee uses irony to make fun of Miss Caroline's teaching: for example when she addresses Scout as "my dear" and then immediately tells her to hold out her hand for punishment.

15. In these chapters, the teacher makes a number of mistakes which leave the children uninterested. Can you identify them?

16. If you were in the teacher's shoes what would you have
    (a) said to Scout when you found out she could read?
    (b) read to the students as a story on their first day in Year 1? (See second page of chapter 2.)
    (c) done with Burris Ewell? (See chapter 3.)

17. In the course of the story Scout "climbs into the skin" of various characters: Walter Cunningham in this chapter, Mrs Dubose in chapter 10 and Boo Radley in chapter 31. As you come across these experiences jot down what Scout learns from each of them. Which of these experiences do you think has the greatest impact on her?

18. (a) Do you consider that "climbing into the skin" of someone is a useful way of gaining tolerance of others? Explain.
    (b) Imagine you are Miss Caroline. Write a letter to a friend, who is also a new teacher, about your experiences of the day.

19. Select a scene which you feel is dealt with humorously, and identify the features that make it humorous.

20. In these chapters we are introduced to the Cunninghams and Ewells. Harper Lee makes us feel a certain way toward them. Find three references to each family. How do these words make you feel about each family?

Chapters 4, 5 & 6

A year has passed and Scout is still disappointed with school. One day, on the way home, she discovers little presents left in the hollow of a tree outside the Radley place. Scout at this stage doesn't realise they are from Boo Radley.

Scout visits Miss Maudie Atkinson. Like Atticus, Miss Maudie stands for reason, open-mindedness and compassion. She speaks wisely to Scout about Boo Radley. She is critical of Miss Crawford, the local gossip, and of the religious bigot Mr Nathan Radley, Boo's brother.

In chapter 5 Miss Maudie, who herself is a Baptist, tells Scout about the "foot-washing" Baptists who consider themselves Christians but are willing to judge and condemn others.

'Foot-washers believe anything that's pleasure is a sin. Did you know some of 'em came out of the woods one Saturday and passed by this place and told me me and my flowers were going to hell?'

'Your flowers, too?'

'Yes ma'am. They'd burn right with me. They thought I spent too much time in God's outdoors and not enough time inside the house reading the Bible.'

21. Why do you think Harper Lee implies that many of the white Protestants in Maycomb are not Christian at all?

Commentary and issues

Although we are left in little doubt about Harper Lee's opinion of religious bigotry, she does not condemn religion. She contrasts the narrow-minded white Christian bigots with the black church community who are shown as "God-caring Christians". Another contrast is provided by Atticus, who tells Scout that his religion obliges him to defend Tom Robinson.

Later, the children are caught by Atticus trying to communicate with Boo Radley by pushing a note on a pole under the door of the Radley house.

> 22. What does Atticus urge them to do? Why?

In chapter 6 the children ignore Atticus' ban and make a night-time visit to catch a glimpse of Boo Radley. They don't get far before a shadowy figure appears and, as they run away, "the roar of a shotgun shattered the neighbourhood". Frightened out of their wits, they make a frantic escape although Jem loses his trousers on the fence. Despite Scout's protestations, Jem goes back later and retrieves his pants.

CHAPTERS 7 & 8

Scout learns that when Jem found his trousers they had been repaired, folded and placed neatly on the fence, possibly by Boo Radley. The mystery of the Radley house remains the focus of the story. Jem suspects that the gifts he and Scout find in the tree are also from Boo. Before Jem can place a "thank-you" note in the tree they discover that Mr Nathan Radley has cemented the hole. Jem is reduced to tears.

When winter descends it is unusually severe. Scout and Jem see snow for the first time and they build a snowman. A fire breaks out in Miss Maudie's house. While the children watch aghast as the house blazes, someone puts a blanket around Scout's shoulders. Later they realise that the kind person was Boo Radley.

Jem and Scout have finally learnt that being different doesn't make a person into a monster. They were wrong to annoy Boo Radley.

Chapter 9

The focus of the novel shifts from the Radley house to the Tom Robinson case. Scout is angry and confused when at school Cecil Jacobs announces that Atticus "defended niggers", and then her cousin Francis calls him a "nigger-lover". Later, Atticus persuades Scout to use her head and not her fists: to be rational and not emotional. He explains he will be defending Tom Robinson, a Negro, in court. Uncle Jack arrives for Christmas. Uncle Jack brings air rifles, which Atticus had asked him to buy as presents for Jem and Scout.

Scout gets into trouble during the day and is punished by Uncle Jack, unfairly in her opinion. Atticus always listens to both sides before coming to a judgement. Uncle Jack provides a contrast to Atticus. Uncle Jack is fun-loving but he doesn't understand children and tends to confuse them. Atticus explains this later to his brother, appearing more and more as the voice of calm reason.

Chapter 10

Chapter 10 gives us our first clue about what the title of the book actually means. It also provides new insights on Atticus.

When he gave us our air rifles Atticus wouldn't teach us to shoot. Uncle Jack instructed us in the rudiments thereof; he said Atticus wasn't interested in guns. Atticus said to Jem one day, 'I'd rather you shot at tin cans in the back yard, but I know you'll go after birds. Shoot all the bluejays you want, if you can hit 'em, but remember it's a sin to kill a mockingbird.'

That was the only time I ever heard Atticus say it was a sin to do something, and I asked Miss Maudie about it.

'Your father's right,' she said. 'Mockingbirds don't do one thing but make music for us to enjoy. They don't eat up people's gardens, don't nest in corncribs, they don't do one thing but sing their hearts out for us. That's why it's a sin to kill a mockingbird.'

Scout and Jem feel disappointed in their father. They see him as old, and embarrassingly different from their schoolmates' fathers. However, an incident occurs that makes them see him in another light.

Tim Johnson, "a liver-coloured bird dog, the pet of Maycomb" is noticed by Jem walking dazedly along the street. Calpurnia realises the dog has rabies, which would cause death to anyone it bites. She spreads the word, and in terror people bolt their doors. Sheriff Heck Tate arrives with Atticus.

Tim Johnson reached the side street that ran in front of the Radley Place, and what remained of his poor mind made him pause and seem to consider which road he would take. He made a few hesitant steps and stopped in front of the Radley gate; then he tried to turn around, but was having difficulty.

Atticus said, 'He's within range, Heck. You better get him now before he goes down the side street — Lord knows who's around the corner. Go inside, Cal.'

Calpurnia opened the screen door, latched it behind her, then unlatched it and held on to the hook. She tried to block Jem and me with her body, but we looked out from beneath her arms.

'Take him, Mr Finch.' Mr Tate handed the rifle to Atticus; Jem and I nearly fainted.

'Don't waste time, Heck,' said Atticus. 'Go on.'

'Mr Finch, this is a one-shot job.'

Atticus shook his head vehemently: 'Don't just stand there, Heck! He won't wait all day for you —'

'For God's sake, Mr Finch, look where he is! Miss and you'll go straight into Radley house! I can't shoot that well and you know it!'

'I haven't shot a gun in thirty years —'

Mr Tate almost threw the rifle at Atticus. 'I'd feel mighty comfortable if you did now,' he said.

In a fog, Jem and I watched our father take the gun and walk out into the middle of the street. He walked quickly, but I thought he moved like an underwater swimmer: time had slowed to a nauseating crawl.

When Atticus raised his glasses Calpurnia murmured, 'Sweet Jesus help him,' and put her hands to her cheeks.

Atticus pushed his glasses to his forehead; they slipped down, and he dropped them in the street. In the silence, I heard them crack. Atticus rubbed his eyes and chin; we saw him blink hard.

In front of the Radley gate, Tim Johnson had made up what was left of his mind. He had finally turned himself around, to pursue his original course up our street. He made two steps forward, then stopped and raised his head. We saw his body go rigid.

With movements so swift they seemed simultaneous, Atticus's hand yanked a ball-tipped lever as he brought the gun to his shoulder.

The rifle cracked. Tim Johnson leaped, flopped over and crumpled on the sidewalk in a brown-and-white heap. He didn't know what hit him.

Mr Tate jumped off the porch and ran to the Radley Place. He stopped in front of the dog, squatted, turned around and tapped his finger on his forehead above his left eye. 'You were a little to the right, Mr Finch,' he called.

'Always was,' answered Atticus. 'If I had my 'druthers I'd take a shotgun.'

He stooped and picked up his glasses, ground the broken lenses to powder under his heel, and went to Mr Tate and stood looking down at Tim Johnson.

Doors opened one by one, and the neighbourhood slowly came alive. Miss Maudie walked down the steps with Miss Stephanie Crawford.

Jem was paralysed. I pinched him to get him moving, but when Atticus saw us coming he called, 'Stay where you are.'

When Mr Tate and Atticus returned to the yard, Mr Tate was smiling. 'I'll have Zeebo collect him,' he said. 'You haven't forgot much, Mr Finch. They say it never leaves you.'

Atticus was silent.

'Atticus?' said Jem.

'Yes?'

'Nothin'.'

'I saw that, One-Shot Finch!'

Atticus wheeled around and faced Miss Maudie. They looked at one another without saying anything, and Atticus got into the sheriff's car. 'Come here,' he said to Jem. 'Don't you go near that dog, you understand? Don't go near him, he's just as dangerous dead as alive.'

'Yes sir,' said Jem. 'Atticus —'

'What, son?'

'Nothing.'

Atticus has become a hero in his children's eyes and Jem begins to understand why Atticus doesn't boast of being known as "One-Shot Finch". Jem ends by saying, "Atticus is a gentleman, just like me!"

Commentary and issues

The concept of courage is explored in the novel. Early in the story courage is portrayed as the ability to overcome physically the fear of something: from Jem overcoming his fear of the Radley Place when he runs and touches the house in chapter 1, to Atticus tackling the danger of the rabid dog in chapter 10.

> 23. Do you think physical courage is the only form of courage, or are there other forms? Explain.

Harper Lee also addresses the idea of social status. To many people in Maycomb it is their family background that gives them their position in society.

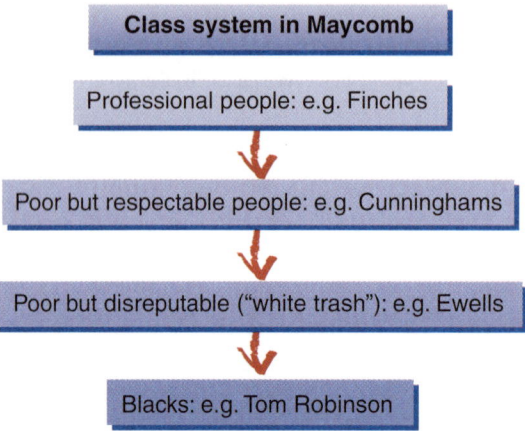

She puts forward the idea that social status should be determined by a person's moral character. For example, this is shown in Miss Maudie's comment about Atticus to the children at the end of the chapter: "If your father's anything, he's civilised in his heart."

The mockingbird is introduced in this chapter. The mockingbird is a symbol of innocence, a source of happiness. Atticus tells his children it is a sin to kill an innocent and beautiful bird. When the rabid dog approaches the mockingbirds go silent, signalling that something sinister or dangerous is about to happen. As the story unfolds the mockingbird helps bind the two parts of the book together. Boo Radley and Tom Robinson are both mockingbird figures. They are both innocent, harmless people and yet are both persecuted by society.

The language of Harper Lee

Effective images are created through the use of similes and metaphors. For example, Scout describes the dog Tim Johnson, mad with rabies: "We could see him shiver like a horse shedding flies."

The atmosphere for this scene is set when Harper Lee writes, "Nothing is more deadly than a deserted waiting street." This builds an air of anticipation in the reader. Note also how the movements at the beginning of this scene are slow and deliberate, in contrast with the final swift shooting of the dog.

Atticus' movements are given a slow-motion effect through Harper Lee's use of metaphor and simile: "In a fog, Jem and I watched ..." "... he moved like an underwater swimmer: time had moved to a nauseating crawl."

Harper Lee creates powerful images in the mad dog scene by using strong words:
- verbs — *cracked, yanked*
- adjectives — *nauseating, rigid*
- adverbs — *vehemently, wickedly*

24. Find three other powerful verbs from this extract, and use them in sentences of your own.

Re-read the last section of the extract. Note that the dialogue throughout this scene is short and sharp to create tension.

CHAPTER 11

Mrs Henry Lafayette Dubose, another neighbour of the Finches, lives alone with her black servant girl. Old, irritable and spiteful, she provides a sharp contrast to the character of Miss Maudie.

Mrs Dubose hurls insults at the children, referring to Atticus as a "nigger-lover". Jem, who is usually calm and level-headed, snaps, and attacks Mrs Dubose's most treasured possession — her camellias. Atticus' punishment is for Jem to read to her daily for a month. Scout decides to accompany him.

We moved our chairs forward. This was the nearest I had ever been to her, and the thing I wanted most to do was move my chair back again.

She was horrible. Her face was the colour of a dirty pillowcase, and the corners of her mouth glistened with wet, which inched like a glacier down the deep grooves enclosing her chin. Old-age liver spots dotted her cheeks, and her pale eyes had black pinpoint pupils. Her hands were knobby, and the cuticles were grown up over her fingernails. Her bottom plate was not in, and her upper lip protruded; from time to time she would draw her nether lip to her upper plate and carry her chin with it. This made the wet move faster.

I didn't look any more than I had to. Jem re-opened *Ivanhoe* and began reading. I tried to keep up with him, but he read too fast. When Jem came to a word he didn't know, he skipped it, but Mrs Dubose would catch him and make him spell it out. Jem read for perhaps twenty minutes, during which time I looked at the soot-stained mantelpiece, out of the window, anywhere to keep from looking at her. As he read along, I noticed that Mrs Dubose's corrections grew fewer and farther between, that Jem had even left one sentence dangling in mid-air. She was not listening.

I looked towards the bed.

Something had happened to her. She lay on her back, with the quilts up to her chin. Only her head and shoulders were visible. Her head moved slowly from side to side. From time to time she would open her mouth wide, and I could see her tongue undulate faintly. Cords of saliva would collect on her lips; she would draw them in, then open her mouth again. Her mouth seemed to have a private existence of its own. It worked separate and apart from the rest of her, out and in, like a clam hole at low tide. Occasionally it would say, 'Pt,' like some viscous substance coming to a boil.

When the month is over, Atticus asks Jem to extend his reading duty by one more week. Soon after, Mrs Dubose dies. Atticus explains to the children that she had been a morphine addict after her doctor had prescribed it as a pain-killer. "She said she meant to break herself of it before she died, and that's just what she did." He also describes Mrs Dubose as a lady, a great lady, much to the amazement of Jem.

'A lady?' Jem raised his head. His face was scarlet. 'After all those things she said about you, a lady?'

'She was. She had her own views about things, a lot different from mine, maybe ... son, I told you that if you hadn't lost your head I'd have made you go read to her. I wanted you to see something about her — I wanted you to see what real courage is, instead of getting the idea that courage is a man with a gun in his hand. It's when you know you're licked before you begin but you begin anyway and you see it through no matter what. You rarely win, but sometimes you do. Mrs Dubose won, all ninety-eight pounds of her. According to her views, she died beholden to nothing and nobody. She was the bravest person I ever knew."

Commentary and issues

Scout learns from Mrs Dubose that there is another type of courage: when a person is faced with a seemingly hopeless situation but still continues to fight on. This test of courage prepares the children for Atticus' fight for Tom Robinson later in the story.

32. Do you think it is courageous or foolish to attempt something "when you know you're licked before you begin"? Explain.

33. Briefly describe a real example of this kind of courage.

Scout begins to realise that people should fight with their heads rather than their fists.

Jem is starting to act more responsibly: he begins to understand what his father is doing and what he stands for. In this way he is a contrast to Scout who, because of her age, does not always understand the significance of what is going on.

The language of Harper Lee

Harper Lee's description of Mrs Dubose is full of detailed imagery. Again powerful similes are used: "inched like a glacier", and "like a clam hole at low tide".

She draws on our senses to bring alive the image of Mrs Dubose, barely alive, ugly in her suffering as she struggles desperately against her morphine addiction. We can see, smell and hear the old lady; we can see the grey, wrinkled face. The sounds of her breathing and the smell of the sick-room come alive in our minds.

Note the short topic sentences that Harper Lee uses to bite into her readers' consciousness. The short sentences are all dramatic entrances to each paragraph:

"We moved our chairs forward."

"She was horrible."

"She was."

34. Why do you think Jem suddenly snapped and attacked Mrs Dubose's camellias?

35. Have you ever been in a situation similar to Jem's and lost your temper? Describe what happened. How do you control a sudden rage when it hits you?

36. Why did Jem find it difficult to accept his father's punishment?

37. Do you feel Scout's decision to accompany her brother reveals something of her character? Explain.

38. What lesson did Scout and Jem learn from this experience?

39. Do you think Atticus showed wisdom in making Jem read to Mrs Dubose? Justify your answer.

40. Which of your senses are drawn upon in the reading scene?
    Support your answer with examples.

41. In pairs, discuss why you think Harper Lee included Mrs Dubose in the story.

42. Compare the courage of Atticus facing the mad dog to the courage of Mrs Dubose.

Chapter 12

The main focus of part 2 of the novel is on the trial of Tom Robinson.

Chapter 12 begins with some insights about the black community of Maycomb. Atticus is away and Calpurnia is looking after Scout and Jem. The children learn that Calpurnia leads two lives and speaks two languages, because she actually lives in two different worlds — the world of whites and the world of blacks. This discovery emphasises the segregation of black and white.

Calpurnia takes the children with her to a Negro church service. Scout and Jem are fascinated by the service and warm to the kindly Reverend Sykes. A collection is taken up for the wife and family of Tom Robinson who is in jail awaiting trial. On returning home they find their Aunt Alexandra has come to stay.

Chapter 13

Jem and Scout reject Aunt Alexandra's snobbish attitudes about "good families" and social status. Her ideas fit in well with public attitudes in Maycomb, however. The children's other concern is that Aunt Alexandra might drive a wedge between them and their father.

Aunt Alexandra at this stage stands as a contrast to Atticus. She emphasises the position of the family in the community while he emphasises the qualities of each individual.

Chapter 14

Pre-trial tension puts the Finch family on edge. Atticus and Aunt Alexandra argue openly, something the children are not used to.

Scout finds Dill under her bed. He feels unwanted and has run away. Scout wants to keep Dill's secret but Jem acts more responsibly and informs Atticus, who arranges for Dill to stay for the summer. Dill's loneliness and lack of family life contrast with the warmth and love Jem and Scout receive. Earlier, in chapter 1, we saw how the lonely Dill was drawn to the lonely figure of Boo Radley "as the moon draws water". In chapter 9 Scout's cousin Francis remarked of Dill, "... he hasn't got a home ... he just gets passed around from relative to relative and Miss Rachel keeps him every summer." His childish desire to marry Scout reflects his desperate need to create the family life he hasn't got at home.

Harper Lee lightens these tragic situations through the use of humour. When Dill says, "Scout, let's get us a baby", Scout answers, "Where?" reminding us of the innocence of the narrator.

CHAPTERS 15 & 16

These chapters expose us to mob scenes. The nightmare begins when Heck Tate and some other friends of Atticus visit him one evening, a week before the trial, to warn him they fear trouble when Tom Robinson is brought to the jail in Maycomb. This scene is defused by an interruption from Jem.

The following night Atticus goes to the jail where he keeps a lonely vigil over Tom Robinson. Outside the jail he reads his paper by the light of a single bulb. He is confronted by a lynch mob, intent on hanging Tom Robinson. Unknown to Atticus, Jem, Scout and Dill have followed him to the jail; when he sees them he commands the children to go home but Jem refuses. The tension builds, and this time it is Scout who breaks it. She sees a familiar face in the mob, Mr Cunningham. When she calls out he doesn't respond so she tries again.

'Don't you remember me, Mr Cunningham? I'm Jean Louise Finch. You brought us some hickory nuts one time, remember?' I began to sense the futility one feels when unacknowledged by a chance acquaintance.

'I go to school with Walter,' I began again. 'He's your boy, ain't he? Ain't he, sir?'

Mr Cunningham was moved to a faint nod. He did know me, after all.

'He's in my grade," I said, 'and he does right well. He's a good boy,' I added, 'a real nice boy. We bought him home for dinner one time. Maybe he told you about me, I beat him up one time but he was real nice about it. Tell him hey for me, won't you?'

Atticus had said it was the polite thing to talk to people about what they were interested in, not about what you were interested in. Mr Cunningham displayed no interest in his son, so I tackled his entailment once more in a last-ditch effort to make him feel at home.

'Entailments are bad,' I was advising him, when I slowly awoke to the fact that I was addressing the entire aggregation. The men were all looking at me, some had their mouths half-open. Atticus had stopped poking at Jem: they were standing together beside Dill. Their attention amounted to fascination. Atticus's mouth, even, was half-open, an attitude he had once described as uncouth. Our eyes met and he shut it.

'Well, Atticus, I was just sayin' to Mr Cunningham that entailments are bad an' all that, but you said not to worry, it takes a long time sometimes ... that you all'd ride it out together ...' I was slowly drying up, wondering what idiocy I had committed. Entailments seemed all right enough for living-room talk.

I began to feel sweat gathering at the edges of my hair; I could stand anything but a bunch of people looking at me. They were quite still.

'What's the matter?' I asked.

Atticus said nothing. I looked around and up at Mr Cunningham, whose face was equally impassive. Then he did a peculiar thing. He squatted down and took me by both shoulders.

'I'll tell him you said hey, little lady,' he said.

Then he straightened up and waved a big paw. 'Let's clear out,' he called. 'Let's get going, boys.'

As they had come, in ones and twos the men shuffled back to their ramshackle cars. Doors slammed, engines coughed, and they were gone.

I turned to Atticus, but Atticus had gone to the jail and was leaning against it with his face to the wall. I went to him and pulled his sleeve. 'Can we go home now?' He nodded, produced his handkerchief, gave his face a going-over and blew his nose violently.

Commentary and issues

Mayella Ewell's alleged rape is not the issue for the lynch mob. Led by Walter Cunningham, they are not defending Mayella's honour; they are defending white supremacy.

The mob is a product of generations of racial prejudice. Even though the Ewell family is "white trash" and Tom Robinson is well respected, the fact is they are white and he is black.

In Southern society of the 1930s two myths existed. One was that white women were goddesses, gentle and fragile, objects to be protected. The other was that all black males desired white women. The two myths combined to turn even the slightest hint of sexual involvement between a black man and a white woman into an emotionally charged situation full of anger.

Another recurring issue is courage. Atticus stands alone before the mob. Scout is not aware of the danger Atticus faces as he confronts Walter Cunningham and the lynch mob outside the jail. Her innocent conversation brings Mr Cunningham back to reality; he is threatening a man who, like him, is a father and who has helped him and his family in the past and extended hospitality to his son Walter. This realisation is stronger than his racial prejudice.

43. Discuss in small groups Atticus' statements:
    (a) "A mob's always made up of people, no matter what. Mr Cunningham was part of a mob last night, but he was still a man."
    (b) ". . . you children last night made Walter Cunningham stand in my shoes for a minute."

44. Write a journal entry describing the lessons Scout learnt from her experiences that night. Share your journal with the class.

The language of Harper Lee

This scene shows the youthful innocence of Scout who has not connected the mob with danger. Note how the first person viewpoint makes the reader see and feel the entire scene through Scout, creating tension in us but not in her.

Despite the tension, the scene has humour: "The men were all looking at me, some had their mouths half-open." In this way Harper Lee contrasts the youthful innocence of Scout with the aggression of the mob. Note how the tension is broken when Mr Cunningham finally speaks: "I'll tell him you said hey, little lady."

45. (a) Do you feel Atticus was brave or foolish in standing alone before the mob? Explain.
    (b) What would you have done in Atticus' situation if you were confronting a hostile mob who wanted to get at someone you were protecting? Would you meet violence with violence, or is there another way?

46. Was Scout aware of the danger? Support your answer with evidence from the story.

47. Atticus would have experienced a number of emotions from the moment the mob arrived to the time he leant against the jail " with his face to the wall". Describe what you think his emotions were. Use words from the story to support your answer.

48. Mr Underwood despises Negroes, yet he was prepared to shoot at the mob to protect Atticus. Imagine you are Scout. Describe how Atticus thanks Mr Underwood, writing the dialogue you imagine takes place.

Now read on

You will need to read to the end of chapter 16 before you can answer questions 49–53.

49. Later Scout becomes aware of the intention of the mob and the danger facing Atticus, "The full meaning of the night's events hit me and I began crying."
    (a) What was Jem's reaction to his sister's show of emotion?
    (b) What does this tell you about Jem?

50. When the "footwashing" Baptists passed Miss Maudie's garden the flowers were in full bloom. One of the "footwashers" shouted, "He that cometh in vanity departeth in darkness". Miss Maudie answered, "A merry heart maketh a cheerful countenance". Explain what you think is the message of each statement.

51. What first impression do you get of Mr Dolphus Raymond? Use evidence from the story to support your answer.

52. Briefly describe the courtroom scene before the beginning of the trial.

53. Why didn't Miss Maudie go to the trial?

Chapters 17 & 18

The courtroom drama unfolds. First the sheriff takes the stand, then Bob Ewell, followed by his daughter Mayella. Atticus' clever cross-examination of Bob Ewell shows he has little concern for his daughter. Atticus confuses Ewell and he is made to look a fool and possibly a liar.

Atticus was trying to show, it seemed to me, that Mr Ewell could have beaten up Mayella. That much I could follow. If her right eye was blacked and she was beaten mostly on the right side of the face, it would tend to show that a left-handed person did it. Sherlock Holmes and Jem Finch would agree. But Tom Robinson could easily be left-handed, too.

Later, Atticus skilfully cross-examines Mayella Ewell and reveals to the court a life of poverty, personal abuse and dreadful loneliness. With a series of penetrating questions, he starts to cut into her story.

'Tell us once more, please, what happened?'

'I told'ja what happened.'

'You testified that you turned around and there he was. He choked you then?'

'Yes.'

'Then he released your throat and hit you?'

'I said he did.'

'He blacked your left eye with his right fist?'

'I ducked and it — it glanced, that's what it did. I ducked and it glanced off.' Mayella had finally seen the light.

'You're becoming suddenly clear on this point. A while ago you couldn't remember too well, could you?'

'I said he hit me.'

'All right. He choked you, he hit you, then raped you, that right?'

'It most certainly is.'

'You're a strong girl, what were you doing all the time, just standing there?'

'I told'ja I hollered'n'kicked'n'fought —'

Atticus reached up and took off his glasses, turned his good right eye to the witness, and rained questions on her. Judge Taylor said, 'One question at a time, Atticus. Give the witness a chance to answer.'

'All right, why didn't you run?'

'I tried to . . .'

'Tried to? What kept you from it?'

'I — he slung me down. That's what he did, he slung me down'n' got on top of me.'

'You were screaming all this time?'

'I certainly was.'

'Then why didn't the other children hear you? Where were they? At the dump?'

No answer.

'Where were they?'

'Why didn't your screams make them come running? The dump's closer than the woods, isn't it?'

No answer.

'Or didn't you scream until you saw your father in the window? You didn't think to scream until then, did you?'

No answer.

'Did you scream first at your father instead of at Tom Robinson? Was that it?'

No answer.

'Who beat you up? Tom Robinson or your father?'

No answer.

'What did your father see in the window, the crime of rape, or the best defence to it? Why don't you tell the truth, child? Didn't Bob Ewell beat you up?'

When Atticus turned away from Mayella he looked like his stomach hurt, but Mayella's face was a mixture of terror and fury. Atticus sat down wearily and polished his glasses with his handkerchief.

Suddenly Mayella became articulate. 'I got somethin' to say,' she said.

Atticus raised his head. 'Do you want to tell us what happened?'

But she did not hear the compassion in his invitation. 'I got somethin' to say an' then I ain't gonna say no more. That nigger yonder took advantage of me, an' if you fine fancy gentlemen don't wanta do nothin' about it then you're all yellow stinkin' cowards, stinkin' cowards, the lot of you. Your fancy airs don't come to nothin' — your ma'amin' and Miss Mayellerin' don't come to nothin', Mr Finch —'

Commentary and issues

Could a black person expect justice from a totally white jury? The blacks are separated by colour, by separate housing, by education and by speech. Scout does not understand that the white community only expects Atticus to give a token defence for Tom Robinson. What they dislike is Atticus' determination to do his best for him.

54. Why does Atticus defend Tom Robinson so strongly?

The language of Harper Lee

Passages of description contrast with the cut-and-thrust of the cross-examination. Atticus' questions are short and sharp and the description has very few adjectives and adverbs. It relies heavily on powerful verbs and nouns.

Within the detailed description of the poverty-stricken squalor in which the Ewells live there is contrast too, in Mayella's "... brilliant red geraniums, cared for as tenderly as if they belonged to Miss Maudie Atkinson ..." This link to Miss Maudie gives the impression that Mayella does have some sense of decency.

The description of the Ewell house just before Bob Ewell gives evidence positions us as readers. The language makes us feel negative towards Bob Ewell before he speaks one word. Note also how the Ewell hovel is contrasted to the homes of the black community: "... their cabins looked neat and snug ..."

Spoken language is also used for characterisation. In court Bob Ewell's language is insulting and indecent: "I seen that black nigger yonder ruttin on my Mayella." In contrast, Atticus is courteous and formal in his speech.

55. What questions make Bob Ewell angry? Why?

56. What impression do you get of Atticus as a lawyer? Include evidence from the story to support your answer.

57. (a) Atticus often pushes up his glasses or pushes up his hat. You can find references to this in chapters 5, 10, 15 and 30, for example. Find these descriptions and describe what each action means.
(b) During the cross-examination of Mayella Ewell Atticus does something else with his glasses. What does he do and what do you feel this action means?

58. (a) Find five words and phrases Harper Lee uses to describe Mayella.
(b) How do they make you feel about her?

59. Describe what you think might have happened to Mayella after the trial was over.

60. In groups act out the trial scene.

61. In the 1930s the Ewells were considered "white trash". How would society view them today? Do you feel they would be treated differently? Explain.

CHAPTER 19

Atticus' only witness is Tom Robinson who testifies that Mayella Ewell often asked him to do odd jobs. Tom Robinson says he feels sorry for Mayella; this, however, is a blunder for no black should feel sorry for a white. As Tom Robinson gives his testimony Scout comes to see that Mayella Ewell "... was even lonelier than Boo Radley, who had not been out of the house in twenty-five years." Having Tom Robinson do odd jobs for her is Mayella's only means of human contact outside her disreputable family. Tom claims that on the occasion of the alleged rape Mayella Ewell made sexual advances to him. He tried to resist, then Bob Ewell appeared at the window and in fright Tom ran out the door. When asked why he was scared, Tom replies: "Mr Finch, if you was a nigger like me, you'd be scared, too."

The cross-examination begins. Dill is so upset by the cruel harassment of Tom Robinson by Bob Ewell's solicitor, Mr Gilmer, that he and Scout have to leave the courtroom.

> 62. In small groups read the evidence of the sheriff, Bob and Mayella Ewell and Tom Robinson.
>   (a) Draw up two columns. In one column list in point form the evidence that you believe helps Tom Robinson. In the other column list the evidence that goes against him.
>   (b) What other questions would you have asked these witnesses?
>   (c) Your group is the jury. Reach a verdict based on the evidence you have heard.

CHAPTER 20

Outside the courtroom Dill and Scout meet Mr Dolphus Raymond who is thought of as the town drunk and who lives with the blacks. He reveals to them the secret of his drinking bag which everyone thinks is full of whisky but really contains only Coke. This is a lesson to Scout not to judge people by rumours but to try to see each person's point of view. She asks him why he has entrusted them with his secret.

'Because you're children and you can understand it,' he said, 'and because I heard that one —'

He jerked his head at Dill: 'Things haven't caught up with that one's instinct yet. Let him get a little older and he won't get sick and cry. Maybe things'll strike him as being — not quite right, say, but he won't cry, not when he gets a few years on him.'

'Cry about what, Mr Raymond?' Dill's maleness was beginning to assert itself.

'Cry about the simple hell people give other people — without even thinking. Cry about the hell white people give coloured folks, without even stopping to think that they're people, too.'

'Atticus says cheatin' a coloured man is ten times worse than cheatin' a white man,' I muttered. 'Says it's the worst thing you can do.'

Mr Raymond said, 'I don't reckon it's — Miss Jean Louise, you don't know your pa's not a run-of-the-mill man, it'll take a few years for that to sink in — you haven't seen enough of the world yet. You haven't seen this town, but all you gotta do is step back inside the courthouse.'

63. What does Mr Dolphus Raymond mean by "the simple hell people give other people"?

64. Why does Mr Raymond pretend to be drunk?

65. What do you think Scout learnt from talking to Mr Raymond?

66. Read Atticus' summing up in the second half of the chapter.
   (a) In his summing up what did Atticus identify as Tom Robinson's "mistake"?
   (b) Why was it a mistake?

CHAPTERS 21 & 22

Although Jem is confident Atticus has won the case the Reverend Sykes prepares him for the inevitable: "... I ain't ever seen any jury decide in favour of a coloured man over a white man ..."

In the courtroom, as Scout waits for the jury to hand down its verdict, she experiences the same dreamlike feeling as on the morning her father shot the mad dog: "when the mockingbirds were still, and the carpenters had stopped hammering ..." It was, she says, "like watching Atticus walk into the street, raise a rifle to his shoulder and pull the trigger, but watching all the time knowing that the gun was empty."

The jury, inevitably, finds Tom Robinson guilty.

Afterwards, at home Jem weeps at the injustice of the court. The people of Maycomb accept the judgement, and gifts from the black community appear on the doorstep in gratitude to Atticus. It is left up to Miss Maudie to explain to the children the significance of the fact that the jury took a long time to convict Tom Robinson. In this there is hope — "... it's just a baby step, but it's a step."

Aunt Alexandra shows qualities of concern and support that appear to help Atticus in defeat.

Bob Ewell spits in Atticus' face and this act introduces the idea of revenge which runs through the last part of the story.

CHAPTER 23

Jem talks about the unfairness of the jury system with his father and is able to carry out a mature discussion with him. Atticus understands Jem's reservations:

'If you had been on that jury, son, and eleven other boys like you, Tom would be a free man,' said Atticus. 'So far nothing in your life has interfered with your reasoning process. Those are twelve reasonable men in everyday life, Tom's jury, but you saw something come between them and reason. You saw the same thing that night in front of the jail. When that crew went away, they didn't go as reasonable men, they went because we were there. There's something in our world that makes men lose their heads — they couldn't be fair if they tried. In our courts, when it's a white man's word against a black man's, the white man always wins. They're ugly, but those are the facts of life.'

'Doesn't make it right,' said Jem stolidly. He beat his fist softly on his knee. 'You can't just convict a man on evidence like that — you can't.'

'*You* couldn't, but *they* could and did. The older you grow the more of it you'll see. The one place where a man ought to get a square deal is in a court-room, be he any colour of the rainbow, but people have a way of carrying their resentments right into a jury box.'

When Jem asks ". . . why don't people like us and Miss Maudie ever sit on juries?"
Atticus answers:

'There are lots of reasons. For one thing, Miss Maudie can't serve on a jury because she's a woman.'

'You mean women in Alabama can't — ?' I was indignant.

'I do. I guess it's to protect our frail ladies from sordid cases like Tom's. Besides,' Atticus grinned, 'I doubt if we'd ever get a complete case tried — the ladies'd be interrupting to ask questions.'

Scout learns that it was Cunningham who stood up for Atticus and delayed the jury decision, and she resolves to have young Walter Cunningham over to dinner and perhaps to stay after school. Aunt Alexandra firmly opposes the idea and states, ". . . he — is — trash . . ." Her snobbishness distresses Scout, who still holds to the view that "There's just one kind of folks. Folks."

Commentary and issues

A combination of "simple hells people give other people" give us an understanding of the character of Maycomb. Central is the hell of prejudice demonstrated by the conviction of an innocent man because of his colour. There is also the hell of family life experienced by Boo Radley, Dill and Mayella Ewell, the hell of religious intolerance and the hell privileged people give to those beneath them. We are also given a glimpse of the hell of sexist attitudes.

The language of Harper Lee

The chapter begins with the words, "I wish Bob Ewell wouldn't chew tobacco", introducing humour into the serious theme of revenge. The conversation between Jem and Atticus uses powerful dialogue as the young boy grapples with the injustice he sees in the jury system. Notice how Harper Lee uses a contradiction for effect: "Atticus was speaking so quietly his last word crashed on our ears."

The language used by Atticus to explain the prejudices of the men is powerful: ". . . you saw something come between them and reason . . ."

69. What do you think Atticus means by this last statement?

70. What are Jem's objections to the jury system?

71. What did Atticus mean when he said, "If you had been on that jury, son, and eleven other boys like you, Tom would be a free man."?

72. (a) Atticus obviously feels strongly about prejudice against blacks. Do you think he feels the same way about prejudice towards women? Support your answer with evidence from the story.

   (b) How would you have reacted to what Atticus said about women and juries?

CHAPTER 24

Scout discovers what it is like to be a lady in polite Maycomb society when Aunt Alexandra holds a tea party for the missionary circle. Scout is guided through the party by the wise Miss Maudie. The women reveal their hypocrisy when they claim to be concerned about distant African tribes and yet condemn the "sulkiness of the darkies" in Maycomb. Miss Maudie, with a sharp tongue, cuts through the snobbishness of the women and earns the gratitude of Aunt Alexandra.

During the tea party Atticus arrives home with the news of Tom Robinson's death; he has been shot while trying to escape. Scout courageously follows her Aunt's example and calmly continues to take part in the tea party. She has learnt that there is much more to being a "lady" than she thought.

CHAPTER 25

"Why couldn't I mash him?" Scout is told by Jem not to kill a harmless insect because "they don't bother you". Later, when we hear Helen Robinson's reaction to being told of Tom's death, the symbol is repeated. She fell: "Like you'd step on an ant." Tom's death passes almost without comment by the townspeople. They are largely unmoved by a scathing editorial by B. B. Underwood in the local newspaper, written "so children could understand . . . He likened Tom's death to the senseless slaughter of songbirds by hunters and children . . ." It is here that the full impact of the mockingbird symbol is emphasised.

Then Mr Underwood's meaning became clear: Atticus had used every tool available to free men to save Tom Robinson, but in the secret courts of men's hearts Atticus had no case. Tom was a dead man the minute Mayella Ewell opened her mouth and screamed.

73. What do you think this means?

CHAPTERS 26 & 27

Scout is now in third grade and shows her growing maturity by realising the nuisance they must have been to Boo Radley.

She learns more about prejudice when her teacher Miss Gates condemns the Nazi persecution of the Jews in Germany. Scout remembers Miss Gates voicing her opinion after the trial that the blacks in Maycomb should be taught a lesson. "How", she asks Jem, "can you hate Hitler so bad an' then turn around and be ugly about folks right at home —?" Atticus represents reason and tolerance while many characters, including Miss Gates, reveal their prejudice which is born out of ignorance and fear.

Bob Ewell breaks into Judge Taylor's house. He also hassles Helen Robinson and boasts he will have revenge on Atticus. The town prepares for the Halloween night; there are to be festivities including a pageant in which Scout will appear in costume.

CHAPTER 28

The children go to the pageant alone. Early in the chapter the mockingbird symbol appears again.

Jem said, 'Boo must not be at home. Listen.'

High above us in the darkness a solitary mocker poured out his repertoire in blissful unawareness of whose tree he sat in, plunging from the shrill kee, kee of the sunflower bird to the irascible qua-ack of a bluejay, to the sad lament of Poor Will, Poor Will, Poor Will.

This time Boo Radley is the solitary mockingbird figure. The bird copying the sounds of other birds symbolises the necessity for the children to step into the skins of other people, to walk around in their shoes, if they really want to understand their point of view.

Scout is humiliated when she misses her cue in the pageant. Jem comforts her as would Atticus. On the way home they are attacked in the dark by a man who tries to kill them. Scout escapes injury by the protection of the wire frame of her costume but Jem suffers a broken arm. During the scuffle Scout is aware of the presence of a fourth person who saves them and carries Jem to their house. Aunt Alexandra calls the doctor and the sheriff. The sheriff tells them he has found the dead body of Bob Ewell under a tree. Scout does not recognise the man who carried Jem to safety.

CHAPTER 29

Atticus had misjudged the extent to which Bob Ewell would seek revenge. It shows that Atticus was sometimes naive in judging people who were so different from him. He had made the same mistake in thinking there were no lynch mobs in Maycomb.

> 74. Do you think Atticus was naive in allowing the children to go to the pageant alone? Explain.

When Scout discovers Boo Radley was the mysterious stranger who saved them she is moved to tears.

CHAPTER 30

Atticus mistakenly believes that Jem killed Bob Ewell and feels that the truth should not be hushed up. He thinks Sheriff Tate is protecting Jem by claiming Bob Ewell fell on his own knife. However, it is Boo Radley the sheriff is protecting from any publicity. To expose him to publicity would be a sin. As Scout says, "it'd be sort of like shootin' a mockingbird . . .".

75. (a) Why does Scout consider Boo Radley to be like a mockingbird?
    (b) Have you known individuals who might be compared with a mockingbird, in the way Scout sees Boo?

CHAPTER 31

Scout takes Boo Radley to see Jem before he leaves. Boo touches the sleeping boy's hair and then Scout escorts him home. Standing on Boo's verandah she is "standing in his shoes". She thinks, "Atticus was right. One time he said you never really know a man until you stand in his shoes and walk around in them. Just standing on the Radley porch was enough."

Interpreting the issues

The novel contains many statements by the characters, each of which could spark off some interesting discussions.

76. In pairs discuss the following questions before writing your answers and sharing them with the class.
    (a) Identify who made each of the following statements, and in what situation.
    (b) In each case, what is the message?
    (c) Do you think the message is still relevant today?

1 'There's nothing more sickening to me than a low-grade white man who'll take advantage of a Negro's ignorance. Don't fool yourselves — it's all adding up, and one of these days we're going to pay the bill for it. I hope it's not in your children's time.'

2 'Children are children, but they can spot an evasion quicker than adults ...'

3 'The one thing that doesn't abide by majority rule is a person's conscience.'

4 'Simply because we were licked a hundred years before we started is no reason for us not to try to win.'

5 'Mr Finch, if you was a nigger like me, you'd be scared, too.'

6 '... people who run public education promote the stupid and idle along with the industrious — because all men are created equal, educators will gravely tell you, the children left behind suffer terrible feelings of inferiority. We know all men are not created equal in the sense some people would have us believe — some people are smarter than others, some people have more opportunity because they're born with it, some men make more money than others — some people are born gifted beyond the normal scope of most men.'

7 'It was her callin' Walter Cunningham trash that got me goin' ... I've got it all figured out, now. I've thought about it a lot lately and I've got it figured out. There's four kinds of folks in the world. There's the ordinary kind like us and the neighbours, there's the kind like the Cunninghams out in the woods, the kind like the Ewells down at the dump, and the Negroes.'

8 'You mean women in Alabama can't —?' I was indignant.

9 'At least we don't have that sin on our shoulders down here. People up there set 'em free, but you don't see 'em settin' at the table with 'em. At least we don't have the deceit to say to 'em yes you're as good as we are but stay away from us. Down here we just say you'll live your way and we'll live ours.'

77. The photographs below are from the movie of *To Kill a Mockingbird*.
    (a) Identify the event you believe each depicts, and the characters involved.
    (b) Place the events in the order in which they take place in the story.
    (c) Write a detailed caption for each photograph, including:
        • what is happening.
        • how the director has used camera angle and lighting to convey the atmosphere of the scene.

A

B

C

D

E

Text response — the analytical essay

There are many different ways that you can respond to this or any other novel; one of the most common is the analytical essay. The purpose of an analytical essay is to show:

- your understanding of the setting, the plot, the characterisation, the style and the themes
- your ability to relate the themes to issues in the wider world
- your ability to structure your ideas in an appropriate way for your audience
- your skill at using the appropriate language for your audience
- your skill at using relevant quotes from the text to support your point of view.

78. Read the following analytical essay by a student. Note the structure and language features.

Structure

Language features

Topic: Explain how Harper Lee develops the symbol of the mockingbird in the novel

Atticus Finch says it is "a sin to kill a mockingbird." This concept, the senseless persecution of an innocent individual, is central to Harper Lee's novel. Mockingbirds are not only symbols of innocence; they are also symbols of happiness and to kill them is evil. Harper Lee uses powerful contrasts to highlight the depth of her symbolism: "happiness and innocence" is contrasted with "death and evil". When a mockingbird falls silent it is a symbol of impending doom. Boo Radley and Tom Robinson are both mockingbird figures, innocent yet condemned through the prejudices of society.

Arthur (Boo) Radley is a prisoner in his own home, kept in confinement by his god-fearing Baptist family. Despite this treatment Boo remains gentle and harmless. However, people tell stories about how he eats squirrels and cats and poisons the pecan nuts in the school yard. To the community Boo is a "malevolent phantom".

Gradually Scout and Jem begin to see things from Boo's point of view. Like the mockingbird Boo gives pleasure: for example, the gifts in the tree, the blanket placed around their shoulders as they watch Miss Maudie's home go up in flames. Finally he saves Scout's and Jem's lives. Scout realises that

Structure annotations:
- Main character and theme are introduced.
- Author is identified.
- comment about style
- Topic sentence introduces new point.
- Details support topic sentence.
- topic sentence
- Details support topic sentence.

Language features annotations:
- Quote supports statement.
- Present tense creates a sense that the novel is still important today.
- Shows how Harper Lee creates her effects.
- Use of nickname shows knowledge of character.
- Adjectives add colour.
- Quote gives support.
- link words

to drag Boo into the limelight would be like "shooting a mockingbird": an evil act.

Tom Robinson is also a mockingbird. A black man with a good reputation, he is accused of raping a white girl. He explains he was only in the house to help her. However, he condemns himself in the eyes of the jury when he says he felt sorry for her. The prosecutor responds in amazement. "*You* felt sorry for *her*, you felt *sorry* for her?"

Harper Lee uses rapid dialogue in the courtroom scene to emphasise the way the prosecutor attacks Tom, like an attack on an innocent mockingbird. Tom, innocent and blameless, is condemned by a prejudiced society. The jury would rather see a black man convicted than see a white woman's word questioned.

As the jury returns to give the verdict, Scout remembers the day Atticus confronted the mad dog. She remembers how the mockingbirds went silent, a symbol that something dreadful was about to happen. Harper Lee uses powerful imagery to emphasise the importance of the symbol: ". . . the mockingbirds are still." Words like "creeping", "cold", "shivered" contrast with the heat of summer. Her use of repetition "guilty . . . guilty . . . guilty" slams into Scout and Jem like the symbolic shooting of the mockingbird Tom.

The mockingbird symbol also involves the broader themes of justice and how it can destroy an innocent person. Harper Lee exposes not just the prejudices of Maycomb but the ugly nature of such beliefs in society as a whole. Atticus and Miss Maudie are presented as characters who represent justice and open-mindedness. Both say it is a sin to kill a mockingbird. Justice is betrayed when the jury ignore the evidence and destroy the mockingbird figure of Tom Robinson.

The novel's title reflects the importance of the symbol of the mockingbird which is best summed up in the words of Miss Maudie: ". . they don't do one thing but sing their hearts out for us. That's why it's a sin to kill a mockingbird."

Tim Gotterson
(student)

Annotations (left margin):
- topic sentence
- Details support topic sentence.
- comment about style
- topic sentence
- comment about style
- topic sentence
- Details support topic sentence.
- Conclusion sums up the writer's opinion.

Annotations (right margin):
- Quote adds support.
- Short, provocative sentence matches Harper Lee's style.
- Pronouns used as Tom's character and actions are analysed.
- Quote gives emphasis.
- Shows how Harper Lee brings her symbols to life.
- strong opinion
- link between two parts of the novel
- Shows how Harper Lee creates the symbols.
- Shows how the characters fit into the theme.
- Links back to the introduction.

Text response assessment sheet

Criteria	Level of achievement — tick the appropriate point on the line.
1. Knowledge of the text • Does the essay show understanding of the various elements of the novel? • Have relevant examples been used? • Is the novel related to aspects of the wider world?	Major problems Highly successful
2. Structure of the essay • Does the essay answer the question? • Is the structure appropriate for the audience? • Is it logical? • Are the different aspects connected effectively? • Does the introduction clearly outline the intent? • Does the conclusion tie together the main ideas?	
3. Language and presentation • Is the language and presentation appropriate for the audience? • Is it fluent and clear? • Are spelling and punctuation correct? • Are the sentences constructed correctly? • Are the paragraphs linked? • Has the correct format been used for quoting from the text?	

Assessment by:... **of essay by:** ....

80. **Your turn.** Complete an essay on the following topic:

> Although Atticus describes Mrs Dubose as "the bravest person I ever knew", it is Atticus himself who is the real hero of the novel. Examine the character of Atticus and comment on whether you believe him to be a hero.

Below is the introduction and conclusion. Complete the essay by writing paragraphs of your own. To help you, a suggested main idea for each paragraph has been included.

Introduction

In the novel *To Kill a Mockingbird*, Atticus Finch is not the typical Maycomb citizen. He is the role model, showing his natural courage, tolerance and fairness towards life and the people of Maycomb. Atticus appears as a hero because he stands up for what is right, has respect for others and is a symbol of reason and justice.

Paragraph 2 — Does not conform to others. Believes in individual conscience.

Paragraph 3 — Teaches respect for other people.

Paragraph 4 — Shoots dog — courageous act.

Paragraph 5 — Defends Tom Robinson — a higher form of courage.

Paragraph 6 — He is a symbol of reason and justice.

Conclusion

Atticus Finch is a figure of justice and fairness in this novel. He dares to be an individual while others conform. He dares to keep an open mind while others prejudge. "So far nothing in your life has interfered with your reasoning process," he says to Jem, referring to Maycomb's conformist disease. Atticus Finch is a role model not only for the unfair and unjust society of Maycomb, but for all societies in all times.

On your own

81. In about 500 words, respond to one of the following topics in essay form. Ensure that you refer to incidents and extracts from the novel to support your view. Before you begin, look again at the assessment sheet on page 70 as a guide to your response.
    (a) Explain the significance of the title, *To Kill a Mockingbird*.
    (b) "I wanted you to see what real courage is, instead of getting the idea that courage is a man with a gun." What kinds of heroism or courage are shown in *To Kill a Mockingbird*?
    (c) Comment on the different forms of prejudice explored in *To Kill a Mockingbird*.
    (d) *To Kill a Mockingbird* traces Scout's growing awareness of the adult world. Identify her experiences and comment on how they affect her.
    (e) The success of Harper Lee's novel *To Kill a Mockingbird* is largely due to her skilful use of language: powerful imagery, interesting symbolism, provocative topic sentences and tight dialogue. Comment on how these and other language features give impact to the story.

82. Make a copy of the assessment sheet on page 70 and have your partner assess your essay. Perhaps you could include this essay in your folio.

SELF ASSESSMENT

Name: ....

1. Can I?

Write "yes" or "no" in the box. If you write "no", go back over your work until you can write "yes".

- Define the elements of the novel *To Kill a Mockingbird* .... ☐
- Give a detailed account of the plot .... ☐
- Comment on the issues and language features .... ☐
- Write an analytical essay .... ☐

2. Your reaction

(a) Which extract did you like best? Say why.

(b) Which activity did you like best? Say why.

(c) Which skill do you need to work on most? What can you do to improve it?

3. For your folio

From the work you have done in this chapter, choose the pieces you want to include in your folio. Each piece of work in your folio should include a cover sheet which shows the date it was completed, the title, the purpose and the audience.

4. Ongoing skills

Complete the table below by:
- placing a tick at the point at which you feel you usually achieve in each skill
- shading in the range of your achievement in each skill.

When you have completed the table place it in your folio.

Am I improving in these skills?	Level of achievement		
	Same as before	Improving	Much better
Example: Oral work		✓	
Reading a novel			
Cooperating in group work			
Explaining my answers			
Writing extended answers			
Discussing issues			
Using powerful language			
Using correct spelling and punctuation			
Seeing things from someone else's point of view			

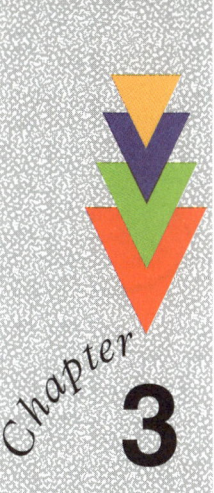

"Poetry is the spontaneous overflow of powerful feelings."

3 POETRY

Content

Skills

- What is poetry?
- What is its purpose?
- What is its relevance?
- Poetic techniques
- Issues
- Ideas, opinions
- Analysing a poem
- Writing poetry

- Understanding poetic techniques
- Knowing different poetic forms
- Expressing ideas, feelings and opinions
- Analysing poetry
- Responding to poetry
- Writing poetry

 # The power of poetry

We all have powerful feelings. Some of us express them in music, some of us express them in art, but all of us can express them in poetry. Words of intense pain or joy are the dawn of a poem, no matter how short, no matter how simple, no matter how personal.

The poem itself is not the experience; it is an exploration of the experience. Read what Gwendolyn MacEwen has to say.

LET ME MAKE THIS PERFECTLY CLEAR

Let me make this perfectly clear.
I have never written anything because it is a Poem.
This is a mistake you always make about me,
A dangerous mistake. I promise you
I am not writing this because it is a Poem.

You suspect this is a posture or an act.
I am sorry to tell you it is not an act.

You actually think I care if this
Poem gets off the ground or not. Well
I don't care if this poem gets off the ground or not
And neither should you.
All I have ever cared about
And all you should ever care about
Is what happens when you lift your eyes from this page.

Do not think for one minute it is the Poem that matters.
It is not the Poem that matters.
You can shove the Poem.
What matters is what is out there in the large dark
And in the long light,
Breathing.

Gwendolyn MacEwen

1. Read the poem and in pairs discuss what you feel it means.

2. Record in your journal your thoughts on the last three lines.

Does poetry matter?

> Most people can't be bothered with poetry ... Somehow they have become convinced that poetry is too difficult, too mysterious, not for them. They haven't had the good fortune to find out that reading poetry can help you live your life.
>
> *Wendy Cope*

Even when you think poetry is not relevant you can still find yourself in the world of poetry, as this student's poem shows. It is filled with defiance, pain and tenderness.

Hot wet pillows

As soon as he entered
I knew he'd attack:

'You
You up the back
Yes you, Josh,
Surly looks
No books
Talking
Clowning
For attention —
— Pay attention!'

Silently I lock him out —
All of them out.

What do I care about
Wordsworth's wussy daffodils
Or Lawson's boring bush.

Do they care
What's in my head
At night
Alone
Anger grown?
Words pour out
On hot wet pillows
Escaping
From the prison
That I lock them in.
No-one knows, no-one knows.

Would Wordsworth have cared?
Would Lawson?
Will you
If I show you this?

Josh Cullen (Student)

3. How do you feel as you read this poem?

4. (a) What sort of student do you think Josh is?
   (b) Why do you think Josh is reluctant to expose his feelings?

5. (a) Why do you think he chose the title "Hot wet pillows"?
   (b) What image does the title convey to you?

6. Who do you think "you" is in the last line?

Sometimes it's hard to open the door to your mind — but if you can open it and show people what's inside you'll be surprised how much they appreciate it and how much you'll learn about yourself.

The door

Go and open the door.
  Maybe outside there's
  a tree, or a wood,
  a garden,
  or a magic city.

Go and open the door.
  Maybe a dog's rummaging.
  Maybe you'll see a face,
or an eye,
or the picture
          of a picture.

Go and open the door.
  If there's a fog
  it will clear.

Go and open the door.
  Even if there's only
  the darkness ticking,
  even if there's only
  the hollow wind,
  even if
        nothing
              is there,
go and open the door.

At least
there'll be
a draught.

Miroslav Holub
trans. *Ian Milner* and
George Theiner

7. What do you think the door represents?

8. What sorts of experiences does Miroslav Holub claim you will have if you open the door?

9. Imagine you could open a door of your own. Describe your discoveries in a poem beginning —
    If I open the door . . .

When you've got something strong or urgent to say, don't mince words —
say it in a poem. Look at how the following poems almost throw themselves
at you.

DOWN THE DRAIN

She curls into a bath
    where only mist
can hold her
    & hide her
eyes dripping like a tap
    as saline water cools

now only the hands
of the clock hold her,
    & they have turned
for two hours

but she is still hot

burning with a rage
her attacker
    may never understand

water subsides with sobs
    while scum —
clings to the gloss of enamel
    & wanders undetected

but all gloss now is dulled

she spins with the suck
of a plughole
    losing some of him —
too much of herself —
    anti-clockwise

while in another hemisphere
    her sisters lose too

clockwise.

          Geoff Goodfellow

The child who walks backwards

My next-door neighbour tells me
her child runs into things.
Cupboard corners and doorknobs
have pounded their shapes
into his face. She says
he is bothered by dreams,
rises in sleep from his bed
to steal through the halls
and plummet like a wounded bird
down the flight of stairs.

This child who climbed my maple
with the sureness of a cat
trips in his room, cracks
his skull on the bedpost,
smacks his cheeks on the floor.
When I ask about the burns
on the back of his knee,
his mother tells me
he walks backwards
into fireplace grates
or sits and stares at flames
while sparks burn stars in his skin.

Other children write their names
on the casts that hold
his small bones.
His mother tells me
he runs into things,
walks backwards,
breaks his leg
while she lies
sleeping.

Lorna Crozier

Hero

'Of course I took the drugs. Look, son,
there's no fair play, no gentlemen,
no amateurs, just winning.
How old are you? Fifteen? Well,
you should know that
no one runs for fun — well, not beyond
the schoolboy stuff, eleven or twelve years old.
I'd been a pro for years;
my job — to get that Gold.

Mind you, we English are an odd lot:
like to believe we love the slob that fails,
the gentlemanly third; so
any gap-toothed yob who gets the glory
also gets some gentlemanly trait:
helps cripples get across
the street, nice to small animals.
You know the kind of thing,
it helps the public feel it's
all legit; that sportsmanship is real and that
it's all clean fun —
the strongest, bravest, fittest
best man won.

Yeah, Steroids . . . Who do <u>you</u> think? . . . Oh, don't be wet —
My coach, of course, he used to get them
through this vet . . . The side effects? Well, not so bad
as these things go — for eighteen months or so
I didn't have much use for girls. But, by then I was training
for the Big One — got to keep the body pure,
not waste an ounce of effort.'

He gives a great guffaw.
A chain of spittle
rattles down the front of
his pyjama jacket.
He wipes his mouth;
His eyes don't laugh at all.

'. . . Do it again? Of course I would —
I'd cheat, I'd box, I'd spike, I'd pay the devil's price
to be that good again
for just one day. You see, at twenty-three
I peaked — got all I ever wanted:
all anyone would ever want from me.
After the race, this interviewer told me
Fifty million people's hopes and dreams had been
fulfilled — a Gold!
How many ever get that chance? I did.
Would you say No to that?
Of course not.

Damn! The bell. You'd better go, they're pretty strict.
Yeah, leave the flowers there on the top,
the nurse'll get some water and a vase.'

Mick Gowar

10. Identify the issues raised in these poems.

11. (a) Which of the issues do you feel most strongly about? Explain.
    (b) In the poem that raises this issue, what emotions has the poet stirred
        in you? Use examples from the poem to support your answer.

12. Write a poem of your own on an issue of your choice. You may wish to use
    one of these poems as a model.

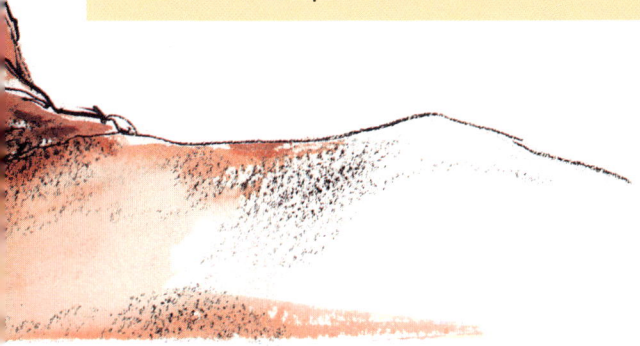

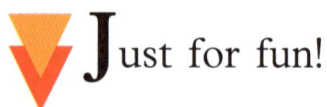 **J**ust for fun!

Cousin Nell
married a frogman
in the hope
that one day
he would turn into
a handsome prince.

Instead he turned into
a sewage pipe
near Gravesend
and was never seen again.

Cousin Daisy's
favourite sport
was standing
on streetcorners.

She contracted
with ease
a funny disease.
Notwithstanding.

Roger McGough

Jennifer Chubb-Challoner
the Cheltenham Ladies
Triple Jump Champion

was first spotted
by a peepingtom talentscout
while still at Junior School

when she won
the 3-legged race
all on her own.

 Poetic techniques

To create the effect that will capture and touch your audience there are many techniques you can use. When you're reading someone else's poem see if you can first feel the depth of their meaning without analysing. As you read the poem again and again you will become aware of the techniques the poet has used to make sure you are gripped; then layer by layer the poem unfolds.

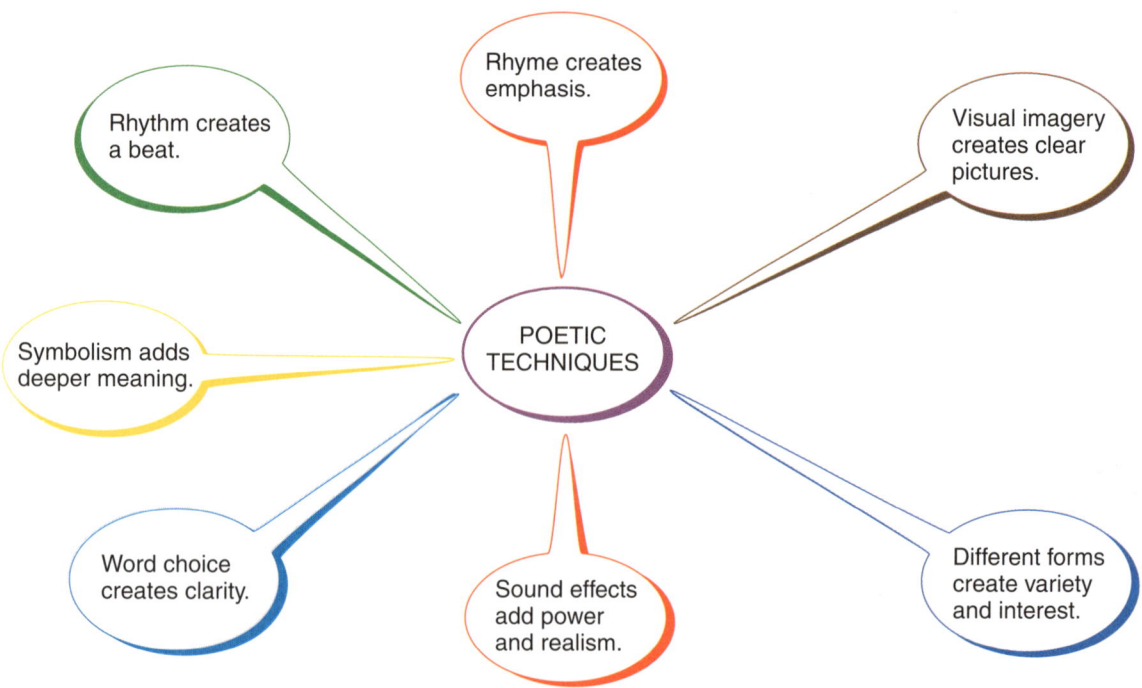

Visual imagery

Metaphors: describing something as something else to create an interesting and more powerful effect.

HEADACHE

It's a lump in your head
it's the blade of a knife
it's your veins bursting
it's your skull squeezing your brain
it's a headache.

Michael Rosen

15. How does the poem make you feel?

16. Which of the metaphors do you like best? Explain.

17. Use metaphors to write a poem with the title "Stomach-ache".

Similes: an interesting way of comparing one thing to something else. This is the most common way of creating an image.

Precious stones

An emerald is as green as grass;
   A ruby red as blood;
A sapphire shines as blue as heaven;
   A flint lies in the mud.

A diamond is a brilliant stone,
   To catch the world's desire;
An opal holds a fiery spark;
   But a flint holds fire.

Christina Rossetti

Personification: treating a non-living object as though it had a life of its own. In its simplest form an object like the moon is given human characteristics.

The moon

The moon was but a chin of gold
A night or two ago,
And now she turns her perfect face
Upon the world below.

Emily Dickinson

13. Which stone do you think Christina Rossetti considers to be the most precious? Why?

14. Which simile do you like best? Why?

18. What are the two human features given to the moon?

19. Use personification to write a poem with the title "The sun".

In Sylvia Plath's poem, "Cut", a cut finger and the poet's blood are described as people.

Cut

What a thrill —
My thumb instead of an onion.
The top quite gone
Except for a sort of a hinge

Of skin,
A flap like a hat,
Dead white.
Then that red plush.

Little pilgrim,
The Indian's axed your scalp.
Your turkey wattle
Carpet rolls

Straight from the heart.
I step on it,
Clutching my bottle
Of pink fizz.

A celebration, this is.
Out of a gap
A million soldiers run,
Redcoats, every one.

personification

Whose side are they on?
O my
Homunculus, I am ill.
I have taken a pill to kill

The thin
Papery feeling.
Saboteur,
Kamikaze man —

The stain on your
Gauze Ku Klux Klan
Babushka
Darkens and tarnishes and when

The balled
Pulp of your heart
Confronts its small
Mill of silence

How you jump —
Trepanned veteran,
Dirty girl,
Thumb stump.

Sylvia Plath

20. Explain the meaning of the two marked examples of personification.

21. What other examples of personification can you find in this poem?

22. Can you find a simile and a metaphor?

23. What effect do you feel these techniques have on the poem?

Word choice

Powerful words create powerful poetry. Look at the striking verbs, adjectives, adverbs and nouns that the Russian poet Yevtushenko uses in this description.

Picture of childhood

Elbowing our way, we run.
Someone is being beaten up in the market.
You wouldn't want to miss it!
We put on speed, racing to the uproar,
scooping up water in our felt-boots
and forgetting to wipe our sniffles.

And stood stock-still . . . In our little hearts something
    tightened,

when we saw how the ring of sheepskin coats,
fur-coats, hooded coats, was contracting.
how he stood up near the green vegetable stall
with his head pulled into his shoulders from the hail
of jabs, kicks, spitting, slaps in the face.

Suddenly someone from the left bashed his forehead
    with a chunk of ice.

Blood appeared — and then they started in, in earnest.
All piled up in a heap they began to scream together,
pounding with sticks, reins,
and iron pins out of wheels.

In vain he wheezed to them: 'Mates, you're my mates —
what's the matter?'

The mob wanted to make a job of it.
The mob were quite deaf. They were raging.
The mob grumbled at those who weren't putting the
    boots in,
and they trampled something that looked like a body
into the spring snow that was turning into mud.

They beat him up with relish. With ingenuity. Juicy.
I saw how skilfully and precisely
one man kept putting the boots in,
boots with greasy tags on them,
right under the belt of the man who was down,
smothered in mud and *dungy* water.

powerful nouns

powerful verbs

powerful adverbs

powerful adjectives

(continued)

Their owner, a bloke with an honest enough mug,
very proud of his high principles,
was saying with each kick: 'We won't let you get away
    with it!'
booting him deliberately, with the utmost conviction,
and, sweat pouring, with a red face, he jovially called
    to me:
'Come on youngster, be in it!'
I can't remember — how many there were, making a
    din, beating him up.

It may have been a hundred, it may have been more,
but I, just a boy, wept for shame.
And if a hundred are beating somebody up,
howling in a frenzy, — even if for a good cause,
I will never make a hundred and one!

Yevgeny Yevtushenko

powerful
participles

24. What drew you into this poem and made you follow it to the end?

25. What message does the poem have for you?

26. Find other examples in the poem of powerful nouns, verbs, adjectives and adverbs.

27. What other techniques can you find that make the poem more powerful?

28. Give the poem a title of your own.

Be specific

Don't say you saw a bird; you saw a swallow,
Or a great horned owl, a hawk or oriole.

Don't just tell me that he flew;
That's what any bird can do;
Say he darted, circled, swooped, or lilted in the blue.

Don't say the sky behind the bird was pretty;
It was watermelon pink streaked through with gold;
Gold bubbled like a fountain
From a pepperminted mountain
And shone like Persian rugs when they are old.

Don't tell me that the air was sweet with fragrance;
Say it smelled of minted grass and lilac bloom;
Don't say your heart was swinging;
Name the tune that it was singing,
And how the moonlight's neon filled the room.

Don't say the evening creatures all were playing;
Mention tree toad's twanging, screeching fiddle notes.
Picture cricket's constant strumming
To the mass mosquitoes humming
While the frogs are singing bass deep in their throats.

Don't use a word that's good for all the senses
There's a word for every feeling one can feel
If you'd want your lines terrific;
Then do make your words specific,
For words can paint a picture that is real.

    The messages brought by the senses
    Are among life's greatest recompenses.

Mauree Applegate

29. Which of the stanzas did you enjoy most? Say why.

30. What is the overall message in the poem?

31. "Words can paint a picture that is real." Which words did this for you?

32. Complete your own stanza starting with:
    Don't ...

Sound effects

Onomatopoeia: using words that sound like their meaning —

   the **crunch** of walking on gravel
   the **pop** of a champagne cork

Onomatopoeia creates powerful sound images. You don't just read what is happening; you can *hear* what is happening.

This poem by Jessie Pope is filled with onomatopoeia. Each one of these sounds evokes striking images.

NOISE

I like noise.
The whoop of a boy, the thud of a hoof,
The rattle of rain on a galvanised roof,
The hubbub of traffic, the roar of a train,
The throb of machinery numbing the brain,
The switching of wires in an overhead tram,
The rush of the wind, a door on the slam,
The boom of the thunder, the crash of the waves,
The din of a river that races and raves,
The crack of a rifle, the clank of a pail,
The strident tattoo of a swift-slapping sail —
From any old sound that the silence destroys
Arises a gamut of soul-stirring joys.
I like noise.

Jessie Pope

33. Which examples of onomatopoeia do you find most striking?

34. (a) Brainstorm and list sounds you enjoy, dislike or find strange.
    (b) Write a short poem of your own starting:
       I like noise ... or
       I dread noise ... or
       Strange sounds ...

Assonance and alliteration: the repetition of sounds for effect

Assonance is the repetition of vowel sounds. For example, you could write:

   Joe drove home so slowly.

The sound does not necessarily have to be spelt the same way in each case; it's the sound that counts!

Alliteration is the repetition of the first letter of a word in the words that follow it; usually the repeated letter is a consonant. An old favourite is:

   Peter Piper picked a peck of pickled peppers.

Both assonance and alliteration are powerful ways to:
- force the poem to flow more quickly as the sounds are repeated
- slow the poem down as each word is emphasised
- create clear images
- add humour
- create a certain mood or atmosphere — either heavy or light, quick or slow.

Look at the poem below. See how Erica Fryberg uses alliteration and assonance for emphasis and imagery.

Friendships

The teacher forced alliances —
Tried to teach 'awareness'.
We were made to expose likes and dislikes, thoughts and feelings.
We played name-games, face-games, voice-games,
Formed outer shells of friendship:
Thin skins, surface gloss, shallow shine,
Veneer!
Plywood performances and laminex laughter
A furniture-display arranged
By her, for her.
And then she left.

The polish dulled . . .
Smeared with embarrassment.
Each face a flimsy chair
Separate
No more the matching suite.
Tentative questions emerged.
I observed, listened, thought and dropped cautious words.
One girl was eager, alert and witty.
I edged closer . . .
          and conversed.
Similar likes! Similar dislikes! Similar opinions!
There *were* irritations
But minor.

Minor became major.
When someone else appeared she reflected *their* ideas . . .
A mirror.
Changing to fit her company
As a beanbag moulds around a rear.

She did *not* think for herself —
She meekly just agreed . . .
A coat-hanger for others' whims.
Very pretty upholstery,
Comfortable padding,
But no firm foundation.
No sound support from supple springs
Thus crumpling under pressure.

I'm secure, I'm dramatic, I'm aggressive.
I need someone who bounces back . . .

A trampoline?

Erica Fryberg (aged 13)

Symbolism

Your poems can become more intriguing and more powerful if you give your words and phrases a double meaning. Perhaps a dark cloud could signify anger, a rose could signify love, a child could signify innocence. This is called using symbols. Look at how William Blake has used a growing apple tree to symbolise his growing anger.

A POISON TREE

I was angry with my friend:
I told my wrath, my wrath did end.
I was angry with my foe:
I told it not, my wrath did grow.

And I watered it in fears,
Night and morning with my tears;
And I sunned it with smiles,
And with soft deceitful wiles.

And it grew both day and night,
Till it bore an apple bright;
And my foe beheld it shine,
And he knew that it was mine,

And into my garden stole
When the night had veiled the pole:
In the morning glad I see
My foe outstretched beneath the tree.

William Blake

Rhythm

Rhythm is the flow of sound created by strong and soft beats. Rhythm creates speed and emphasis, strength and tension in a poem. As you read let the rhythm come naturally; don't try to understand every word. Sometimes the rhythm helps to make the meaning of the poem clear.

Working out the rhythm in a poem is called **scanning**. This allows us to see what the pattern of heavy (/) and light (×) beats is. Each individual pattern is called a "foot".

Classical patterns

The names given to the rhythmic patterns in poetry are mostly derived from Ancient Greek and Latin words. In Greek and Roman poetry, scanning was very important because the sense often depended on the stress given to particular syllables.

- A pattern beginning with a light beat followed by a heavy beat is called **iambic** and makes the rhythm skip along:

  ×　／　×　／　×　／　×　／
  He clasps the crag with crooked hands …

- A pattern beginning with a heavy beat followed by a light beat is called **trochaic** and gives the feeling of a march:

  ／　×　／　×　／　×　／
  Twinkle twinkle little star…

- A pattern which has a heavy beat followed by two soft beats is called **dactylic** and creates the rhythm of a waltz — 1 2 3, 1 2 3, 1 2 3:

  ／　×　×　／　×　×　／　×　×　／
  Twirling and whirling and dancing all night …

- A pattern which has two soft beats followed by a strong beat is called **anapaestic** and makes the rhythm leap along:

  ×　×　／　×　×　／
  It's a lump in your head

  ×　×　／　×　×　／
  it's the blade of a knife …

- The number of times these patterns are repeated in a line is called the **meter**. If it is repeated:

  once — it is called a **monometer**
  twice — it is a **dimeter**
  three times — it is a **trimeter**
  four times — it is a **tetrameter**
  five times — it is a **pentameter**.

  For example, the first line of the poem "Be specific" on page 85 is an iambic pentameter:

  ×　／　×　／　×　／　×　／　×　／
  Don't say you saw a bird; you saw a swallow.

Most poets vary the patterns in a poem; otherwise it can become very boring. So when you are scanning a poem be prepared to see a variety of patterns in both feet and meter. But why scan at all? How does it help you to appreciate what someone else is saying? How does it help *you* to express your thoughts and feelings in a more powerful way?

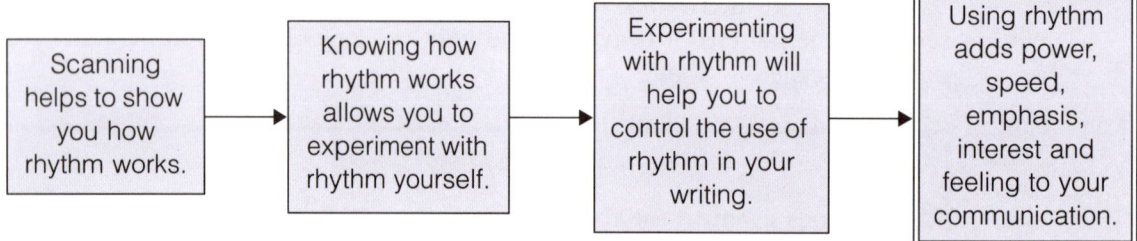

| Scanning helps to show you how rhythm works. | → | Knowing how rhythm works allows you to experiment with rhythm yourself. | → | Experimenting with rhythm will help you to control the use of rhythm in your writing. | → | Using rhythm adds power, speed, emphasis, interest and feeling to your communication. |

Rhythm is a powerful force in poetry. It is like music — it can move people because it creates a certain feeling. John Masefield has used rhythm to create not only the movement of the sea but also the feeling of longing.

Sea fever

I must go down to the seas again, to the lonely sea and the sky,
And all I ask is a tall ship and a star to steer her by,
And the wheel's kick and the wind's song and the white sail's shaking,
And a grey mist on the sea's face, and a grey dawn breaking.

I must go down to the seas again, for the call of the running tide
Is a wild call and a clear call that may not be denied;
And all I ask is a windy day with the white clouds flying,
And the flung spray and the blown spume, and the sea-gulls crying.

I must go down to the seas again, to the vagrant gypsy life,
To the gull's way and the whale's way where the wind's like a whetted knife;
And all I ask is a merry yarn from a laughing fellow-rover,
And quiet sleep and a sweet dream when the long trick's over.

John Masefield

43. In pairs, scan the first two lines of "Sea fever". To do this look again at page 89. Read the poem, marking the strong (/) beats first. Then add the soft (x) beats.

44. What type of rhythm is used? Again check with the examples on page 89 to see which one matches the pattern you have marked.

45. How does the poem make you feel about the sea?

46. Read the poem in pairs, concentrating on the rhythm.

47. (a) Find a poem of your own choice in which the rhythm strongly appeals to you.
    (b) Write it in your journal, noting title, poet's name and the title of the anthology where you found it.
    (c) Note why the rhythm appeals and explain the feeling it conveys.

Rhyme

Rhyme is the repetition of sounds. It helps to control the rhythm of your poem by forcing an emphasis on certain words. Rhyme can be at the end of the line (end rhyme), or within the line (internal rhyme). When you are describing a rhyming pattern you refer only to end rhyme — look at Roger McGough's poem, "Streemin".

Roger McGough

Streemin

Im in the botom streme   A
Which seems Im not brigth   B
dont like reading   C
cant hardly write   B

but all these divishns   D
arnt reely fair   E
look at the cemtery   F
no streemin there   E

Roger McGough

rhyming pattern

48. Write out the words that rhyme in the poem.

49. Do you think this poem has a serious message? What is it?

50. Write your own poem of four lines using the same rhyming pattern.

Notice how the rhyming pattern in Oodgeroo's poem forces you to pause at the end of each second line. The poet's anger comes through passionately this way.

Colour bar

When vile men jeer because my skin is brown,
This I live down.

But when a taunted child comes home in tears,
Fierce anger sears.

The colour bar! It shows the meaner mind
Of moron kind.

Men are but medieval yet, as long
As lives this wrong.

Could he but see, the colour-baiting clod
Is blaming God

Who made us all, and all His children He
Loves equally.

As long as brothers banned from brotherhood
You will exclude,

The Christianity you hold so high
Is but a lie,

Justice a cant of hypocrites, content
With precedent.

Oodgeroo of the tribe Noonuccal
(*formerly known as Kath Walker*)

51. Describe the rhyming pattern in this poem.

52. Why do you think Oodgeroo becomes angry when "... a taunted child comes home in tears"?

53. "Could he but see, the colour-baiting clod is blaming God". What meaning do you get from this part of the poem?

54. How does this poem make you feel?

Free verse

Free verse is the most modern of all forms. It does not have a patterned rhythm or rhyme. It does, however, have the natural rhythms of ordinary speech. The flow of the verse rises and falls as the emotions of the poet rise and fall. Free verse seems much more natural to us and gives the poet tremendous freedom and flexibility. However, there are many skills to develop when using free verse:
- When creating imagery you must have tight control over your words or the poem will seem sloppy.
- When creating mood you must have tight control over your rhythm or the poem will sound awkward.
- When exploring an idea or feeling you must have tight control over your structure or the poem will seem confusing.

The following poem by Steven Herrick is in very natural, but carefully constructed, free verse. When you read it you can almost hear him speaking.

To my son Joe

for the first five years
you'll be like your Dad
you'll fall over a lot
always be on the bottle
& stay awake all night.
then your Mother, who
until now
you've always trusted, will
send you off to a place
where men in shorts & long socks
named Mr Duffy will
teach you i comes before e
except after c
other boys will think of
stupid names to call you
when you get out for a duck
in the Final.
names like Slow Joe
or Boofhead.
your mother will tell you
to ignore them.
your Dad will tell you
to kick them in the guts.
thankfully
you never listen to him.
at thirteen
you'll get a cramp
in your stomach when you sit
next to Wendy Spencer.
don't worry.
this always happens around girls.
it will disappear when you turn 75.
when you leave school
relatives will ask you
what you want to do.

you'll tell them you
want to be like your Dad
they'll say A POET
you'll say NO, UNEMPLOYED.
around this time your Father
will ask you
to pay back the pocket-money
for the past 15 years
with Interest.
you'll tell him to
speak to your Mother.

Steven Herrick

55. Did you enjoy this poem? Explain.

56. Write out the part you feel has a natural rhythm.

57. What impression do you get of the father in this poem? Quote from the poem to support your answer.

58. How old do you think Joe is? Explain.

59. What part of the poem did you find most humorous?

60. Imagine you were writing a poem to your son or daughter. Write the first 5–10 lines.

In this poem by Bruce Dawe notice how you are carried along at a rapid pace by the natural rhythm and the internal rhyme created by the words, "I said".

Mrs Swipe speaks out

So I said to her I said
I'm not one to complain
I said as you know only too well
I said but if you think I'm going to
put up with this nonsense indefinitely
you've got another think coming oh yes I said
please don't think you can come the bounce
on me I said because I've had just about
enough thank you very much I said
you can walk the whole length and breadth
of Varicose Street I said and you won't find
a more long-suffering and charitable
person than yours truly I said
but like the Good Book says every worm
must have its day and mine is
just around the corner I said so you needn't
stand there looking four-eyed and fish-faced
as if Meadow-Lea wouldn't melt in your mouth
since I have not the slightest intention of
prolonging this conversation any further
live and let live I said even though it seems
to me there's some as would be hard-pressed
to justify their miserable
existence naming no names of course
and I dropped the paper parcel of prawn-shells
over her side of the fence I believe
these are yours madam I said and although
it was a horrible cold day the look on its face
as I walked away kept me warm as toast
for the rest of the morning!

Bruce Dawe

61. Practise reading the poem to yourself, then read it aloud to a partner.

62. What effect does reading the poem aloud have on the poem?

63. Suggest a title of your own for this poem.

64. Write several lines of a poem beginning:
    So I said to him I said . . .

Different forms of poetry

Although modern writers tend to use free verse, there are many other structures that you can use depending on what you want to say and the mood you want to create.

SOME POETIC FORMS

Ballad

A ballad tells a story — usually of love or tragedy. It has a regular rhythm and rhyme which help the poem to flow. The ballad usually has verses four lines long with a rhyming scheme of A B A B.

Dramatic monologue

This is the words of one person speaking alone to an audience, and tells us about a dramatic experience.

Elegy

An elegy can have any structure but is always sad and serious. It is often a lament about the death of a loved one.

Epic

This is a long poem describing a heroic adventure. It usually describes important events and people and often contains supernatural beings. The lines are of equal length and there are no stanzas.

Haiku

This is a Japanese verse form which looks simple but is packed with information, moods and ideas. It consists of only three lines with a total of seventeen syllables.

Lyric

Traditionally these were meant to be sung and so usually had a repeated verse. A lyric is an outpouring of the thoughts and feelings of the poet.

Ode

An ode is a rhyming poem describing the good qualities of a person or object. Each stanza has a regular pattern. The ode is usually divided into three sections.

Pastoral

Pastoral poetry is about country scenes, people or events, described in idyllic ways.

Sonnet

A sonnet has fourteen lines. The sonnet form is often used to express and comment on an idea. Various rhyming patterns can be used; probably the most familiar is the Shakespearian form of three quatrains followed by a couplet (see chapter 7, *Romeo and Juliet*).

A ballad

Read the following song, a ballad by Don McLean. It describes the life and painting of the famous artist Vincent Van Gogh, who was considered by many to be insane. He cut off part of his ear in a fit of despair. The song also shows us McLean's feelings about the artist and his work and the way he was so misunderstood by the rest of the world.

Vincent

Starry, starry night,
Paint your palette blue and grey,
Look out on a summer's day,
With eyes that know the darkness in my soul.
Shadows on the hills,
Sketch the trees and the daffodils,
Catch the breeze and the winter chills,
In colours on the snowy linen land.
Now I understand
What you tried to say to me,
And how you suffered for your sanity,
And how you tried to set them free.
They would not listen,
They did not know how;
Perhaps they'll listen now.

Starry, starry night,
Flaming flowers that brightly blaze,
Swirling clouds in violet haze,
Reflect in Vincent's eyes of china blue.
Colours changing hue,
Morning fields of amber grey,
Weathered faces lined in pain,
Are soothed beneath the artist's loving hands.
Now I understand
What you tried to say to me,
And how you suffered for your sanity,
And how you tried to set them free.
They would not listen,
They did not know how;
Perhaps they'll listen now.

For they could not love you,
But still your love was true.
And when no hope was left inside
On that starry, starry night,
You took your life as lovers often do.
But I could have told you, Vincent
This world was never meant for one as beautiful as you.

Starry, starry night,
Portraits hung in empty halls,
Frameless heads on nameless walls,
With eyes that watch the world and can't forget,
Like strangers that you've met.
The ragged men in ragged clothes,
A silver thorn, a bloody rose,
Lie crushed and broken on the burning snow.

Now I think I know
What you tried to say to me
And how you suffered for your sanity,
And how you tried to set them free.
They're not listening still,
Perhaps they never will.

Don McLean

Vincent Van Gogh
The Starry Night. **Saint Rémy, June 1889**
Museum of Modern Art, New York

65. Read the ballad, then have it read aloud.

66. Summarise what you feel is the meaning of each stanza of the ballad.

67. How does Don McLean feel about Van Gogh?

Haiku

Here Roger McGough has some fun with the haiku form.

Two haiku

only trouble with
Japanese haiku is that
you write one, and then

only seventeen
syllables later you want
to write another

Roger McGough

Two sonnets

Bruce Dawe likes to break the rules! Here he has written a sonnet which, although it has fourteen lines, certainly does not have a traditional rhyming pattern or rhythm. Yet it captures the essence of a sonnet as it explores so poignantly his relationship with his brother. Compare Bruce Dawe's sonnet with the one by Judith Wright which is much more traditional.

My brother

The other day you were driving through town
on one of the new freeways,
doing a steady forty-five as usual,
minding your own business, miles away,
and the traffic kept cutting you down,
the young kids in the big unpaid-for cars,
and the older men going flat out to keep ahead
of their life insurance payments,
and I didn't have the heart to tell you
that they didn't drive at that speed any more
(well, not in the middle-lanes, anyway)
and I wished to Hell I was back twenty years ago
when the roads were free and you were as fast
as the best of them.

Bruce Dawe

Magpies

Along the road the magpies walk
with hands in pockets, left and right.
They tilt their heads, and stroll and talk.
In their well-fitted black and white

they look like certain gentlemen
who seem most nonchalant and wise
until their meal is served — and then
what clashing beaks, what greedy eyes!

But not one man that I have heard
throws back his head in such a song
of grace and praise — no man nor bird.
Their greed is brief; their joy is long.
For each is born with such a throat
as thanks his God with every note.

Judith Wright

72. What has happened to Bruce Dawe's brother?

73. What is he saying about other people on the road?

74. How do you think he feels about his brother? Quote from the poem to support your answer.

75. What poetic technique has Judith Wright used to describe the magpies?

76. What effect does this have on you?

77. What do you feel is the message of the sonnet?

78. Illustrate the poem.

79. Write a sonnet of your own.

 # Analysing a poem

There are two ways of looking at a poem: from the inside out, where you try to *feel* how the poet feels, or from the outside in, where you *evaluate* how the poet feels. The best understanding would come from doing both. One way of responding to a poem is to ask some questions.
• What is the poem about?
• What is the setting?
• What is its theme?
• What emotions does it convey?
• Who was it meant for?
• What is its form?
• What is the style?
• What techniques have been used?

Mid-term break

I sat all morning in the college sick bay
Counting bells knelling classes to a close.
At two o'clock our neighbours drove me home.

In the porch I met my father crying —
He had always taken funerals in his stride —
And Big Jim Evans saying it was a hard blow.

The baby cooed and laughed and rocked the pram
When I came in, and I was embarrassed
By old men standing up to shake my hand

And tell me they were 'sorry for my trouble';
Whispers informed strangers I was the eldest,
Away at school, as my mother held my hand

In hers and coughed out angry tearless sighs.
At ten o'clock the ambulance arrived
With the corpse, stanched and bandaged by nurses.

Next morning I went up into the room. Snowdrops
And candles soothed the bedside; I saw him
For the first time in six weeks. Paler now,

Wearing a poppy bruise on his left temple,
He lay in the four foot box as in his cot.
No gaudy scars, the bumper knocked him clear.

A four foot box, a foot for every year.

Seamus Heaney

The audience could be young or old as this experience would touch anyone.

The form is free verse in three-line stanzas.

The settings are the boy's school, outside his home, and the bedroom.

The language is simple and direct.

The techniques include:
- alliteration
- repetition
- strong adjectives
- short phrases
- strong verbs
- irony
- punch line.

The theme explores the effects of a child's death.

80. (a) How did the young boy die?
    (b) Try to express the poet's feelings about the death of his brother.

81. (a) How did the poem make you feel?
    (b) What part of the poem did you find most powerful?
    (c) Choose another poem that conveys strong emotions. In pairs, analyse it by the same method.

Unlocking the poem

We can never be sure that we understand and feel everything that a poet meant to include in a poem. Sometimes we can see things that the poet may not even be aware of. The more we look and listen to a poem the clearer it becomes. Unlocking the poem is like unlocking the mind and heart of the poet. Let's look closely at a poem by Tennyson who was shattered by the death of his friend. Once we have analysed what Tennyson is saying and what techniques he has used to create the atmosphere, we can write a response to his poem.

Title and first line are repetitious, creating a sad rhythm. The word "break" is harsh, creating a feeling of anger.

Assonance creates a mood of anger.

Break, break, break

Break, break, break,
   On thy cold grey stones, O Sea!
And I would that my tongue could utter
   The thoughts that arise in me.

O well for the fisherman's boy
   That he shouts with his sister at play!
O well for the sailor lad,
   That he sings in his boat on the bay!

And the stately ships go on
   To their haven under the hill;
For O for the touch of a vanished hand,
   And the sound of a voice that is still!

Break, break, break,
   At the foot of thy crags, O Sea!
But the tender grace of a day that is dead
   Will never come back to me.

Alfred, Lord Tennyson

Strong adjectives create imagery.

Strong verb shows anguish.

The happiness of the young people in this stanza creates a contrast.

Exclamation marks create tension.

Pause intensifies contrast.

Strong rhythm creates a sad mood.

Strong noun emphasises despair.

Rhyme makes the poem flow.

The last two lines run on and leave a feeling of ongoing pain.

The word "day" symbolises the friend who has died also.

Soft adjective and noun create a sense of gentleness.

A student's text response to "Break, break, break"

Tennyson's poem is powerful, sensitive, angry and tender. The anguish he feels for the loss of his friend can be seen not just in the words but in the imagery and in the use of pauses. Although the poem is short it is very powerful. Tennyson paints a clear picture: the sea, the children at play, the ships and he, the poet, standing alone, silently gazing across the sea. The last two lines with their haunting rhythm sum up exactly how he feels.

The words "break", "cold", "utter" and "crag" are harsh words that seem to lash the reader. In contrast words like "voice", "vanished", "tender" and "grace" are soft words which create a sense of despair. The lilting rhythm that Tennyson uses is almost hypnotic as though he is staring out to sea in a state of shock. The rhyming pattern supports this. The flow of the poem is therefore very smooth.

The contrast between the first and second stanzas is deliberate as it makes us feel annoyed at the children playing and singing while he is in such anguish. The children perhaps symbolise the rest of the world that goes on as though nothing has happened, "And the stately ships go on".

The echoing effect of the first and last stanza creates a sense of heavy repetition like a weight pressing him down, a weight that he cannot lift and will recur again and again.

Kirri Withers

What about your own?

Analysing your own poem is a good way to learn how to analyse other people's poetry. Look at how Karen, a student, has done this with one of her poems. Here, first, is the poem.

The spirit of the night sea

As the shimmering sun surrenders
to the enchantment of the night,
the skies' battling colours of crimson gold
abruptly end their mystical fight.

The golden strands of sunlight,
once glistening upon the sea,
are replaced by haunting shadows,
dancing endlessly.

Echoes from howling winds
stretch far beyond the sea,
whilst voices murmuring in the waves,
set the spirit of the night sea free.

Sudden cries from seabirds
pierce the crisp night air,
and ragged rocks on which waves plunge,
stand looming and silently stare.

Like angry spirits of the sea,
the waves rage towards the shore,
and plunge and crash upon the beach,
while birds above freely soar.

Throughout the night the sea spirit lives,
alive and full of zest,
before the beckoning sun sheds light,
and the night sea spirit comes to rest.

Karen Sank

ANALYSING MY POEM

Using a descriptive approach, I have attempted to capture a theme expressing the enchantment and mystery that surrounds the sea at night.

Instead of telling a story, the poem is a series of feelings and emotions expressed through imagery and rhyme.

The rhyming pattern I used is ABCB. This indicates the first and third lines of each stanza are blank verse, while the second and fourth lines rhyme.

In various parts of my poem, personification and similes can be identified. An example of personification lies in the third stanza, in the third and fourth lines. These are "Whilst voices murmuring in the waves, set the spirit of the night sea free." Though we know that the ocean is incapable of speaking, I have given it this human characteristic to describe the way the waves in the sea do seem to speak.

In the fifth stanza, there is an example of a simile: it appears in the first and second line which are "Like angry spirits of the sea the waves rage on towards the shore ..." I used this specific simile as I feel an angry spirit would be rough and uncontrollable: just as the waves in the sea are at times.

Throughout the poem, I have attempted to create an eerie or mysterious atmosphere, an atmosphere which enables the reader to actually picture and appreciate the wonders of nature and its existence in the sea at night.

My reasons for writing this particular poem stem from the fact that I find the ocean a vast and superior place, which is both mystifying and beautiful. When I have the opportunity to visit the ocean, I seize it, just to watch the waves roll onto the shore.

Karen

Structure annotations:
- overall theme
- techniques used
- tone
- aim
- purpose

Language features annotations:
- First person creates an informal tone.
- Terms show the writer knows poetic techniques.
- Quote from poem makes comments clearer.
- Words match the tone of the poem.
- Conclusion provides the personal source of inspiration for the poem.

Peer assessment

You could assess each others' poems and analysis by copying and completing the table below. Of course, not all of these requirements will be appropriate in every poem.

Text response assessment sheet

Criteria	Level of achievement		
1. The poem	**Major problems**		**Highly successful**
• Is it interesting?			
• Is it clear?			
• Does it use rhythm?			
• Does it use rhyme?			
• Does it create an appropriate tone and mood?			
• Does it use imagery?			
• Does it use pauses?			
• Does it use powerful verbs?			
2. The analysis			
• Is the meaning examined?			
• Is tone referred to?			
• Is imagery highlighted?			
• Is there comment on rhythm and rhyme?			
• Is word choice considered?			
• Are pauses referred to?			
• Is a clear opinion given?			

Assessment by: .... **of poem by:** ....

Take care — don't shed blood!

Don't destroy the poem with too much analysis, especially analysis which is cold and distant as though you are dissecting it.

Be careful

not

to

kill

the

poem.

Integration as a process

I once saw a man
Sneaking up on butterflies.
He caught them,
Quietly killed them,
And pinned them to a board.
I saw the man again,
Analysing poetry.
Piece by meaningless piece,
He cut it up,
Catalogued it,
Until it died.
Like an old photograph,
Studied closely,
Merely a collection of dots.
But step back!

Liam O'Connor

Look at the poem below and the one on page 106. The first is by Judith Wright and the second by a student who has written a parody on analysing Wright's poem.

THE OLD PRISON

The rows of cells are unroofed,
a flute for the wind's mouth,
who comes with a breath of ice
from the blue caves of the south.

O dark and fierce day:
the wind like an angry bee
hunts for the black honey
in the pits of the hollow sea.

Waves of shadow wash
the empty shell bone-bare,
and like a bone it sings
a bitter song of air.

Who built and laboured here?
The wind and the sea say
— Their cold nest is broken
and they are blown away.

They did not breed nor love.
Each in his cell alone
cried as the wind now cries
through this flute of stone.

Judith Wright

A SONNET — 14 LASHES FOR THE OLD PRISON

What are the metaphors in stanza 1?
What does line 2 mean?
What type of imagery is used in stanza 2?
What does line 4 mean?
List the adjectives in stanza 2.
What is the meaning of line 2 stanza 3?
List the adjectives in stanza 3.
What is the atmosphere of the first three stanzas?
What is the meaning of line 3 stanza 4?
Explain the first line of the last stanza.
What is the tone of the last two stanzas?
What is the link between the first and last stanza?
Scan the poem.
What is the rhyming scheme?

Nick Mercer

82. Read Judith Wright's poem.

83. What is her poem about? Could you suggest a setting?

84. Read Nick Mercer's sonnet aloud, making each line sound like a cracking whip. Each student could read one line.

85. Do you think the student's sonnet is meant to be taken seriously? Explain.

86. How would you feel about Wright's poem if you had to analyse it this way? Explain.

87. Suggest an alternative way to analyse Judith Wright's poem.

88. Now analyse Judith Wright's poem (but be sensitive!) in paragraph form and share your analysis with a partner.

Creating your own poetry

If we look at the peer assessment table on page 104 it shows us what an audience might be looking for when they read a poem.

Have you made it interesting?

Whatever you're feeling inside is of great interest to you. But how can you make it interesting to others? How can you let others see inside you? Even the most ordinary experience can be made interesting if you describe it in an unusual way, a powerful way, a sensitive way.

Have you made it clear?

Being able to understand your poem is very important to the audience. Simplicity is the key. Sometimes symbols and poetic techniques can confuse rather than clarify what you are trying to say.

Check with friends and family to see if they understand what you are trying to say.

Have you used poetic techniques?

Poetic techniques make your poem more powerful, more startling, more unusual, more visual. Poetic techniques allow you to slip into the reader's head and heart without them realising you are there.

Poetic techniques are the keys to unlocking the powerful feelings in you:
- Have you released the rhythm that you feel inside?
- Have you painted the images that you see?
- Have you created the tone that you feel?
- Have you used the words that will hammer out your meaning?

Ted Hughes, a poet famous for his powerful, wild and violent poems, feels that there is one thing that is more important than anything else when writing a poem.

That one thing is to imagine what you are writing about. See it and live it. Do not think it up laboriously, as if you were working out mental arithmetic. Just look at it, touch it, smell it, listen to it, turn yourself into it. When you do this, the words look after themselves like magic. If you do this you do not have to bother about commas or full-stops or that sort of thing. You do not look at the words either. You keep your eyes, your ears, your nose, your taste, your touch, your whole being on the thing you are turning into words. The minute you flinch, and take your mind off this thing, and begin to look at the words and worry about them ... then your worry goes into them and they set about killing each other. So you keep going as long as you can, then look back and see what you have written. After a bit of practice, and after telling yourself a few times that you do not care how other people have written about this thing, this is the way you find it; and after telling yourself that you are going to use any old word that comes into your head so long as it seems right at the moment of writing it down, you will surprise yourself. You will read back through what you have written and you will get a shock. You will have captured a spirit, a creature ...

Now read Trang Ly's brief poem.

When I am angry
I feel something inside of me angry
too.
That thing cries;
I cry.
When it's hungry,
I am hungry.
So when it dies
I die.
That thing is part of me.

Trang Ly

89. What do you think Trang Ly is describing?

90. Consider the comment by Ted Hughes and write a poem of your own.

Poem about writing a Poem

'Write a poem,' she says
'About anything you like.'
You can practically feel the class all thinking,
'On your blooming bike!'

A poem! I'll tell you one thing:
Mine's not going to rhyme.
A poem between now and playtime!
There's not the time.
In half an hour she'll say,
'Have you done? Hand papers in
And go out.'
I mean, does she have the slightest idea
What writing a poem's about?
I mean, it's agony:
It's scribbling thoughts
And looking for rhymes
And ways to end and begin;
And giving it up in total despair —
'I'm chucking it in the bin.'
But tomorrow it pulls you back again,
And hey, a bit of it clicks!
And you sweat with the words
But it's hopeless again
And it sticks.
And you put it away for ever . . .

But it nags away in the back of your head
And the bits of it buzz and roam,
And maybe — about a century later —
You've got a kind of a poem.

Eric Finney

S E L F

ASSESSMENT

1. Can I?

Write "yes" or "no" in the box. If you write "no", go back over your work until you can write "yes".

- Understand the value and purpose of poetry .... ☐
- Identify poetic techniques .... ☐
- Identify different forms of poetry .... ☐
- Analyse a poem .... ☐
- Write poetry .... ☐

2. Your reaction

(a) Which poem did you like best? Say why.
(b) Which activity did you like best? Say why.
(c) Which skill do you need to work on most? What can you do to improve it?

3. For your folio

From the work you have done in this chapter, choose the pieces you want to include in your folio. Each piece of work in your folio should include a cover sheet which shows the date it was completed, the title, the purpose and the audience.

4. Ongoing skills

Complete the table below by:
- placing a tick at the point at which you feel you usually achieve in each skill
- shading in the range of your achievement in each skill.
When you have completed the table place it in your folio.

Am I improving in these skills?	Level of achievement		
	Same as before	**Improving**	**Much better**
Example: Oral work		✓	
Reading poetry			
Discussing poetry			
Cooperating in group work			
Explaining my answers			
Oral work			
Discussing issues			

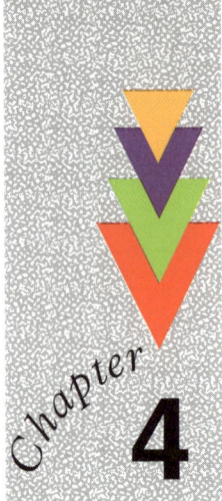

Chapter 4 HUMOUR

A smile increases your face value.

Content

- Creating humour
- Humour in cartoons
- Humorous devices
- Funny essays
- Parody
- Captions
- "Female" humour?
- Humour and issues

Skills

- Identifying styles of humour
- Creating cartoons
- Creating funny essays
- Writing a parody
- Writing humorous captions
- Investigating points of view
- Investigating issues

Humour has the power to change our lives. As well as entertaining us, it can focus our attention, alter our moods, make us feel better and it can greatly improve our ability to communicate. One way to learn how to harness the power of humour is to study how other people have used it. But be careful — close analysis of humour *can* take away the fun.

Creating humour

What things do you laugh at? Do you find that you and your friends laugh at different things? What is funny for one person may not be funny for another, but there are types of humour for everyone, and many different techniques and methods of presenting it.

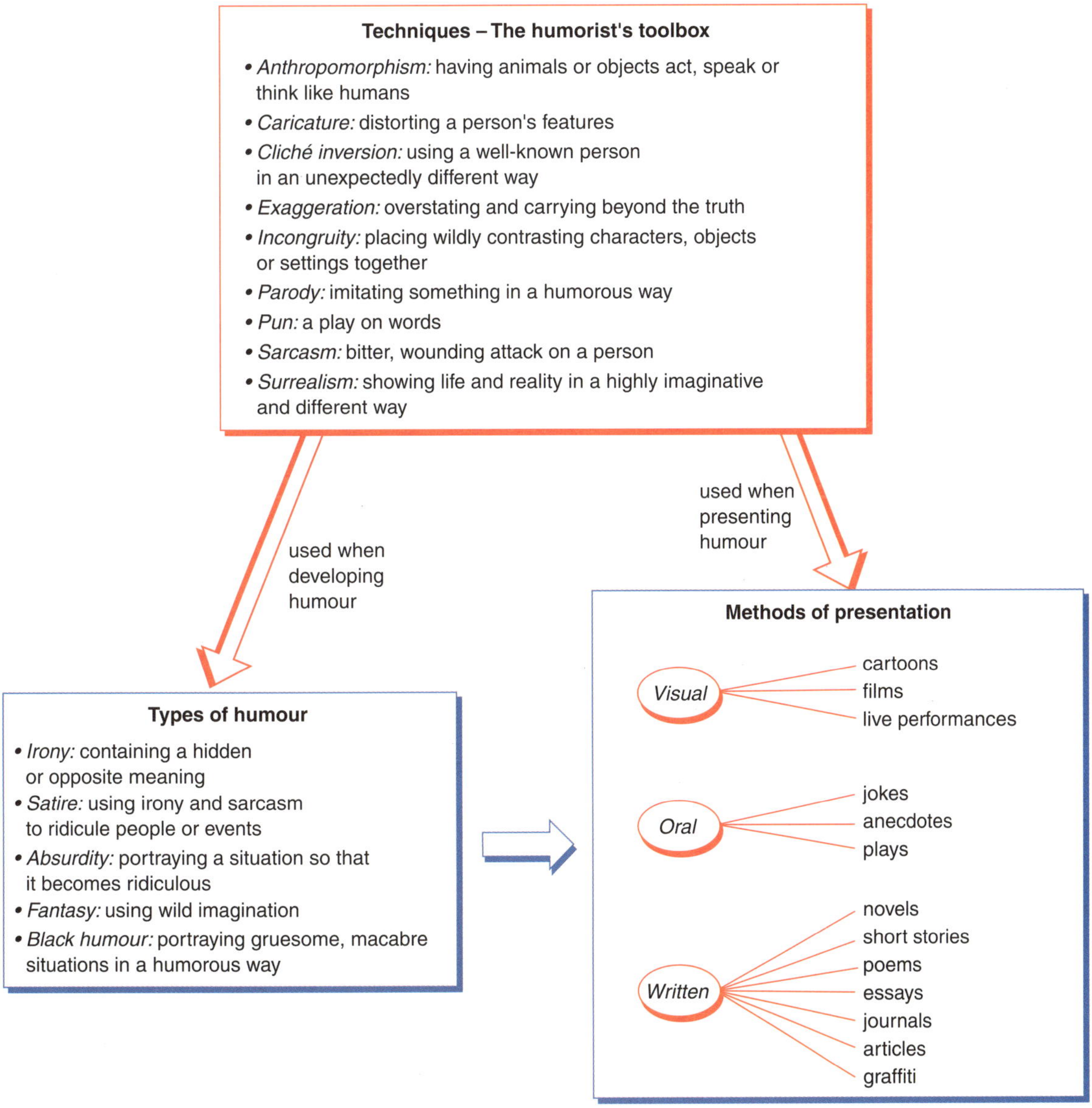

Techniques – The humorist's toolbox

- *Anthropomorphism:* having animals or objects act, speak or think like humans
- *Caricature:* distorting a person's features
- *Cliché inversion:* using a well-known person in an unexpectedly different way
- *Exaggeration:* overstating and carrying beyond the truth
- *Incongruity:* placing wildly contrasting characters, objects or settings together
- *Parody:* imitating something in a humorous way
- *Pun:* a play on words
- *Sarcasm:* bitter, wounding attack on a person
- *Surrealism:* showing life and reality in a highly imaginative and different way

used when developing humour

used when presenting humour

Types of humour

- *Irony:* containing a hidden or opposite meaning
- *Satire:* using irony and sarcasm to ridicule people or events
- *Absurdity:* portraying a situation so that it becomes ridiculous
- *Fantasy:* using wild imagination
- *Black humour:* portraying gruesome, macabre situations in a humorous way

Methods of presentation

Visual
- cartoons
- films
- live performances

Oral
- jokes
- anecdotes
- plays

Written
- novels
- short stories
- poems
- essays
- journals
- articles
- graffiti

Cartoon magic

One of the most popular forms of humour is the cartoon. Often simple and easy to understand, cartoons are drawn to make us laugh. However, they may also contain a serious message. The cartoons below, representing the five general types of humour, were all drawn by Phil Somerville, one of Australia's leading cartoonists.

The genesis of a cartoon

An important step in understanding how a cartoonist conveys the message is to be aware of how the cartoon is created. Many cartoonists feel that the most difficult task in creating a cartoon is coming up with the initial idea. Phil Somerville has two ways of generating his cartoons:

- doodling
- word association.

Perhaps one of them will work for you!

Method 1: Doodling

Because cartoonists are "visual" people, many of their creative ideas begin with doodling. This is how Phil Somerville describes it.

STEP 1: To get the cogs turning I like to grab a soft pencil and simply doodle. It's a painless way of freeing up subconscious thoughts. From these, often, the germ of a cartoon reveals itself. Curved objects seem to be the theme in this crop.

STEP 2: I like the shape of that rainbow. It would be nice to make it the central "character" in a drawing. The rainbow is such a well-known image that there is a real challenge to do something quite different and humorous with it. I now try sketching a bunch of simple, more disciplined ideas.

STEP 3: Out of these comes the idea of rainbows in unexpected situations. I try the idea of placing one in a room where someone is watching television.

STEP 4: However, I feel the idea hasn't been taken "all the way to the end of the street". It doesn't feel completed — not interesting enough. I realise that the rainbow should be outdoors. I recall the leprechaun and pot of gold from my earlier doodlings and try to combine all of these elements. However, it still doesn't feel right.

STEP 5: The TV set outdoors is too jarring somehow. I decide to eliminate it. It is at this moment that the "solution" to this cartoon suddenly drops into place. I decide to have the rainbow itself behave like a TV set in need of repair. In this case the problem will be a lack of colour. Finally I come up with the words. This acts as the last nail that holds the whole cartoon together. I do a grey wash over the final pencil rough.

"Sorry, your whole colour control's stuffed. I'm going to have to take it back to the shop."

STEP 6: I do final artwork in pen, waterproof ink and watercolour washes done in many layers to give a lush depth to it. I instruct the publisher to have the caption typeset underneath for design neatness. Voilà, a cartoon is born.

2. Take five minutes to create your own page of doodles. Let your creativity flow freely and try not to focus on any one topic.

3. Study your drawings and try to identify anything which might form the basis of a cartoon. Work with these ideas until you have a central "character".

4. Continue to try different settings, events, captions or speech bubbles to suit your "character".

5. To help make your cartoon funny, refer to the humorist's toolbox on page 111.

6. When you are happy with the evolution of your work from doodle to cartoon, display it on the class noticeboard. Perhaps you could also submit it for the school magazine. Humour is always best when it is shared.

Method 2: Word association

Somerville's second method for getting started involves word association — using connections between words to generate ideas.

STEP 1: I begin by compiling several word lists. Then I cross-match words from different lists and hope that some humorous bell will ring. I keep mixing and matching words until ideas begin to form.

THE LISTS

Characters
pirate
extraterrestrial
Noah
snake
octopus
Humpty Dumpty
clergyman
King Arthur
angel
Loch Ness Monster

Objects
computer
bicycle
quicksand
road sign
camera
wall
bathtub
telephone
book
television

Settings
underwater
snowscape
jungle
desert
the Pyramids
golf course
cinema
hell
bookshop
beach

Activities
reading
eating
talking on phone
childminding
commuting
holidaying
bankrobbing
jogging
sleeping
swimming

STEP 2: Eventually I choose a central character, in this case Humpty Dumpty. I like the mythical aspects and he is visually attractive. For a setting I choose the pyramids. Perhaps he is holidaying. What have we got?

STEP 3: Hmmm — not much hilarity there, perhaps a new setting. A bookshop where Humpty stumbles across relevant titles.

STEP 4: Some humour is starting to emerge but it is not strong enough to stand by itself yet. The pyramids bring to mind other tourist spots. Then the "wall" idea points to a "great" place to put Humpty on holiday.

STEP 5: With a few detail changes, such as Humpty being drawn as the guide, the final cartoon is taken to its full potential and completed in pen, ink and watercolour wash. And of course, signed!

7. (a) What type of humour do you think Somerville has used in this cartoon? Explain. (Refer to page 111.)
   (b) What techniques do you think he has used? Explain.

8. Try using Somerville's method of word association to help you generate ideas. If it works for you, develop it through until you have created your own cartoon. Display this with the others you have created, and submit them to the school magazine.

9. Which of the two methods works for you when creating a cartoon? Explain.

 # Picture stories

Picture stories provide another form of visual humour. They are often done as parodies, which are humorous imitations of a serious piece of literature or fairytale.

Snow White in New York

a picture story by Fiona French

This picture story closely imitates the classic fairytale of Snow White and the Seven Dwarfs. Snow White in New York *is set in the 1920s, the evil stepmother now uses the "New York Mirror" to see how beautiful and popular she is, the seven dwarfs have been replaced by the seven jazz-men, and the role of the handsome prince is now played by an equally handsome newspaper reporter.*

Although neither the original nor the modern story is humorous in itself, the modern version is so similar to the original that it creates amusing comparisons.

Look at the following two scenes from the traditional story of Snow White. Then turn the page and see what Fiona French created from them.

"Mirror, mirror on the wall, who is fairest of them all?"

The Queen was jealous of Snow White's beauty and soon she began to hate her.

All the papers said that Snow White's stepmother was the classiest dame in New York. But no one knew that she was the Queen of the Underworld. She liked to see herself in the New York Mirror.

NEW YORK MIRROR

QUEEN OF DIAMONDS!

QUEEN OF HIGH SOCIETY

EXTRA!

But one day she read something that made her very jealous

'Snow White the Belle of New York City.'

And she plotted to get rid of her stepdaughter.

While the humour in *Snow White in New York* is very subtle, the strikingly powerful impact of the illustrations is a good example of visual language, where the pictures say more about the story than the words do. Both Snow White and the Queen are presented as stereotyped characters: the Queen is totally evil, while Snow White is totally good.

Look at the drawings of the Queen. Traditionally seen as the colour of evil or death, the black associated with the Queen gives her a sinister appearance. Her hard facial expressions, narrowed green eyes and raised eyebrows also add to the feeling of evil. The harsh, straight lines behind her and the angry-faced men surrounding her seem to make the Queen an even more menacing figure.

10. Make a list of five ways that *Snow White in New York* imitates *Snow White and the Seven Dwarfs*.

11. What are the main differences between the two styles of illustration?

12. Find examples in the story of the following techniques of humour:
    (a) pun
    (b) exaggeration
    (c) caricature
    (d) surrealism.

13. Study the picture of Snow White on page 118. In a paragraph describe what impressions we are given about her from the illustration. Consider the following points:
    • use of colour in the background, and in her make-up, eyes, hair and clothes
    • style of clothing
    • body language.

14. How has Fiona French used lighting to create the atmosphere in the story? Consider the use of silhouettes, shadows, shading and line technique.

Something extra

15. There are various factors that affect the way we interpret visual images:
    • **previous knowledge** — most readers will be familiar with *Snow White and the Seven Dwarfs*
    • **personal values and attitudes** — in this case, the way we feel about the struggle between good and evil
    • **the context of the pictures** — here the visual images are presented in the form of a picture book story so we expect stylised characters and plot
    • **written information** — the captions, verbal text, headings or speech bubbles add meaning to the pictures.
    Obtain a copy of *Snow White in New York*. How does your knowledge of *Snow White and the Seven Dwarfs* affect your response to it?

16. Find another example of a humorous picture story book.
    (a) Without reading any of the captions or dialogue, study the humour of the visual language and try to write down what you think is happening.
    (b) Then re-read the book including captions and dialogue. Compare your second interpretation of the story with your first.

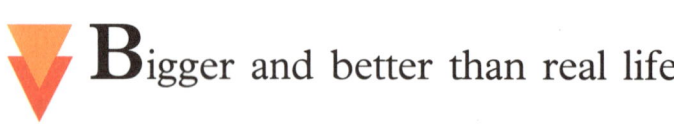

Bigger and better than real life

Students have had to write essays about holidays since holidays were first invented. Here are two examples of such essays that use exaggeration to create humour. In both, the setting is realistic, but the characters and events are highly exaggerated to create a humorous sense of unreality.

The first essay uses a dash of sarcasm as Amanda Prescott paints a picture of herself as the perfect goody-goody. In the second essay correct grammar and spelling are totally forgotten as Kylie Mole tells a tale of unbelievable boredom.

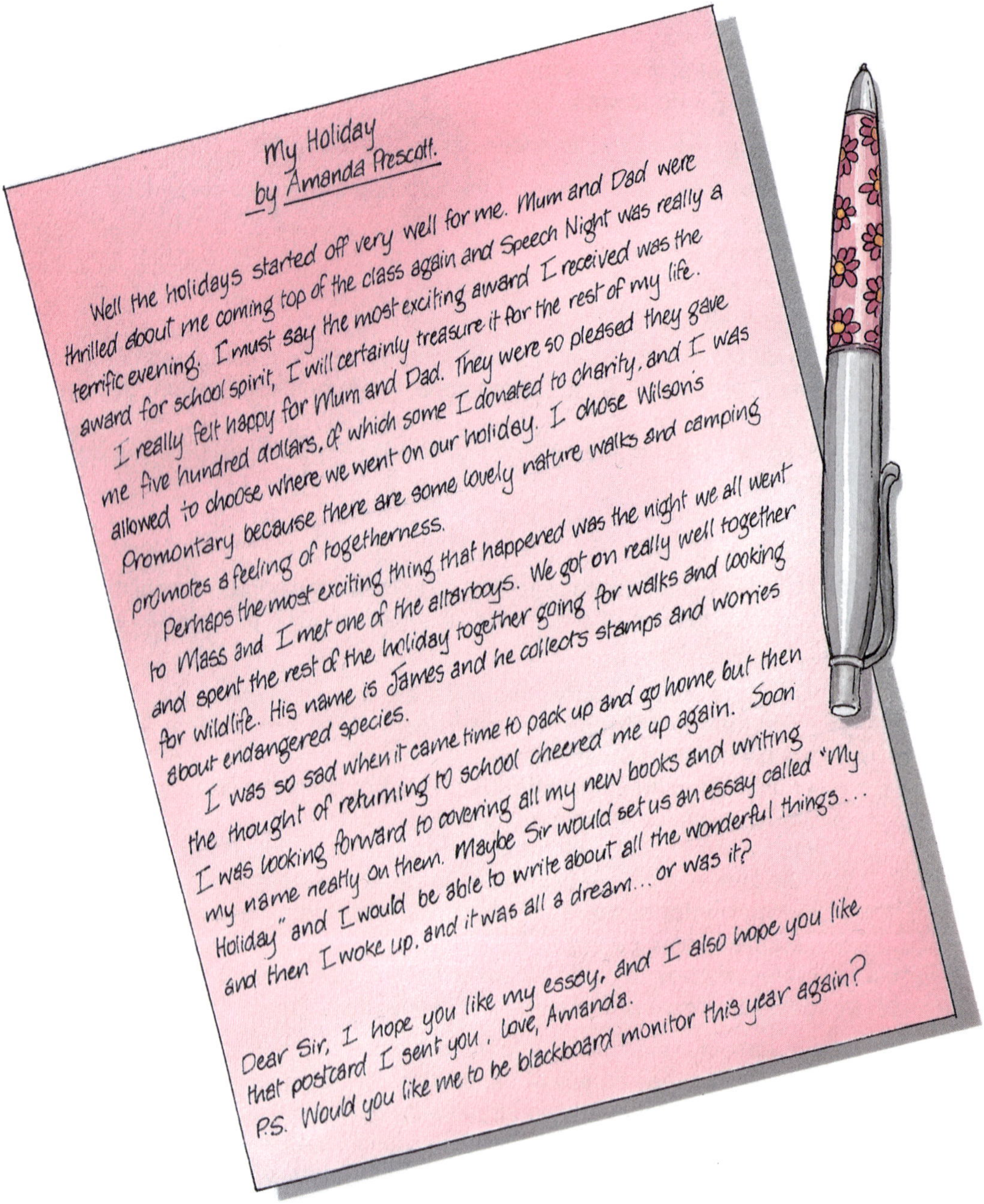

My Holiday
by Amanda Prescott.

Well the holidays started off very well for me. Mum and Dad were thrilled about me coming top of the class again and Speech Night was really a terrific evening. I must say the most exciting award I received was the award for school spirit, I will certainly treasure it for the rest of my life.

I really felt happy for Mum and Dad. They were so pleased they gave me five hundred dollars, of which some I donated to charity, and I was allowed to choose where we went on our holiday. I chose Wilsons Promontary because there are some lovely nature walks and camping promotes a feeling of togetherness.

Perhaps the most exciting thing that happened was the night we all went to Mass and I met one of the altarboys. We got on really well together and spent the rest of the holiday together going for walks and looking for wildlife. His name is James and he collects stamps and worries about endangered species.

I was so sad when it came time to pack up and go home but then the thought of returning to school cheered me up again. Soon I was looking forward to covering all my new books and writing my name neatly on them. Maybe Sir would set us an essay called "My Holiday" and I would be able to write about all the wonderful things... and then I woke up. and it was all a dream... or was it?

Dear Sir, I hope you like my essay, and I also hope you like that postcard I sent you. love, Amanda.
P.S. Would you like me to be blackboard monitor this year again?

Amanda
is a
bogan

My Holiday   by Kylie Mole

(I wood of writ new paragrafs for evry
new thought but i didnt hav any new thoughts)

My holiday was so boring it was almost as
bad as bein at school but not quite coz nothin
could be as borin as that. the furst week of
the hols i just complained all the time and
went i'm bored theres nothink to do so mum
goes kylie if you keep complainin all the
time you wont be comin down the caravan
wif us so i kept complaining but they still
made me go parents are so unfair so then we
had to drive down to the caravan and adam
picks his nose the whole way with both hands
and then harfway there we had to turn around
and go back coz adam says we left his imaginry
frend behind spewin there was only one good bit at the
caravan when dino hitched down and we went
to the beach and it was so funny cos there was
this sign sayin NO DOGS ALLOWED and dino
goes to me you better get off the beach kylie it was
so funny fair dinkum we just larghed so much.
so ace then we went lookin for people who were
gettin with each other and threw watermellon at them
it was so excellent then dino saw this rooly
old couple in their forties getten wif each other and
we spat six pips at them and will you believe it
it was my mum and dad so embarrassing! I was goin
to be grounded but they coodnt coz i was grounded
already and that was my holiday the end.

17. Which essay did you find the more humorous? What did you find funny?

18. The essays are vastly different and yet they were written to be read together and compared. How does the comparison add to their humour?

19. Write your own humorous essay using exaggeration. Choose one of the following fantastically funny topics. (?!)
    • Our family picnic
    • A visit to the dentist
    • Washing the dishes
    • Mowing the lawn
    • The spit bomb war
    • Bathing my dog
    Use word association techniques (page 115) to make a list of all the wild things that might happen. Use these "over-the-top" ideas to help you write your essay. Be daring, adventurous, crazy — but above all, exaggerate.

The ready-made essay

Of course there are times when even the funniest writers don't feel like putting creative pen to paper. The following "ready-made" essay is designed for just such an occasion.

You simply cross out the sections that don't suit your usual creative style and . . .

BINGO

. . . after just a few moments your "ready-made" essay is ready to be handed in.

20. Photocopy this page and complete your own "ready-made" essay by crossing out the unwanted sections below. Share your essay with a partner.

My weekend at the beach/zoo/farm

Last weekend we all went to the (beach/zoo/farm.) We stayed in a (caravan/shearing shed/cage) because (Mum and Dad wouldn't pay for a unit/Mum and Dad wouldn't pay for anything/Grandpa hates kids.) The food was (awful/terrible/only fit for animals.) We spent most of the time (sweeping out the shed/avoiding the tourists/hiding from the animals.) Each day after breakfast I had to (wash the dishes/shear the sheep/spread new hay over the floor of the cage.) The best part of the weekend was (avoiding Grandpa/avoiding the tourists/avoiding being eaten.) My family were asked to (feed the lions/take photographs of a busload of tourists/clean out the sheep dip.) Unfortunately they (were fed to the lions/fell into the sheep dip/were trapped in the tourist bus) and I missed out on dinner. All in all it was a (lousy weekend/great weekend/time I will never forget) and I hope that (I can go again soon/ I find the tourist bus that took Mum away.) (I'm hungry/This is all I need to write for the essay.)

21. What did you enjoy about "writing" this style of essay?

22. What type of humorist's techniques are used in a "ready-made" essay? Discuss your ideas with a partner.

23. Try to create your own humorous "ready-made" essay on the topic "Going out to the takeaway/movies/disco". To help you with some ideas, photocopy and fill out the following activity sheet by brainstorming ideas with a partner. Some examples have been included to get you started.

Funny places to go for a school excursion:

- *sewage treatment works*
- ....
- ....
- ....
- ....

Strange activities for a school excursion:

- *a barbecue beside one of the treatment ponds*
- ....
- ....
- ....
- ....

Our school excursion

Unusual names for teachers and students:

- *Mr Phew*
- ....
- ....
- ....
- ....

Highly exaggerated events:

- *Mr Phew is grabbed by something from out of treatment pond.*
- ....
- ....
- ....
- ....

24. Use your lists of words and ideas to write your "ready-made" essay.

25. Share your funny "essay" with some of your classmates and let them experiment with it.

THE SMART DOG

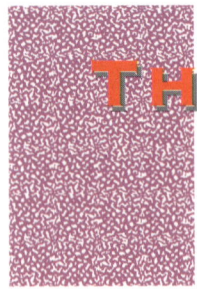

a short story by Dal Stivens

Humour needs to be quick. A joke may last for a number of minutes but it is only in the brief moment of hearing the punch line that the real humour is released. Even in a funny story or novel, once a humorous section is read it is quickly passed over as the story progresses. Because humour moves so quickly, the short story is a perfect medium. Without lengthy character or plot development, the reader is brought quickly to the humorous heart of a funny short story.

In The Smart Dog, *Dal Stivens introduces the idea of a talking dog and quickly brings the reader to the humorous conclusion of his very funny tale.*

There was once a dog who discovered that he could talk, but he didn't lose his head. It happened when he was gnawing a bone on the dining-room carpet. His master saw this and began complaining: 'How many times have I got to tell you not to eat on the carpet?'

'Ah, pull your head in,' said the dog. 'It's about time you got rid of this old carpet.'

When he realised that he had spoken the dog turned tail and bolted.

'Don't you answer me back!' snapped his master after the dog.

The dog came back hastily.

'Excuse me, but I forgot this,' he said, snaffling his bone and bolting outside again.

As soon as he was outside the dog was very worried. He thought: That's torn it! As soon as that mug inside wakes up and realises that I can talk, he'll lead me a man's life. I can kiss my old carefree life good-bye. Every evening and two afternoons a week I'll be on the halls. The only thing to do is to scram!

So he did, just in time, because the 'mug' came rushing out with his eyes as big as oranges, and calling after the dog: 'Hey, stop! I want to talk to you!'

Don't you answer me back..!

'Not on your life!' said the dog, and kept on going. His master hailed a cab and after a few minutes he drew level with the dog.

'Stop and talk this over,' he pleaded. 'We can make a fortune.'

The dog galloped a little faster, and then replied over his shoulder: 'And spend all my life working as hard as a film star? I'm happy as I am.'

The cabby was so shocked at hearing a dog speak he ran his cab up on the footpath, and after the cabby and the dog's master had smoothed out three old ladies, the dog was half a mile ahead. When they drew level again the master said: 'One performance a week. I promise!'

'I know all about your promises,' panted the dog.

The man tried another approach.

'Towser! Come to heel! Come to heel!'

'I'm finished with that stuff!' said the dog, and doubled up a lane where the cab couldn't follow. He'd gone about two hundred yards when a bag was flung over him, and when he was released he found himself with a dozen other dogs in a yard with a high fence. His new owner was a trainer in a circus.

'Just my luck!' said the dog. 'If this man discovers I can talk, I'm done for, I'll play dumb.'

And he did. He played so dumb that every day the trainer beat him because he wouldn't learn the simplest tricks. After a week of this the dog lost his temper.

'You hit me again and I'll bite you!' he snapped at the trainer.

The trainer dropped his stick.

'A miracle!' he shouted. 'My fortune is made. A talking dog at last, though I always reckoned I was on the verge of achieving it.'

He rushed in to embrace the dog, which was still angry and shouted back: 'Keep your smelly hands off me, you big ape!'

'Smelly, are they?' cried the trainer. 'Ah, well, I'll let it pass. What else do you think about me?'

'I could go on for five minutes,' said the dog, and began. But at the end of three minutes he realized he had fallen into a trap, and suddenly shut up and wouldn't say any more.

The trainer fell to beating him again after a time, but the dog remained silent under all the blows, and in the end the trainer gave it up and went away.

'I ought to kick myself,' said the dog. 'I'm a goner unless I can think of something.'

Next morning the trainer was all smiles and love when he returned.

'I'm sorry I lost my temper, but the shock, you know, at hearing you speak —'

'Forget it,' said the dog.

'If there's anything I can do,' said the trainer. 'Just anything.'

'I don't think there is anything,' said the dog. 'Unless —'

'Yes?' said the trainer eagerly.

'It's nothing much, but I wonder if I might be moved near the lions?' said the dog. 'It may sound odd, but I have always wanted to make a study of the king of beasts.'

It was done immediately, and for the rest of the day, apart from amiable conversation with the trainer, the dog gazed contemplatively at a very large and bad-tempered lion.

The next morning the trainer was again all love and smiles, but the dog refused to speak. After half an hour of futile arguments he would again have beaten the dog if his hand hadn't been stayed by hearing a voice from the lion's cage saying: 'Why the devil do you want to waste your time on a talking dog? There's nothing very remarkable about it. Everyone says dogs almost talk, so I ask you!'

"You, too?' he gasped.

'Why not?'

The trainer went over to the lion's cage, and the lion began growling.

'Don't take any notice of my growls. Sometimes I get confused with my two voices, but I'll improve.'

'Well, I'll be —'

'Come closer,' said the lion, 'so that I can whisper. I don't want the dog to hear this.'

The trainer did so, and the lion killed him with a fearful smack of his huge paw.

Soon afterwards the little dog escaped. But never again did he speak. And as for telling anybody that he was a ventriloquist — well, who'd believe him?'

26. What part of the story did you find most humorous? Why?

27. What type of humour is used in this story?

28. What techniques has the author used to create the humour?
(See page 111.)

29. (a) Did the ending surprise you?
(b) How did it add to the overall impact of the humour in the story?

Funny poetry

Oh no, I got a cold

Sniff...
groan...

I am sitting on the sofa,
By the fire and staying in,
Me head is free of comfort
And me nose is free of skin
Me friends have run for cover,
They have left me pale and sick
With me pockets full of tissues
And me nostrils full of Vick.

That bloke in the telly adverts,
He's supposed to have a cold,
He has a swig of whatnot
And he drops off, good as gold,
His face like snowing harvest
Slips into sweet repose,
Well, I bet this tortured breathing
Never whistled down his nose.

I burnt me bit of dinner
Cause I've lose me sense of smell,
But then, I couldn't taste it,
So that worked out very well,
I'd buy some, down the café,
But I know that at the till,
A voice from work will softly say
'I thought that you were ill'.

So I'm wrapped up in a blanket
With me feet up on a stool,
I've watched the telly programmes
And the kids come home from school,
But what I haven't watched for
Is any sympathy,
Cause all you ever get is:
'Oh no, keep away from me!'

Medicinal discovery,
It moves in mighty leaps,
It leapt straight past the common cold
And gave it us for keeps.
Now I'm not a fussy woman,
There's no malice in me eye
But I wish that they could cure
the common cold. That's all. Goodbye.

Pam Ayres

30. Is Pam Ayres' poem a good description of how a cold makes you feel? What memories does it stir within you? What words are most effective in describing the feeling of a cold?

31. How does the poet make you feel about the cold sufferer?

32. What introduces and develops the humour in this poem? Give examples to support your answer.

33. Create your own version of the fourth verse of this poem in the same style and rhythm as Pam Ayres uses, starting with:
    So I'm wrapped up in a blanket …

34. (a) Who was telling the story?
    (b) How would it change if it was told by someone else? Some examples might be:
    • her husband
    • a friend
    • her children.

35. Imagine you are one of these others. Write a humorous poem about someone else suffering from a cold. Exaggerate their symptoms, how they look and how they sound. People suffering from colds are sometimes short-tempered or grumpy, so emphasise this too. Try to build your description and the humour throughout the poem. Share your poem with a partner.

In his poem "superwog", Komninos parodies the introductory theme of the old television program "Superman". By changing words and phrases but not the basic style or structure of the original, he brings to light the amazing powers of Con Pappas, alias superwog.

superwog

look!
up in the sky.
it's a bird.
it's a plane.
no . . .
it's SUPERWOG.
strange visitor from a european country
with powers and abilities far beyond those
or normal anglo-saxons.
who can gut and fillet mighty man-eaters,
pick up hot dim-sims in his bare hands.

faster than a squirt of vinegar,
more powerful than tsatsiki,
able to use the lifts in tall buildings.

and who,
disguised as con pappas,
mild mannered fish monger
at a great metropolitan shopping complex

fights a never ending battle
against macdonalds,
kentucky fried chicken,
and the american take away.

komninos

36. List the fantastic feats of superwog.

37. Superman fought against criminals and kept the world free from danger. Does Komninos have a serious message behind the humour in his poem? Explain.

Now read the original Superman theme, taking note of how Komninos has altered it to create his poem.

Look
up in the sky.
Is it a bird?
Is it a plane?
no . . .
it's Superman.
Strange visitor from another planet
with powers and abilities far beyond those
of mortal men.
Faster than a speeding bullet.
More powerful than a locomotive.
Able to leap tall buildings in a single bound,
and who,
disguised as Clark Kent,
mild-mannered newspaper reporter
for the Daily Planet,
fights a never ending battle,
for truth,
justice,
and the American way.

38. Compare this to Komninos' poem. What makes his poem humorous?

39. Write your own humorous Supersomething poem — maybe "Supermum", "Superteacher" or "Superstudent"? The topic is up to you, but once you have chosen it, brainstorm with a partner to come up with a list of funny describing words and phrases, actions and thoughts to use in your poem. Try to include a serious message in your poem.

40. Read your poem to the class, illustrate it, place it on your class notice board and perhaps submit it for your school magazine.

A play on words

A pun is a play on words designed to create humour. In "You tell me", Michael Rosen creates a poem of puns using the names of English soccer teams and places.

You tell me

Here are the football results:
League Division Fun
Manchester United won, Manchester City lost.
Crystal Palace 2, Buckingham Palace 1
Millwall Leeds nowhere
Wolves 8 A cheese roll and had a cup of tea 2
Aldershot 3 Buffalo Bill shot 2
Evertonill, Liverpool's not very well either
Newcastle's Heaven Sunderland's a very nice place 2
Ipswhich one? You tell me.

Michael Rosen

41. What do you feel creates the humour in this poem?

42. "You tell me" asks you to create a pun for the last line. Do so and share it with the class.

43. (a) Could Australian place names be used in the same way? Grab an atlas and start exploring for the names of Australian towns or cities which could have funny double meanings or be used in some other humorous way. Write down ten towns or cities. Here are some to get you started.

    Innisfail, Alice Springs, Wood Head, Seaspray, Longreach

    (b) Working with a partner, write your own humorous sports results poem.

She, shis and shim

The English language is a mixture of many languages and is constantly growing and changing. The following poem is a witty look at why English is so hard. Wit is the clever expression of ideas in a way designed to create humour.

Why English is so hard

We'll begin with a box, and the plural is boxes;
But the plural of ox should be oxen, not oxes.
Then one fowl is goose, but two are called geese;
Yet the plural of moose should never be meese.
You may find a lone mouse or a whole lot of mice,
But the plural of house is houses, not hice.
If the plural of man is always men,
Why shouldn't the plural of pan be called pen?
The cow in the plural may be cows or kine,
But the plural of vow is vows, not vine.
And I speak of a foot, and you show me your feet,
But I give you a boot — would a pair be called beet?
If one is a tooth and a whole set are teeth,
Why shouldn't the plural of booth be called beeth?
If the singular is this, and the plural is these,
Should the plural of kiss be nicknamed kese?
Then one may be that, and three may be those,
Yet the plural of hat would never be hose.
We speak of a brother, and also of brethren,
But though we say mother, we never say methren.
The masculine pronouns are he, his, and him,
But imagine the feminine she, shis, and shim!
So our English, I think you will all agree,
Is the trickiest language you ever did see.

Anon

EEEK!!
Mouses.... er meeces ※ ~more than one mice!

Moosen sure are dumb.

44. What did you enjoy about this poem? Explain.

45. Just for fun, create humorous plurals of the following words:
    child, genius, bacterium, thesis, I, she, he.
    Compare your answers with others in the class.

46. Write a humorous poem using some of the following words:
    bow, bough, beau, cough, though, rough, thought, caught, court, sort, cow, tow.

Parody

Throughout history adventurers have set out on dangerous journeys to discover the unknown, chart new lands and to go to where no-one has ever gone before. At the end of each day the explorers would record their experiences in a journal. They were usually serious and factual: a great opportunity for a humorist to poke fun.

Across the Andes by Frog

a journal by Knud Svenson

The following journal entries are the personal records of heroic Danish explorer Knud Svenson as he attempted in 1971 to be the first person to cross the Andes Mountains by frog. Svenson, having already tried (and failed) to sail around the world on a rabbit, and to cross the Spitzbergen on a fish, saw this arduous crossing as his most dangerous journey ever.

Iquique, Jan. 19
Expedition delayed by three days after the frog was squashed when I sat on it. We wait around in the sultry heat of this coastal town whilst another frog is found.

Iquique, Jan. 21
A perfect day to set off. The sunshine was bright, but a strongish north-easterly wind kept us cool. The baggage porters had at last settled their differences over pay, and the forecast was good. However, as soon as I mounted the frog, I squashed it again. Oh, the frustrations! We must reach the Andean foothills by mid-February, or the vicious South American winter will set in.

Iquique, Jan. 26
I have tried mounting frogs without a saddle and even tried with my haversack off, but they always squash as soon as I sit down on them.

Have decided to try a different approach. I will walk and the frog can carry the baggage. It will be hard work, especially in the mountains, but I would rather suffer some discomfort than give up now.

Iquique, Jan. 27
The frog has proved incapable of carrying even the lightest hold-all. Seven or eight were squashed in succession last night while we were trying to load up.

Iquique, Jan. 28
Today at last we set out from the main square here in Iquique, on the 500-mile journey to Santa Cruz in Bolivia. The frog, unladen by any baggage, set a furious pace, and we lost it through a hole in the wall not ten yards from where we started.

Iquique, Feb. 6
The days pass in a long frustrating week, whilst we design a special frog harness. The Andean winter gets closer as every day goes by. Conditions in the mountains could be hell.

Iquique, Feb. 7
The frogs are so slippery that any harness is almost impossible to fit. They are sending to Belgium for a specialist.

Iquique, March 30
At last, the Belgian specialist has arrived. He says that frogs are totally unsuitable for this sort of journey. The man is a complete fraud. We refuse to pay his return fare.

Iquique, March 31
Wake up with a huge Malaysian Leper Frog at my throat. The Belgian specialist eventually calls it off, after we promise to pay his fare back.

Iquique, March 32
Decide to set off with frog in a box. The weather holds out, and we make good progress. We reach the outskirts of Pozo Almonte before I discover someone has let the frog out of the box.

Pozo Almonte, March 33
I am beginning to have suspicions about my Chilean calendar.

Pozo Almonte, March 34
Success! I discover a frog in my lunch, so I put him in the box and set out again.

Iquique, March 35
I misread the map. Simple mistake. Bump into the Belgian specialist in the street. He hits me with a South American Singing Toad, which he was taking to the vet. I report him to the RSPCA.

Iquique, March 35
RSPCA man arrives from London. He says he has called about a matter of sixteen frogs squashed while under my care.

Iquique, March 37

How the frogs have let me down, making a mockery of the oft-repeated maxim: "a man's best friend is his frog". Decide to take up a new challenge with a more reliable creature. Decide to attempt the first crossing of the Skaggerak by maggot.

London, March 43

So my Chilean calendar was right. It really is March 43rd.

47. Explain what you found humorous about this explorer's journal.

48. (a) Which humorous techniques are used? Refer to the toolbox on page 111.
    (b) Which technique do you think is most effective?

49. Do you feel the illustrations add to the humour? Explain.

50. If you've ever tried to climb the Great Divide on a cane toad, or cross Bass Strait on an echidna, then you really do have a story to tell. However, even if you've only been on the usual old "run-of-the-mill" family holiday you may still have the makings of a ripping yarn — if you tell it humorously.
    (a) Think about a holiday that you have been on. List the things you did, the places you visited, the sights you saw.
    (b) Now add to this list some incredible, crazy, mixed-up, made-up things that could never have really happened. Create some imaginary places and unbelievable sights.
    (c) Use these to write your own humorous journal entries.

51. Choose one of the following ways to share your humorous journal.

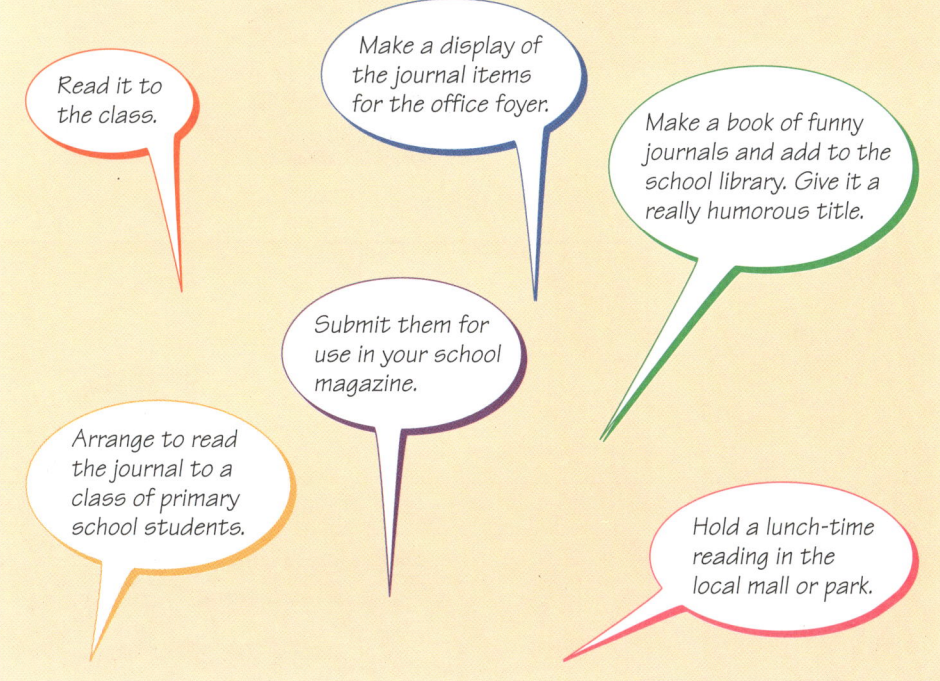

Read it to the class.

Make a display of the journal items for the office foyer.

Make a book of funny journals and add to the school library. Give it a really humorous title.

Submit them for use in your school magazine.

Arrange to read the journal to a class of primary school students.

Hold a lunch-time reading in the local mall or park.

Captioning the moment

You can add humour to virtually any image with a humorous caption or speech bubble. When writing these it is helpful to remember the following points.

• Focus on the part of the picture with the greatest visual impact.
• Try to come up with a comment which gives a totally new meaning to what the visual image is saying.
• Be brief and to the point.
• Consider the style of humour best suited to the picture.

52. Look at the following pictures. Write your own funny captions or speech bubbles for them.

A

B

C

D

A different point of view

Most people agree that there is no such thing as strictly "male" or "female" humour. What individuals find as funny is more likely to be determined by their likes or dislikes, past experiences, values, and feelings for themselves and for others, rather than by their gender.

But what of the people who tell the jokes? Male and female comedians do seem to use a different style of humour in their acts.

Noted Australian comedian, Wendy Harmer, put the following question to a group of professional comics: "What, if any, differences are there between men's and women's humour?"

The answer may be as simple as a different point of view . . .

It seems to me that if something is funny, it's funny regardless of whether it comes from a man or a woman. One thing I have noticed, however, is that Victoria Wood picks subject matter that has been overlooked by men. Everyday stuff like waiting in queues at the supermarket, dealing with doctors' receptionists and so on. I guess the reason it has been overlooked is that it isn't deemed "important". She's also a keen observer of women. Her observations are acute and funny, but there's real warmth in the characterisation.

Angela Webber

Women are more interested in character portrayal and setting up the character to be laughed at . . . perhaps a more vulnerable position than that of men who tend to direct the humour at others. (Please omit Joan Rivers from this analysis.)

Liz Sadler

It's hard to know really, because up till now we've had a predominance of male humour and to me that's like getting a funny look at the world through one eye — a sort of a Cyclops view if you like! Women comedians pick up on a lot of things men don't see, don't want to see or have no interest in seeing. Though, in general, people mostly laugh at the same things. I don't think we'll ever know if there are any real differences between male and female humour until we're equal!

Geraldine Doyle

Female cartoonists

A

B

C

55. (a) Which cartoon do you find the funniest? Why?
    (b) Compare your answer to others.
    (c) Which of the cartoons is the class favourite?

56. Do you feel the comments made by Sadler, Webber and Doyle on page 135 about female humour are relevant to these cartoons?

Humour and issues

Pollution, racism, poverty, human rights — these are issues that arouse
strong emotions in people. Humour can often take the stress out of a tragic
situation but still communicate a powerful social comment. Look at the
following cartoons and decide what issues they focus on.

A

B

C

D

57. What do you think is the issue shown in each cartoon? Explain.
    Remember, your response may be different from that of others.

58. Which of the cartoons holds the most powerful message for you? Why?

59. Do you feel that humour is a good way to comment on important social
    issues? Explain.

60. (a) Find another cartoon that deals with a social issue. In class, discuss
       its meaning.
    (b) Put all of these cartoons and their commentaries into a book to
       present to another class.

S E L F

ASSESSMENT

Name: ....

1. Can I?

Write "yes" or "no" in the box. If you write "no", go back over your work until you can write "yes".

- Identify the different types of humour .... ☐
- Identify the techniques of humour .... ☐
- Understand how a cartoonist creates humour .... ☐
- Explain how a picture storybook works .... ☐
- Create humorous poetry .... ☐
- Create humorous captions and speech bubbles .... ☐
- Understand the role of humour in issues .... ☐

2. Your reaction

(a) Which extract did you like best? Say why.

(b) Which activity did you like best? Say why.

(c) Which skill do you need to work on most? What can you do to improve it?

3. For your folio

From the work you have done in this chapter, choose the pieces you want to include in your folio. Each piece of work in your folio should include a cover sheet which shows the date it was completed, the title, the purpose and the audience.

4. Ongoing skills

Complete the table below by:

- placing a tick at the point at which you feel you usually achieve in each skill
- shading in the range of your achievement in each skill.

When you have completed the table place it in your folio.

Am I improving in these skills?	Level of achievement		
	Same as before	Improving	Much better
Example: Oral work		✓	
Writing creatively			
Cooperating in group work			
Interpreting visual images			
Creating cartoons			
Writing creative essays			
Writing journal entries			
Oral work			

© J. Eshuys, V. Guest and P. Phelan 1994

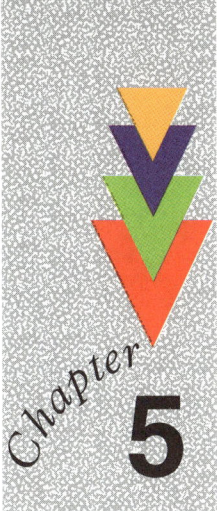

Chapter

5 THE VISUAL IMAGE

Content

- Visual language
- Features of an image
- Symbols in an image
- Techniques in creating a still image
- Words with an image
- Techniques in creating a moving image

Skills

- Identifying the features and symbols in an image
- Understanding the techniques used to create a still image
- Increasing the impact of an image with appropriate wording
- Understanding the techniques used to create a moving image

Our world is full of visual images which give us information and strongly influence our thoughts, feelings, attitudes and behaviour. Photographs in newspapers and magazines and the moving images on TV, for example, are powerful means of communication. It is important that we understand the "language" of such a strong influence in our lives.

How does visual language work?

To understand how visual language works and the effect it has on us we need to look at the image in many different ways:
- the image itself
- the features of the image
- the symbols in the image
- the techniques used to create the image
- the words that go with the image.

The image itself

Ask yourself these questions —

1. What are the objects in the image — people, animals, plants, buildings, cars, food …?
2. Where does the image come from — a magazine, newspaper, book, photo album, TV show, film …?
3. Is it linked to other images?

1. Describe what you can see in this image.

The features of the image

The way the person behind the camera wants to present the image is very important. The photographer creates the image keeping in mind:

- **the size** of the objects, which indicates what is most important in the image
- **the position** of the objects, which tells us what to focus on. Usually the most important object is near the centre; but if the main object is placed near the edge of the image it can create a feeling of anticipation, as though something is about to happen.

2. What, in your opinion, is the most important object in the image? Explain your choice.

3. Why do you think the photographer has chosen to place the ballerina at the edge of the photograph?

4. Explain the feelings you get from this image.

5. (a) Find an example of an advertisement in a magazine where size and/or position of objects have an impact on the message.
   (b) Cut it out, paste it in your workbook and write a short explanation of the effect you think the advertiser wanted to have on the audience.

Eye direction

What is the person or animal in the picture looking at: you, or another person or object? If a person in a picture is looking directly at you, you in turn will tend to look at them. On the other hand, if they are looking at an object or into the distance then your attention tends to be drawn towards that object or into the distance.

Picture A

6. Look carefully at the two pictures on this page.
   (a) When you look at picture A who are your eyes drawn to?
   (b) When you look at picture B where are your eyes drawn?
   (c) Compare your answers with those of a partner.

7. How do you think this feature can be used in advertising?

Picture B

The symbols in the image

A symbol is something that adds a deeper meaning to an object than may be obvious at first sight. Symbols may be simple or very complex.

Common symbols are ones we recognise easily: a horseshoe meaning good luck, a crown meaning royalty, a skull meaning death, champagne meaning a celebration.

Colours can also have symbolic meaning, although it can vary from culture to culture. Europeans use black as a symbol of mourning, for example, whereas in India the colour symbol for mourning is white.

Body language is an important symbol in any image. Body language is the subconscious way we relate to people. The way we stand or sit, how much distance we put between others and ourselves, the way we move our head and hands, the expressions on our face — all these send signals. They tell people how we really feel about them without our saying a word. Nearly 80 per cent of your everyday communication is through body language.

8. (a) How do you think the three people in the photograph feel about each other?
   (b) There are lots of body language signals that tell you this. How many body language signals can you find in this image?

9. (a) What is happening in this image? What body language signals tell you this?
   (b) Create a dialogue that suits their body language. Compare what you have written with a partner.
   (c) Imagine this photo is to be used in an advertisement for a teenage magazine. Write a caption or speech bubble that would promote a product of your choice.
   (d) Collect an example of an advertisement where body language speaks strongly. Cut out, paste in your workbook and write a brief caption on the body language and how it would promote the product.

Clothing

Clothes and hairstyles often symbolise people's attitudes towards society and their position within it.

Symbols of authority

Anti-authority symbols

10. Look at the images below. In each case what do you think the clothing symbolises?

11. Turn each image into an advertisement for a magazine of your choice.

12. Cut out an advertisement you like. Identify some of the symbols the advertiser has used to attract you.

A

B

The techniques used to create the image

A photographer can use a number of techniques to create an image according to the way the audience is intended to feel. Each technique positions the viewer to respond in a certain way.

Which angle?

Viewing the subject from a particular angle will create certain effects.

- **Eye-level** — looking at the subject on the same level as yourself — can help create a feeling of equality and honesty.
- **Low angle** — looking up at the subject — gives the feeling that the subject is strong and important.
- **High angle** — looking down on the subject — gives the feeling that the subject is less powerful. It is also used to create an impression of loneliness or fear.

A. An eye-level shot positions the viewer to feel equal to the subject.

B. A low-angle shot positions the viewer to feel the importance of the subject.

C. High-angle photography positions the viewer to feel superior to the subject.

13. Which of the images would you use in the following situations? Explain your reasons.
    (a) A recruiting campaign for surf lifesaving.
    (b) A community awareness campaign about the importance of lifesavers on our beaches.
    (c) A magazine article describing the difficulties faced by lifesavers.
    (d) An advertisement about why it is important to obey a lifesaver's directions on the beach.
    (e) Accompanying a feature article about this particular lifesaver.
    (f) A fundraising campaign.

Which view?

A photographer uses a range of lenses to create different feelings about the subject or event.

A standard lens — as the eye sees it — gives a feeling of naturalness.

A wide-angle lens gives a feeling of space and also makes the viewer feel distanced.

A telephoto lens gives a feeling of being close to the subject or event and makes the viewer feel part of the action.

14. Describe what you can see in each photo.

15. Which one gives you a feeling of being involved? Explain.

16. If you were to write a magazine article on the fun of playing netball, which type of lens would you use? Why?

A fisheye lens allows a very wide image. It can also have an unusual bending effect. It gives the feeling of being able to see more than normal — almost a dreamlike experience.

17. Note how this cityscape is depicted as "crowding in", overbearing or even threatening. In pairs, imagine you are writing an article on cities and the effect they have on society and you want to include this image. Decide what your article is about and then write a heading for the article, an opening sentence and a caption for the image. Make an oral report on what you have written and what you would plan to write.

18. Suggest purposes for which a fisheye effect would be appropriate.

Where to place the object

Framing means placing an object in a particular spot in the image. Psychologists have discovered that most people tend to look at an image in a certain way. They look along invisible vertical and horizontal lines about one-third of the way in from the edges. Anything placed on these lines is more likely to catch the eye of the viewer. This technique is called using the "rule of thirds" and creates a balanced picture by dividing the frame into 3 equal parts horizontally and three vertically. Dividing the image into three also allows for objects in landscape pictures to be placed in the foreground, middle or background according to their importance.

background

middle

foreground

A landscape

A couple

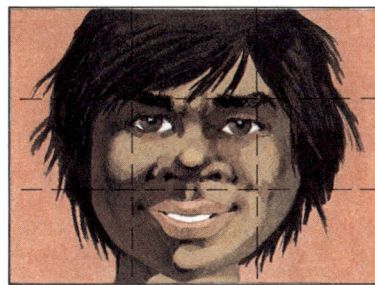

A portrait

19. What did the photographer want to draw attention to in each photo?

Another important aspect of framing is to make sure you give your object some natural space in the frame, unless you are deliberately creating a confining effect.

Confined — no space to look into

Open — space to look into

20. What feeling does this photo give you?

21. What techniques has the photographer used to achieve this feeling?

What to show

The photographer can also decide what is going to be in the frame by cropping, either when taking the photograph or during printing.

22. First, cover over page 149; then look at the photo below. What do you think is happening in this photo?

23. Now compare the two photographs. How has cropping affected your interpretation of this photograph?

24. Make two photocopies of an interesting photo. Crop part of one photocopy to change the impact of the image. Paste both in your workbook, explaining what you have aimed to achieve.

Calvin & Hobbes

How close?

Photographers can use different types of shots according to what they wish to highlight. A distant view will emphasise the setting, whereas a close-up concentrates on a much smaller subject.

Extreme long shot (ELS): emphasises the setting.

Long shot (LS): emphasises a subject in the setting.

Medium shot (MS): emphasises the subject, with some setting shown.

Close-up (CU): emphasises the subject.

Extreme close-up (ECU): emphasises subject detail.

When making movies cinematographers also use different types of shots to influence the audience. Close-ups create a feeling of being involved, while long shots create a feeling of looking on from outside the action.

25. Explain what type of shot you would use in the following cases:
    (a) a photo for the family album of your family in front of your house
    (b) a photo of a famous person to go in their biography
    (c) a shot in a travel film showing the vastness of the Great Barrier Reef
    (d) a shot for a mouthguard commercial.

26. Select (a), (b), (c) or (d) above and cut out a photograph from a magazine that would suit the purpose. If appropriate add your own caption.

How fast?

Shutter speed is the length of time the shutter in the camera stays open when you press the button. Varying the shutter speed can either freeze an action or create a feeling of movement by blurring the action.

27. Which of the photos above might be used in a cycling magazine to show technique? Why?

28. Imagine you are a magazine photographer. When would you use the slow shutter speed for effect?

29. Look at the photograph on the left.
    (a) Suggest a magazine that you feel might use the photograph. Say why.
    (b) Suggest how the photo could be used: e.g. front cover, feature article, advertisement.
    (c) Give it a caption or title.

Focus

Photographers pick out what they want the observers to believe is important in a photograph by bringing one object into focus and blurring out other details.

Foreground focus   **Background focus**

Lighting

Lighting techniques help create the atmosphere the photographer wants. The use of lighting can also make part of a photograph stand out while the rest is in shadow, directing attention to one aspect of the image.

Look at the two photographs below. They were both taken for advertisements — the one on the left for shampoo, the one on the right for make-up.

Backlighting behind the girl makes her hair a golden halo.

Frontlighting emphasises the face.

33. Explain whether you think these are effective techniques for advertising.

34. Find an advertisement in which this technique has been used.
    (a) What features have been highlighted? Why?
    (b) Who do you think is the intended audience for this advertisement?

Special effects

Photographers have special filters that can create some wild effects. The effects in the photograph below have been achieved using a combination of techniques including filters, special lenses and clever lighting.

35. Describe the feeling you get from the photo.

36. How could the photo be used in an advertisement?

37. Write an advertising caption for the photo.

The words that go with the image

A caption, a speech bubble, a headline, an article all add meaning to an image. The words can be serious or funny, factual or creative.

38. Collect an example of each.

Notice how the meaning of the image changes, depending on what words you use with the image.

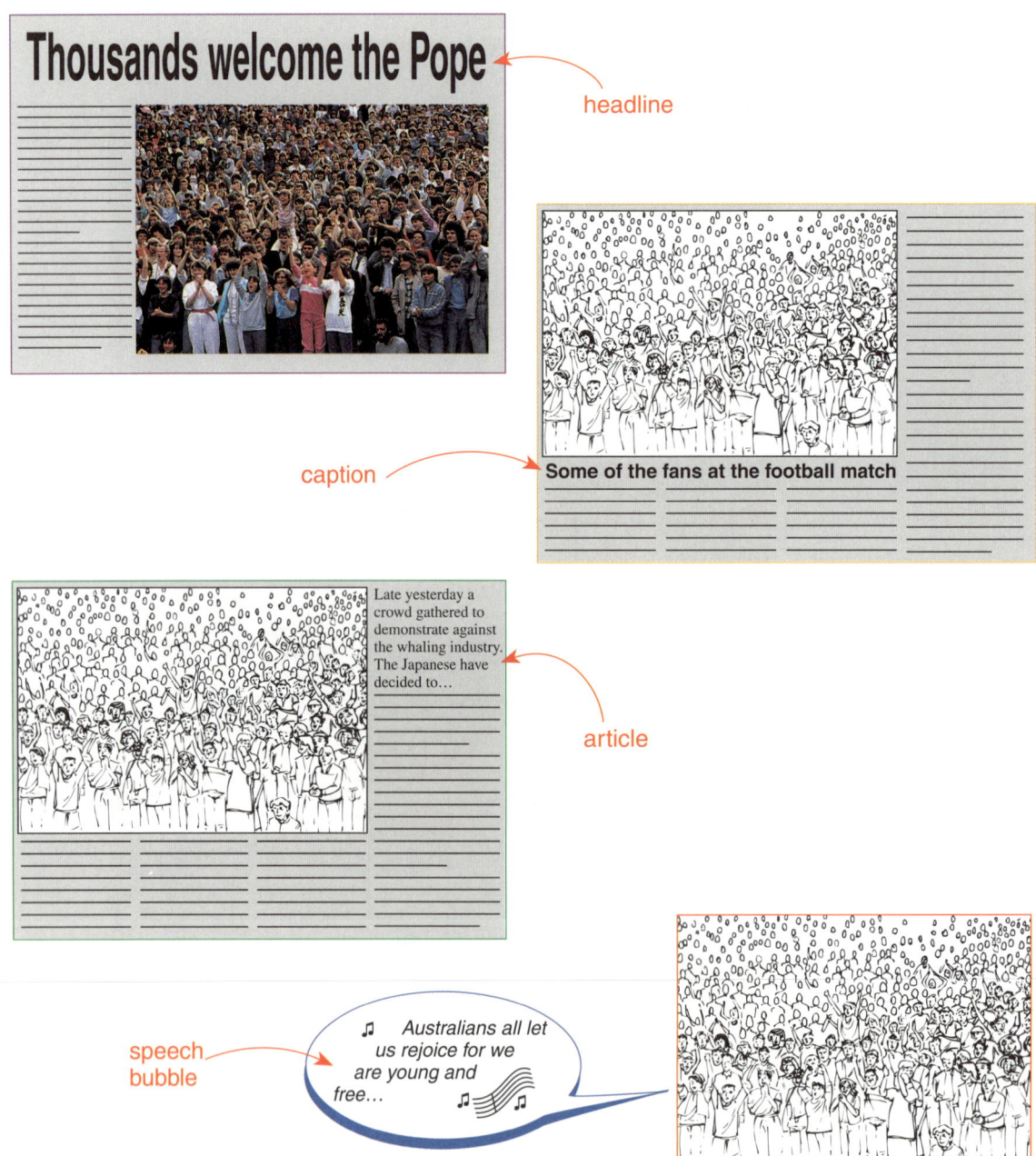

Thousands welcome the Pope — headline

Some of the fans at the football match — caption

Late yesterday a crowd gathered to demonstrate against the whaling industry. The Japanese have decided to… — article

♫ Australians all let us rejoice for we are young and free… ♫ — speech bubble

39. Look at the image on the left.
    (a) Imagine you are creating a magazine advertisement for babies' nappies. Decide whether you want to use a speech bubble, a headline or a caption to get your message across. You may feel a combination of these would be most effective.
    (b) Use the same image as an illustration for an article on women in the workforce. Give your article a headline and a caption, and write a short description.
    (c) Give an oral report to your class.

Putting it all together

A

B

40. Describe the objects in images A and B.

41. How important is the setting in each image?

42. Identify any symbols, including body language, in both of the images and explain what they mean to you. How is shutter speed used for special effect?

43. Images A and B each have their own impact. Which one appeals to you more? Why?

44. You have been asked to use these images in the media. Use a chart like the one below to present the following information.
    (a) Decide where you would use each image — as a book cover, in a magazine, on a poster, in an advertisement or on a video cover.
    (b) For each one decide on your audience: for example, a book cover for teenage fiction or a cover on a video for PG viewing.
    (c) Decide whether to include caption, title, speech bubble, lead to an article, blurb or a combination of these.

	Image A	Image B
(a) Where used		
(b) Audience		
(c) Type of wording		

 # The moving image

The moving image we see on TV and in the cinema is the most powerful of all media influences, whether it be for advertising, information or entertainment. For this reason it is very important that we understand the techniques of the film-makers and how we are positioned by them. These techniques include:

- camera movement
- camera viewpoint
- shot length
- fades and cuts
- shot sequence
- special effects
- sound effects
- editing.

How the camera moves

Imagine a scene where a child is lost in a storm. The camera operator starts with a close-up of the child's tiny feet, wet and muddy, then tilts slowly up to show the terrified face and tearful eyes. The camera zooms out, revealing a vast windswept plain. A crane is then used to lift the camera high above, and looking down on, the child who seems so weak and small in this empty place.

In this way the cinematographer has created a feeling about the child, created an atmosphere and given us information about the story. The cinematographer uses five basic camera movements to create effects in a moving image. All these movements combine to involve the audience and create emotional effects.

Dolly shot

The camera is placed on a device with wheels called a **dolly** so that it can be moved smoothly towards or away from the object being filmed. This action allows the audience to feel as if they are moving into or away from the objects in the film.

Crane shot

Cranes, cherry pickers and even see-saws can be used to create this shot, moving the camera up or down, and towards or away from the object. This can give the audience a feeling of being high above the action.

Panning

The camera is mounted on a tripod and swung horizontally, allowing the audience to experience a wide view of the scene.

Tilting

The camera is swung vertically on the tripod to create a view that moves either up or down. This allows an audience to view the scene from below or above.

Tracking shot

The camera moves along with the object being filmed, allowing the audience to keep abreast of the action. The camera is rolled along a small railway track, or sometimes a dolly can be used.

45. Which of these basic camera movements would you use to film each of the following scenes? Say why.
    (a) a rock band on stage
    (b) ski jumping
    (c) a car chase
    (d) a beach scene
    (e) a basketball game

46. Watch a scene from a movie, TV show or advertisement. Identify the different camera movements used.

Camera viewpoint: the subjective and objective views

As you sit watching a film you see what is happening through the "eyes" of the camera. The camera can influence your feelings. Imagine if, for example, in the scene with the child in the storm, the camera showed us the view of the storm through the eyes of the child — the lashing wind, the swirling clouds, the wide open plain. It would give a very powerful insight into what was frightening the child.

This type of shot is called a **subjective** shot because it is from the point of view of the person or **subject**. On the other hand, if the camera was looking at the child in the storm it would be like a third person looking on the scene. This is called the **objective** shot.

47. Consider three of the following scenes and decide whether a subjective or objective view would dominate. Explain the effect you are trying to achieve in each case.
    (a) a person being chased by a violent criminal on a dark night
    (b) a student arriving at school on the first day
    (c) a person climbing a mountain
    (d) a dog trying to find its way home
    (e) the life of a cricket stump or netball hoop

Shot length

Imagine again the scene of the child in the storm. The camera operator can control how long each part of the scene takes. The length of the shot can help control the atmosphere in the film: too long, and the scene can become tedious and boring, too short, and the tension and feeling can be lost. Surprisingly most shots are only 3–20 seconds long.

Fades and cuts

At the end of each shot the film has to move on to the next shot or scene. This can either be done quickly with straight cuts or smoothly by fades. Shots can also be blended from one to another by superimposing the new shot over the old.

Shot sequence

Imagine how the cinematographer could have changed the impact of the lost child scene by altering the sequence of the shots. Imagine, for example, if the opening shot was from the crane showing a distant child overwhelmed by a wild storm. The viewers' overriding impression would be of the power of the storm and the loneliness of the small figure. Then the next shot is of the child's muddy feet, followed by a tilting shot of the teary face. The overall result may still make us feel the same towards the child but our senses and emotions may have been jolted differently.

48. Create another shot sequence of this scene explaining what effect and emotions you are trying to create. If you have access to a video camera, experiment with this.

Special effects

Special effects have an enormously powerful impact upon the atmosphere of a film, shocking the senses of the audience as they experience wild, often surreal worlds.

Special effects can lull us into a sense of tranquillity and romance in one scene, then dramatically jolt our senses a split second later.

Sound effects

Music is possibly the most powerful of the sound effects. Music can often control the whole mood of a film. There is a tremendous amount of symbolism in music as it creates softness, peace, romance, fear, anger, tension, and many other emotions.

Other sound effects also help to create the atmosphere of a movie: the trickling of water creates a sense of calm, the revving of a car engine creates excitement or anxiety, the thump of a boxing glove on flesh creates a sense of power and tension.

49. What sort of emotions do you think are created by the following sound effects?
   (a) a clap of thunder
   (b) a police siren
   (c) a clock ticking
   (d) soft music
   (e) a child crying
   (f) howling wind
   (g) a loud burp
   (h) a scream
   (i) screeching brakes
   (j) a trickling stream

50. (a) Watch a movie, taking note of the sound effects in a particular scene. Choose a scene where there is no dialogue. What impact do the sound effects have on you?
   (b) Watch the same scene with the volume off. What effect does this have?

Editing

This is the last stage of making a film, and a very important one. The editor has to cut perhaps 50–60 hours of film down to a 90 minute movie. Editing involves putting everything in the right sequence, and deciding on cuts, fades and shot length. Good editing makes the difference between a sequence of shots and a meaningful film where the language of the images can be understood.

The language of images

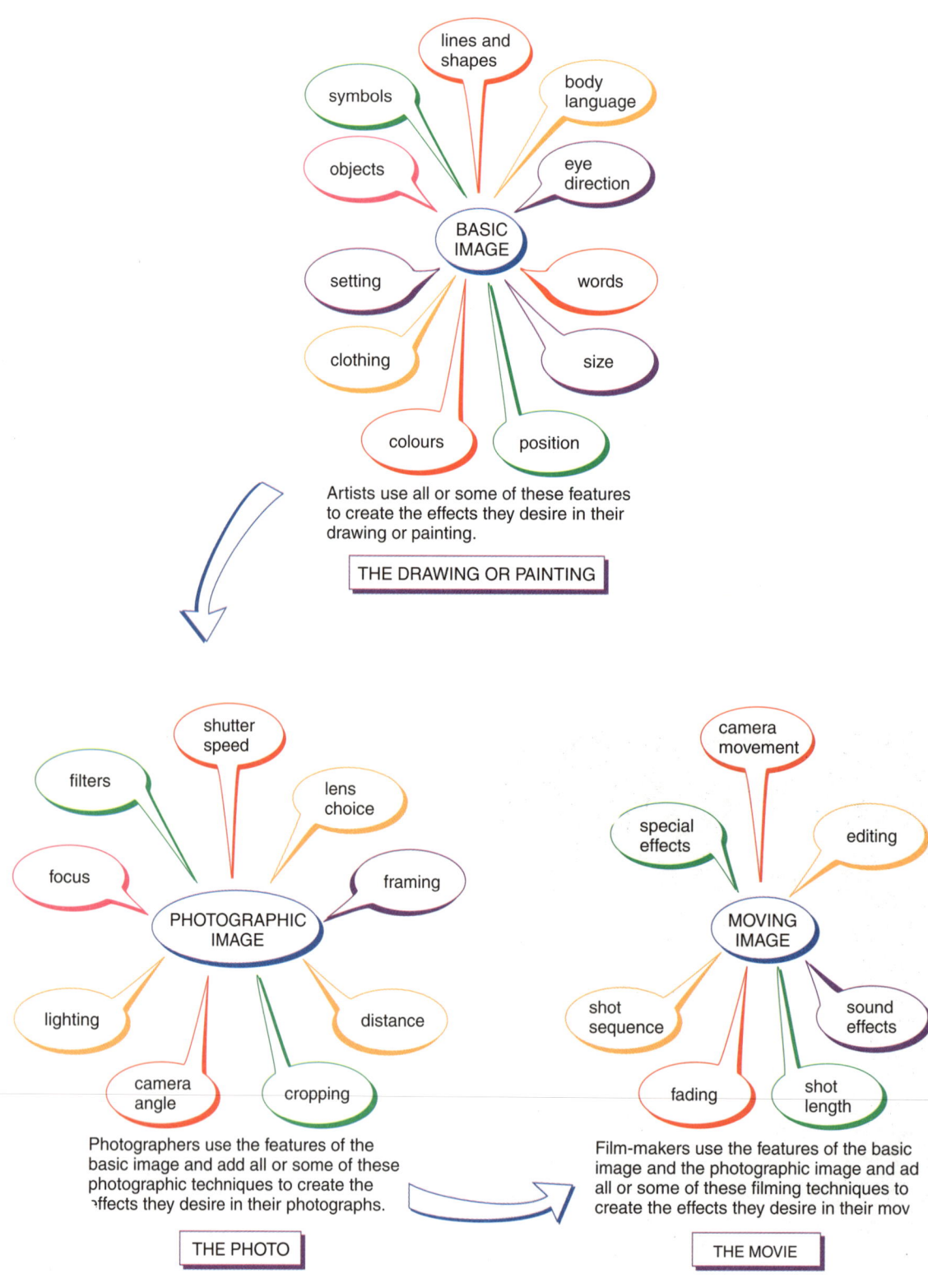

BASIC IMAGE
- lines and shapes
- body language
- eye direction
- words
- size
- position
- colours
- clothing
- setting
- objects
- symbols

Artists use all or some of these features to create the effects they desire in their drawing or painting.

THE DRAWING OR PAINTING

PHOTOGRAPHIC IMAGE
- shutter speed
- filters
- lens choice
- framing
- focus
- distance
- lighting
- cropping
- camera angle

Photographers use the features of the basic image and add all or some of these photographic techniques to create the effects they desire in their photographs.

THE PHOTO

MOVING IMAGE
- camera movement
- special effects
- editing
- sound effects
- shot length
- fading
- shot sequence

Film-makers use the features of the basic image and the photographic image and ad all or some of these filming techniques to create the effects they desire in their mov

THE MOVIE

S E L F

ASSESSMENT

Name: ....

1. Can I?

Write "yes" or "no" in the box. If you write "no", go back over your work until you can write "yes".

- Identify the features of an image .... ☐
- Identify the symbols in an image .... ☐
- Identify the techniques used to create a still image .... ☐
- Use words to add meaning to an image .... ☐
- Identify the techniques used to create a moving image ...... ☐
- Understand how an audience is positioned .... ☐

2. Your reaction

(a) Which image did you like best? Say why.
(b) Which activity did you like best? Say why.
(c) Which skill do you need to work on most? What can you do to improve it?

3. For your folio

From the work you have done in this chapter, choose the pieces you want to include in your folio. Each piece of work in your folio should include a cover sheet which shows the date it was completed, the title, the purpose and the audience.

4. Ongoing skills

Complete the table below by:
- placing a tick at the point at which you feel you usually achieve in each skill
- shading in the range of your achievement in each skill.

When you have completed the table place it in your folio.

Am I improving in these skills?	Level of achievement		
	Same as before	Improving	Much better
Example: Oral work		✓	
Using visuals to communicate			
Expressing my feelings			
Cooperating in groups			
Writing paragraphs			
Writing captions and speech bubbles			
Oral work			

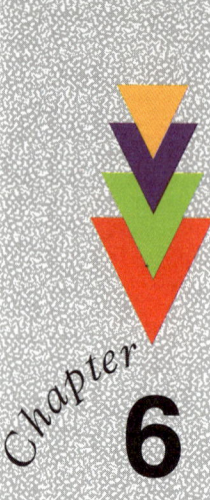

Chapter

6 FILM AS TEXT

Content

- The film-makers
- The actors
- Types of films
- Elements of a film
- Case study — *Dead Poets Society*
- Film review

Skills

- Understanding how a movie is created
- Understanding how visual language techniques are used to control audience response
- Discussing films as text
- Writing a film review
- Assessing a film review

In someone else's world

A movie can hit you like a truck and leave you shattered, can lift you like a soaring bird and leave you ecstatic, can caress you like a child's hand and leave you calm, can twist your heart like a cyclone and leave you anguished. Why? How can a movie — a couple of hours of moving images — have such power over you? When we walk into a theatre, sink into a seat, feel the lights go down and the darkness surround us, our senses become part of someone else's emotional and physical world. The big screen, the enveloping sound and the darkness create a cocoon and we enter an imaginary yet real world: a world full of powerful emotions. We can see the beauty and horror, we can hear the laughter and screams, we can almost taste and smell the sweetness and stench. Sometimes we wish it wouldn't end; sometimes we feel drained by the experience.

Films are a very powerful form of communication. They can change people's attitudes and influence their behaviour. Yet all of this happens not by accident, but because film-makers have learnt the techniques of touching our souls. When we look closely at how film-makers do this we can see that films are not made just to entertain us but to affect us, to make us take sides, to make us feel how the film-maker feels. In short, we are positioned to respond in a certain way.

Who are the people involved in making a film and what techniques do they use to position us?

The film-makers

When the Oscars are presented each year for the world's best movies there is not just one award per movie. There are awards for:

- Best Movie
- Best Director
- Best Cinematographer
- Best Editor
- Best Actor
- Best Supporting Actor
- Best Musical Score
- Best Scriptwriter
- Best Wardrobe Designer
- Best Special Effects

This shows that when an audience watches a movie they are watching the results of many people coming together and blending creativity with skills, technology and organisation.

The scriptwriter creates the screenplay which is often based on a novel, play or true life story. It includes directions, dialogue, shot descriptions and information about sound. For complicated scenes the script is converted to a storyboard which is like a comic strip with dialogue and camera instructions. It can also include sound details. There is an example of a storyboard on page 165.

The producer is the driving force behind the project. A producer's main job is to organise the finance and personnel to make the movie. The producer is the one responsible for the movie from beginning to end and is often involved in the film at all stages.

The director is in charge of the actors, the acting, the types of shots, the type of sound and costuming. The director coordinates the entire production crew. Generally the director has the final say in how a scene will look on film.

The assistant director is the organiser in charge of all schedules — the order in which the scenes will be shot, who needs to be there, what locations are needed, and so on.

The production designer heads the team that creates all the sets, wardrobe, props, vehicles and make-up.

The director of photography is sometimes called the DOP, but more often the cinematographer, and is in charge of how the image appears on film. It is a very technical and creative position. The cinematographer knows all about lenses, lighting, filters and shot composition. It is the cinematographer who creates the breathtaking scenery, the haunting silhouettes, the frightening close-up.

The sound recordist records all the sound including dialogue, music and effects.

The continuity person is very important for providing linking from shot to shot. This person must make sure that all props, sets, wardrobe, performance, lighting and composition are the same for any shots or scenes that connect to another, even if the takes are shot days or weeks apart. It is amazing how quickly an audience will pick up an error in continuity.

The editor is the last person in the creative chain and is in charge of putting together all aspects of the film including sound and dialogue. The editor decides on shot length, sequence and transition from shot to shot. On average an editor can put together about five minutes of final film per day.

Storyboard for scene 38 of *Dead Poets Society*

1. STATIC SHOT OF LIGHT IN STAIRWELL—
SHADOWS MOVE ACROSS THE FRAME AS
BOYS MOVE DOWN STAIRS. EERIE MUSIC.

2. CLOSE UP OF MURAL SHOWING OLD BOYS
—SOUND OF DOOR OPENING AND LIGHT IS
CAST ACROSS THE WALL — DOG BARKS.

3. CLOSE UP SHOT OF HOUSEMASTER IN HIS
ROOM. HE HEARS THE DOG BARK AND LOOKS
SUSPICIOUS — CLOCK ON WALL SHOWS ELEVEN.

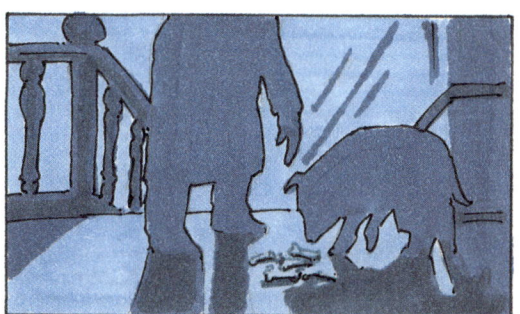

4. CLOSE UP OF SILHOUETTE OF BOY'S
LEGS AND DOG AT THE TOP OF STAIRS — HE
GIVES THE DOG BISCUITS—WHISPERS 'LET'S GO'

5. SHOT DOWN THE HALLWAY AS HOUSE
MASTER COMES OUT OF HIS ROOM AND
SHINES HIS TORCH AROUND—EERIE MUSIC CONT.

6. LOW SHOT—ARCHED CEILING IN SHADOWS, BOY
WHISPERS 'WHAT'S THE TIME—TILT DOWN, BOY WHISPERS,
'11 O'CLOCK—ANOTHER WHISPERS 'ALL RIGHT, LET'S GET OUT, GO'

7. SHOT OF ARCHED DOORWAY—SOUND OF DOOR OPENING,
LIGHT ENTERS AND BOYS AS DARK SHADOWS
GLIDE OUT SILENTLY, SOUND OF DOOR SOFTLY CLOSING

8. SHOT OF SILHOUETTES OF THE BOYS LEAVING
THE SCHOOL BUILDING AND RUNNING ACROSS
THE FOGGY GROUNDS — BLUE LIGHT.

The others

There are many others involved in the four steps to making a movie.

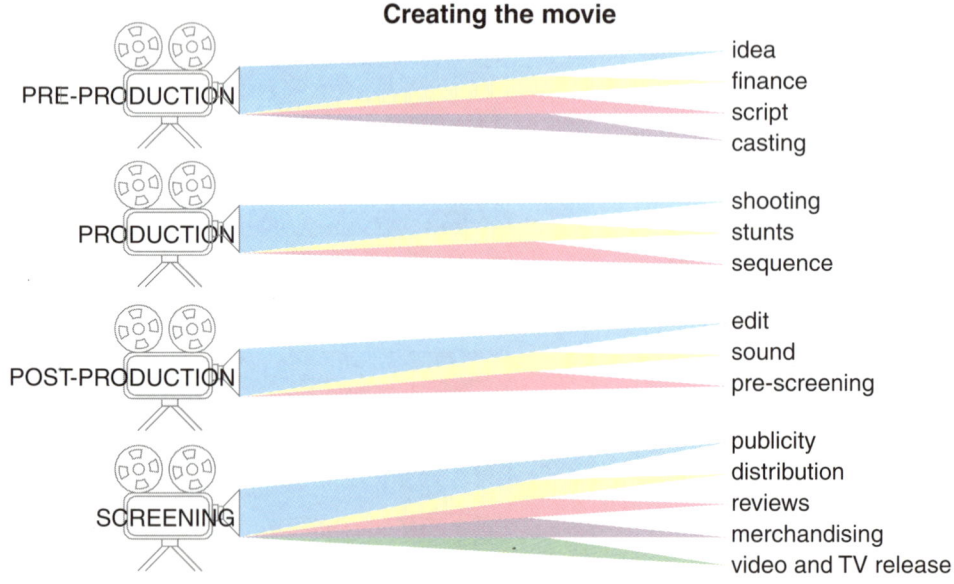

Creating the movie

PRE-PRODUCTION
- idea
- finance
- script
- casting

PRODUCTION
- shooting
- stunts
- sequence

POST-PRODUCTION
- edit
- sound
- pre-screening

SCREENING
- publicity
- distribution
- reviews
- merchandising
- video and TV release

1. If you were offered a job on a film set, which one would you choose? Why?

The actors

The actors are the most visible part of the team. The audience learns to love or hate, support or oppose, accept or reject the actors in the film. The audience ignores the actors' real personalities and identifies only with the characters they are portraying. The role of the actor is to "live" the character.

A "character" is developed by:
- appearance, including clothing
- body language
- possessions
- surroundings
- relationships with others
- language — words, accent, tone, volume.

Producers of big-budget movies employ "stars" in the hope that they will attract a bigger audience. The star has an aura that is carried from film to film. This aura of fame develops out of their personality, their skill, their looks, their image and their publicity machine. Robin Williams is such a star. He is zany, eccentric, friendly, unpredictable, humorous and sensitive. His fame began with the TV show "Mork and Mindy", grew in *Garp*, *Awakenings* and *The Fisher King* and skyrocketed in *Good Morning Vietnam*. He was the ideal choice for the romantic, unpredictable teacher, John Keating, in *Dead Poets Society*. *Mrs Doubtfire* was another great success.

2. List five films you have enjoyed. Who were the stars in each film?

Types of films

Walk into any video shop and you will find films are classified into a wide variety of types.

A film-maker knows that the way a film is classified will give an audience particular expectations. Although the different types often overlap, each follows certain conventions. An audience watching a musical would be confused and upset if, halfway through, it changed to a war movie or a science fiction adventure.

3. (a) Which type of film do you like best?
   (b) What features of that type do you enjoy?

4. (a) When you see the classifications G, PG, M, MA and R, what do you understand by them?
   (b) What expectations do you have for a PG film compared to an MA film as regards sex, language, violence?

Elements of a film

Most movies have a storyline, sometimes called a narrative pattern, similar to that of a novel. It usually begins with an orientation — setting the scene and introducing the main characters. This is followed by a series of complications which create conflict and tension. This conflict might be within one person, between different people, or between a person and society. In most movies the conflict is resolved by some means at the end.

Each part of the narrative is linked to the next so that the audience does not have to piece the movie together. The audience is carried along by the storyline step by step until the climax. Even though the climax may be horrific, and the audience may be angry, shocked, upset and even stunned, the film-makers are usually clever enough to make the audience accept it as a natural step in the storyline.

The invisible links

The narrative links the events and issues in the film in an obvious way. But there is also a series of invisible links that tie the emotions in the movie tightly together. These links are not obvious; if they were, the audience would feel manipulated and the movie would lose its credibility. Instead, the audience is emotionally positioned by a variety of techniques such as the following.

The choice of shots. Has a long shot been used to establish the setting and give us information? Has a low-angle shot given us a sense of threat or fear? Has a close-up been used to create tension? Has a high-angle shot been used to give us a sense of power over the events? Has the camera taken a subjective view to get us involved in the action?

The sequence of shots. In a dialogue scene does the camera stay focused on one person or does it cross from one to another? Does the scene contain flashbacks? Is a close-up of one person under stress followed by a medium shot of another quietly relaxed?

A Russian film-maker, Kuleshov, did an experiment using an unemotional close-up of the famous Russian actor Mosjukhin and connecting the close-up to three different sequences. Exactly the same close-up was used before each sequence. In the first, the close-up was followed by a shot of a plate of soup. In the second it was followed by a shot of a dead woman in a coffin. In the third it was followed by a shot of a little girl playing with a funny toy bear. When the three combinations were shown to an audience who had not been let into the secret they raved about how good an actor he was — the heavy thoughtfulness when gazing at the soup, the deep sorrow when looking at the dead woman, the happy smile when watching the girl at play. Yet in all three cases the face was exactly the same. The power of sequencing was amazing.

The use of sounds and music. How does the music make you feel: romantic, frightened, anxious, relaxed? Do the lyrics reinforce the storyline? Is the music loud or soft? Are the sound effects realistic? Do they jolt you or soothe you? Is the music repeated throughout the film like a theme? Music is one of the most powerful yet subtle links in the whole movie.

5. Name a film theme you really like. Why does it have such impact on you?

The lighting. Is the lighting bright and clear to create a feeling of openness and security or is it low-key to give a sense of fear and drama? Is it hard with strong shadows to create tension or is it soft to create a sense of romance?

Use of symbols. Does the clothing or make-up indicate a certain type of person? Does body language tell us how they feel? Does colour have a special meaning? Are certain actions, sounds, signs symbolic? These are the most subtle of all the links, yet they can profoundly affect the way we feel.

DEAD POETS SOCIETY

This famous movie, released in 1989, won an Oscar in the Academy Awards for Best Original Screenplay and was nominated for Best Picture, Best Actor and Best Director.

The team

Producers — Steven Haft, Paul Junger Witt and Tony Thomas
Director — Peter Weir
Screenplay — Tom Schulman
Director of photography — John Seale
Editor — William Anderson
Music — Maurice Jarre

The cast

Characters	Actors
John Keating	Robin Williams
Neil Perry	Robert Sean Leonard
Todd Anderson	Ethan Hawke
Knox Overstreet	Josh Charles
Charlie Dalton	Gale Hansen
Richard Cameron	Dylan Kussman
Mr Perry	Kurtwood Smith

Running Time 129 minutes, USA 1989 Warner Bros. Video Release by Touchstone Pictures.

Elements of *Dead Poets Society*

Setting

An exclusive private school, Welton Academy in rural Vermont, USA. The year is 1959.

Plot or storyline

The new English teacher, John Keating, encourages the boys to grab life with both hands, to take risks, to be different. The boys re-form the "Dead Poets Society" and explore their own hopes and dreams. One of the boys, Neil, commits suicide. Keating is blamed for this and is dismissed.

Characters

John Keating: witty, lively unusual
Neil Perry: artistic, sensitive, expressive, dominated by his father
Todd Anderson: shy, insecure, naive
Knox Overstreet: emotional, romantic, impulsive
Charlie Dalton: rebellious, strong-willed, popular
Richard Cameron: conservative, hard-working, unemotional
Mr Perry: hard, authoritarian, concerned

Themes

- Boys striving for self-realisation
- Authority versus non-conformity
- The power of charismatic leaders
- Realism versus idealism
- The effect of family pressure

Style

- Narrative
- Lots of short scenes to create a fast-moving story – 112 scenes in 129 minutes
- Lots of symbolism
- Powerful use of panoramic shots and low-key hard lighting
- Dialogues short and sharp

Before you watch the movie

Look at "themes" in the diagram on page 169 and answer the following questions. Then discuss your answers with others.

6. How much influence should adults have in deciding goals for teenagers?

7. Why are parents and schools concerned about young people who don't conform? Do you think this is reasonable? Explain.

8. What characteristics do you admire most in a teacher?

9. What sort of power do you think a popular teacher has over students? Could this be dangerous? Explain.

10. "Idealism versus realism" — in groups discuss the following.
    (a) What do these words mean?
    (b) Which do you think is more important? Explain.
    (c) Is it possible to have both? Explain.

11. How do you respond to pressures put on you by your family? Are you happy with the way you respond? Explain. If your answer is "no", what could you do to improve the situation?

The movie — scene by scene

The action in each scene of the film is summarised in the pages that follow. For most scenes, issues and visual language are discussed in the purple boxes on the left, and there are activities arising from this discussion in the cream boxes on the right.

1 Opening — preparing for Assembly.

The whispering creates a feeling of awe and formality.

2 Assembly hall. The traditional ceremony of lighting candles is performed. The headmaster praises the school, its tradition and its performance. John Keating is introduced.

The camera crosses backwards and forwards from headmaster to parents to students.

12. What is the significance of this?

13. What is the significance of establishing the "four pillars" of the school so early in the film — tradition, honour, discipline, excellence?

3 School grounds — parents are saying goodbye.

4 Assembly hall foyer. Todd Anderson is introduced to the headmaster. He is expected to do as well as his brother, who had previously attended the school. Neil Perry is greeted by the headmaster. Mr Perry says, "He won't disappoint you". Neil says, "I'll do my best, Sir".

The pressure is on for both Todd and Neil. Todd seems unhappy to have this thrust upon him. Neil seems confident and anxious to please. Mr Perry seems tough and humourless.

14. What feelings does this scene give you?

5 School grounds — younger students — teary farewells.

6 Wide scenic shot of countryside.

Note the autumn colours.

15. What could this shot symbolise?

7 Dormitory. Neil and Todd realise they are to be room-mates.

Again Todd is made aware of his brother's reputation.

16. Imagine you are Todd. Write a diary entry after your first day at school.

8 Dormitories — Neil's and Todd's room. Neil is welcomed back, obviously popular. Other boys drop in. Cameron, Charlie Knox, Meeks. Cameron is referred to as a "bootlicker". Todd is again compared to his brother.

The boys' own "four pillars" are Travesty, Horror, Decadence, Excrement. We are being positioned to see Cameron in a negative light. Todd feels the pressure to be as good as his brother.

17. What is the significance of letting us know Neil has been to summer school?

9 Neil and Todd's room and corridor. Neil's father tells Neil to drop extra-curricular activities. Neil disputes him but is cut short: "Don't you ever dispute me in public. When you finish medical school you can do as you please, but until then you do as I tell you."

This scene is full of contradictions. Neil's father refuses to listen to his son and yet finishes by saying, "If you need anything you let us know." There is great tension here as Neil is torn between his father's wishes and his own needs. Even a reference to his mother's hopes for him adds more stress.

18. How do you think you would have responded in this situation?

10　Corridor. The boys ask Neil why he doesn't stand up to his father, but all agree they don't stand up to theirs either. Neil is obviously upset at not being able to work on the school magazine but says, "I don't care a damn about any of it."

Idealism versus reality. The boys know they have to obey authority; that is the system. Note the stress on the word "any" in Neil's statement: a hint that it is all becoming too much.

19. Imagine you are Neil. Write a diary entry of your first day back at school.

11　Neil's and Todd's room. Todd is setting his alarm clock, and checks his watch.

12　Clock tower. The bell sounds.

Note the link from watch to clock.

13　Huge flock of birds scatter in the autumn sky.

Note the link from clock to birds.

20. Do the birds symbolise freedom, order or rowdiness?

14　School staircase crowded with boys making a racket.

Note the link from birds to the low-angle shot of boys, both in visuals and sound.

21. What do you think is the significance of the link?

15　Classroom. Chemistry lesson.

These three scenes are short and show the formality and conformity of the normal lessons at Welton. The four pillars of learning are clearly shown.

16　Classroom. Latin class.

17　Classroom. Trigonometry — "Your study requires absolute precision."

18 Classroom — English. Keating enters, whistling; he walks through and out the other door. The boys are stunned. His first words are "Well, come on!" Bewildered, the boys follow.

In strong contrast to previous three lessons this one promises to be unusual, interesting and daring. Notice how Cameron is the first to obey.

19 In foyer. Keating asks the boys to be daring: "Call me Captain! My Captain!" They consider him strange but like his clever wit and sharp mind. He draws attention to the photo of the Old Boys and says, "We are food for worms, lads ... We must all carpe diem ... Seize the day, make your lives extraordinary."

There is symbolism in "Captain! My Captain!" which emerges right at the end of the film. It is a quotation from the American poet Walt Whitman.

This is the longest scene so far. Note the crane shot to allow us to see the whole group and their body language towards Keating. Notice how he identifies with the boys by calling Welton "Helton", as they do. A quick close-up of Neil shows him smile. Note tracking and panning shots to make us feel part of the group. One of the main issues of the movie is presented here, strongly and clearly yet with humour and sensitivity.

22. Why do you think the film-makers made this the longest scene so far?

23. What do you think "Seize the day" means?

20　School grounds. The boys talk about the lesson — "That was weird" … "spooky". Cameron says, "Will he test us on that?" The other boys shake their heads in disbelief at his question.

Keating has obviously affected the boys in different ways. They have begun to think.

24. What does Cameron's question tell us about him?

25. How would you have responded to Keating's first lesson?

21　Showers. Knox announces he is going out that night to visit friends of his family, the Danburrys, for dinner. Todd is invited to join the study group by Neil. He refuses, preferring to remain alone.

Notice how a single line by the teacher creates the impression that Charlie Dalton is a troublemaker.

26. What is this line?

22　Todd's room. He writes, "Seize the day", but throws it in the bin and begins homework.

Quick cut links the scenes.

27. Is the quick cut a symbolic rejection of Keating's ideas? Explain.

23　24　Knox is taken to Danburrys' by one of the schoolmasters. Beautiful autumn scene and setting sun.

There is a calmness about these images.

28. (a) Do these images of calm represent the peace of autumn? Explain.
    (b) Is it the calm before the storm? Discuss in small groups.

25　26　At Danburrys'. Knox is stunned by the beautiful Chris. He meets the Danburrys.

This is the beginning of Knox's journey into self-realisation.

27 Later that night — boys at study. Cameron is conscientious. Knox arrives; says that dinner was "terrible ... Tonight I met the most beautiful girl I have ever met in my entire life ... She is practically engaged ... All the good ones go for jerks."

Cameron's personality is continually being presented to us. We are made to think of him as being only concerned about study and results. Knox is in direct contrast to this. He can think only of Chris.

29. What do the boys' comments about girls tell us about their attitude to women?

28 The teacher dismisses the boys. Dalton says to Knox, "Did you see her naked?" The teacher questions the boys about their secret radio.

Dalton's personality is also being consolidated for us — he is a rebel. The teacher's comments show how the school disapproves of any unauthorised experimenting.

29 Classroom. Keating's English lesson begins with reading the introductory chapter in a poetry book called *Understanding Poetry* by Pritchard. Keating claims this is "excrement" and tells the boys to rip these pages from the book.

Cameron responds immediately by copying down the graph. We are made to feel that he sees all study as merely following orders. Keating's outburst of "excrement" refers back to one of the pillars of knowledge that the boys use. The word is a powerful contradiction to what Cameron is doing. Notice that Dalton is the first boy to tear out the page. The boys are shocked but excited by this unusual approach.

30 Classroom. The Latin teacher McAllister enters, shocked at what is going on, but does not dispute Keating's authority. Keating creates a huddle: "We read and write poetry because we are members of the human race and the human race is filled with passion. The powerful play goes on and you may contribute a verse."

Although in disagreement McAllister conforms to the traditional attitude of not interfering with another teacher's class. Note the camera focuses on individual boys and finally rests on Neil whose eyes are bright and eager and Todd whose eyes are confused.

30. Notice the body language: close, friendly, almost a conspiracy — what is it a conspiracy against?

31. Keating's statement is one of the keys to the whole film. What do you think it means?

31 Mealtime. McAllister claims Keating is misguided. He says, "I'm not a cynic but a realist. Show me the heart unfettered by foolish dreams — and I'll show you a happy man." Keating replies, "But only in their dreams can men be truly free".

Notice the link here from the previous scene with the words, "May the Lord make us truly thankful." The argument between McAllister and Keating is one of the main issues in the film — "realism versus idealism".

32. (a) Which do you support: realism or idealism?
   (b) How have the film-makers positioned you to feel this way?

33. Can we excuse the sexist language in this scene? Explain.

32 Mealtime. Neil shows the boys an old school magazine which includes Keating. It also mentions that he was a member of the "Dead Poets Society".

Dalton's rebellious nature is further developed. He picks up on Keating's "hell-raising" days.

33 School grounds. The boys ask Keating about the Dead Poets Society. He says they were dedicated to "sucking the marrow out of life. We didn't just read poetry; we let it drip from our tongues like honey." The boys decide to reconvene the Dead Poets Society.

The Dead Poets Society was obviously unacceptable to the administration. Camera focuses on Neil. It's as though he has made up his mind to do something. Again this scene is done as a huddle — secretive, warm, supportive.

34. Why was the original Dead Poets Society unacceptable to the administration?

34 **35** Study room. Boys check map for the original meeting place of the Dead Poets Society. Todd wants to join but lacks the confidence to read poetry aloud. Neil offers to talk the boys into letting him join anyway.

Todd's character is becoming clearer. We are slowly made to see his major problem with speaking in public.

36 Shower room. Boys preparing for bed.

37 Neil's and Todd's room. Neil discovers a book on his desk: Keating's copy of *Five Centuries of Verse*, which Keating has secretly left there for him.

Again the sense of conspiracy emerges. The issue — should Keating be encouraging the boys to embark on this plan or even think in this way?

35. Do you think Keating should have taken this initiative? Explain.

38 Late at night. The boys sneak out; the dog barks; the housemaster is suspicious.

Powerful use of symbols: mist, silhouettes, darkness, unexpected noises, crow. This creates a feeling of daring, excitement even fear. This is a new and frightening world they are about to enter.

36. Which symbol do you feel is the most powerful in creating the atmosphere?

| 39 | 40 | Boys, monk-like, run through the forest to the cave.

| 41 | 43 | Cave. Neil leads the group and reconvenes the Dead Poets Society. He tells a horror story and the others all read poems or stories. They dance the conga to the poem "Congo".

Neil shows that he is a good actor. The boys are spellbound by his ability. Each boy's story tells us something about him. Neil's lines from Tennyson — "It is not too late to seek a newer world . . ." — are important to him. There is a powerful feeling that the Dead Poets Society is critically important to Neil.

| 44 | Back to school.

Note the use of "Congo"/conga as the visual link here.

37. Are the chimes of the clock tower another symbol. If so, of what?

| 45 | Classroom. Keating encourages boys to use powerful, not insipid language. The purpose of language? "To woo women". He mimics Shakespearian actors and has all the boys in fits of laughter. He stands on his desk and encourages the boys to do so on theirs. "We must constantly look at things in a different way . . . Strive to find your own voice." The students have to write a poem of their own.

The issue of powerful language is important — "Use 'exhausted' rather than 'very tired'" — and shows his desire to teach the boys to be more powerful communicators. He gains their respect with his wit and skill. Lateral thinking is one of the major challenges facing the world of conformity. Again Keating threatens the establishment. Notice how the camera angle moves from high to low in this scene.

38. How does Keating threaten the establishment?

39. What is the effect of the shift in camera angle during this scene?

46 Boys rowing on river.

47 School grounds. Pitts and Meeks get the secret radio going. Rock music blares out and boys dance in jubilation.

This contrasts starkly with the highly organised precision of the rowing practice.

48 In Neil's and Todd's room. Todd is writing a poem of personal anguish. Neil announces he is going to be an actor — a very strong but stressful decision. He decides he may have to deceive his father. The scene ends with Todd chasing Neil and others joining in.

Todd is apprehensive; Neil is filled with hope — he feels strong enough to disobey his father. Has the theme, "Strive to find your own voice" begun to work on him? Notice high-angle shots on Todd, low angle on Neil. The lighthearted behaviour of the boys changes the mood; 360° panning shot in a confined space adds to the excitement.

40. What effects are achieved by the high-angle, low-angle and 360° panning shots?

49 School grounds. Knox, on his bike, in a wild moment of passion, decides to visit Chris.

The ducks scatter as Knox yells.

41. What could the symbolism of the ducks scattering be?

50 The football match. Knox sees Chris dance and then cuddle her boyfriend. He is disappointed.

51 School soccer field. Keating uses poetry to teach determination and aggression.

Keating plays powerful music to support his ideas and actions.

42. How is the music designed to affect the audience?

52 The dormitory. Excitedly Neil announces that he has won the important role of Puck in the play *A Midsummer Night's Dream*. He decides to forge a letter from his father to give him permission to go in the play. He is exhilarated. "This is great!"

The exuberance of Neil is contrasted with Todd's quiet concern. Neil seems almost out of control.

53 Evening — outside. A solitary piper plays a melancholy tune.

A very ominous, haunting contrast to Neil's joy. This is a deliberate link to the formality of the opening scene. Note the downward tilt shot and the long still shot of the piper, creating the feeling of loneliness.

43. What do you think is the symbolism of the solitary piper?

54 Neil's and Todd's room. Todd cannot get his poem right.

The bagpipe music links through to this scene.

55 Classroom. Boys reading their poems. Keating makes the comment, "Just don't let your poems be ordinary." Todd has not written a poem. Keating understands. "I sound my barbaric YAWP [a powerful scream]". Todd is asked to get up and gradually succeeds in producing a spontaneous powerful poem.

This is the moment of truth for Todd. For a moment he breaks through the barrier of self-doubt and all the boys know it. This is Keating at his best. It is also a breakthrough for him.

56 School grounds. Keating and boys playing soccer. All very happy and excited.

The cut to Beethoven's *Ode to Joy* is a striking conclusion to the emotional celebration of the previous scene. Note the fast tracking shots and quick cuts to add a sense of elation. The body language is close, affectionate and open.

44. What do you think the visual images of boys running and jumping and carrying Keating on their shoulders are intended to mean?

57 Cave. Boys smoking pipes — a new experience. Dalton plays soulful sax. Knox says, "If I can't have Chris, I'm going to kill myself."

The sad music affects Knox who is pining for Chris. Camera focuses on Neil when Knox makes the statement.

45. What do you think is the significance of focusing on Neil at this moment?

58 At the phone Knox hesitates but is encouraged by the boys: "Carpe diem [seize the day]" — and Chris invites him to a party!

Keating's influence on Knox is clear, giving him the audacity to ring Chris. The "yawp" is used in triumph.

59 A poetry lesson in the quadrangle. The boys learn about conformity: "You must trust your own beliefs."

Another main theme — conformity — is explored. Notice Dalton's response; also the high-angle shot to the headmaster as he watches from his "superior" perspective.

46. Do you believe it is possible not to conform in some way? Explain.

47. Conformity can be comfortable. Do you agree? Discuss.

60 Outside. It is Todd's birthday and Neil encourages him to throw away the present given to him by his parents: a desk set the same as they gave him last year.

This is a symbolic gesture of freedom and independence — painful but liberating. The relationship between Neil and Todd becomes very close.

61 The cave. Charlie Dalton brings two girls: the boys are overawed. Charlie decides he wants to be called Nuwanda.

The feeling at the meeting is different — the girls add tension and uncertainty. Charlie seems to be going too far.

62 63 The party at Danburrys' house. Knox can't get to Chris and he is made to drink alcohol with the boys.

Note the musical link from the previous scene.

64 The cave. Charlie is dominating the events, reciting poetry for the girls.

The party and cave scenes are alternated to create the effect of both events happening at the same time. Charlie's poetry recitation is a clear link back to Keating's comment that poetry is for wooing women.

48. What do you feel about Keating's remark?

65 The party. Knox "seizes the day" and kisses Chris. However, she is shocked and he gets beaten up by Chris' boyfriend. Chris protects Knox.

Note the song here: "Hey Little Girl, How's About a Kiss?"

49. What feeling does the song give to the scene?

66 The cave. The boys are drinking and smoking. Charlie tells them he has written an article in the school paper on behalf of the Dead Poets Society about allowing girls into the school. The boys are horrified.

A crucial step. Charlie takes their newfound ideals into reality, but the other boys are not prepared to follow him.

50. What does this say about Charlie?

51. What does it say about the other boys?

67 Assembly. The headmaster speaks to all staff and students. Charlie breaks the tension with a ridiculous phone call.

A very formal and threatening scene — almost militaristic. Again Charlie is taking a risk.

68 The headmaster's office. Charlie is physically punished.

Charlie is not broken by authority. He refuses to conform.

52. What do you think you would have done in this situation?

69 Corridor. The boys await Charlie and are relieved to hear he did not inform on them.

This is a direct contrast to what happens later on.

70 Classroom. The headmaster talks to Keating about "unorthodox teaching methods". He connects Keating to Charlie and reminds Keating that the boys are impressionable. Keating talks about "dangers of conformity".

The issue of conformity is raised again, this time between two adults. Keating is seen as challenging authority. But Keating continues to stress the importance of thinking for oneself.

53. Who do you think the film-makers intend the audience to support?

71 Students' common room. Keating tells Charlie that "there is a time for daring and a time for caution".

Even at a serious moment Keating creates humour.

54. Do you think Keating is giving Charlie good advice? Explain.

72 Neil, on bike, rides to rehearsal.

Note that clock chimes connect this scene.

55. What symbolic significance do the clock chimes have throughout the film?

73 Hall. Neil at rehearsal.

Neil's eyes shine with anticipation. A low angle shot is used here.

56. What effect does the low-angle shot have?

74 Stairway/Neil's room. Mr Perry very angrily forces Neil to abandon the play. He forbids him to perform in it "even if the world comes to an end tomorrow night".

The boys excitedly run to dinner, in direct contrast to the quiet menace in Mr Perry's voice. He is concerned about image and obedience. Neil's look of determination gives the impression that although he is saying "yes" to his father, he does not mean it. Mr Perry's words are ominous.

57. How would you have responded to Mr Perry in this situation if he was your father?

75 In Keating's room. Neil discusses his problem and Keating tells him to be honest with his father. Neil's words, "I'm trapped" and Keating's response, "No you're not" end the scene.

Notice the low-angle shots for Keating and the high-angle shots for Neil.

58. Do you agree with Keating's advice?

59. (a) Why does Neil feel trapped?
    (b) Who is responsible for this?

60. What are Neil's options?

76 Outside. Knox rides his bike in the snow.

Winter has set in: pure but cold, white but signifying death — a powerful symbol.

77 **78** Chris' school. Knox finds Chris but she rejects him. Knox reads a poem and gives her flowers.

In both these scenes Knox is prepared to take a risk — to make a fool of himself — to be hurt again. He has "seized the day".

61. Do you think Knox is stupid or noble? Explain.

62. What do you think Keating would have thought of his actions?

79 Kitchen at Welton. Knox passes through. He is happy and confident.

80 Dormitory. Knox tells the others what happened: "I did it!"

He is happy, not so much because he succeeded but because he had the courage to do it.

63. Do you think you would do something like this? Explain.

81 Classroom. Keating speaks to Neil who tells him his father has given him permission to act in the play.

Body language and eye contact tells us that Neil is lying.

64. Does Keating believe what Neil is telling him? Explain.

65. What is the effect of the shot angles in this scene?

82 Bathroom. Boys are getting ready to go to the play. Charlie has a tattoo of red lightning on his chest.

Charlie's rebelliousness is growing.

83   Foyer. Knox sees Chris.

84   Outside. Knox and Chris talk. She agrees to go to the play with him.

Knox shows determination and strength. Dead Poets' honour will later be tested.

85   Inside the theatre the play is in progress; Neil "is really good". He is excited, but then sees his father. He continues, but we know his anguish. Knox holds Chris' hand.

The symbolic gesture of Chris' hand squeezing Knox's means we know he has finally succeeded.

86   Theatre. Puck's (Neil's) final speech.

The words of the final speech and the quick cuts to Neil and his father suggest that the words are meant for him. The body language speaks volumes.

66. Describe the feelings created by Mr Perry's body language.

87   Theatre. Standing ovation.

The "barbaric YAWP" is sounded by the boys.

88   Backstage. Neil is elated, but his joy is ended when his father demands he come home.

The positioning of Neil and his father are important — a whole theatre apart — Neil with an apprehensive smile, his father with a disapproving frown.

89 Outside the theatre. Keating congratulates Neil but Mr Perry is furious. "Keating, you stay away from my son."

The anger that is shown through Mr Perry's eyes, body language and words creates great tension in this scene.
There is a sense of violence.

90 Perrys' home. Mrs Perry waits.

Note the symbols of tension and of the important issue of family loyalty.

67. What are these symbols?

91 Neil's father lays down the law. Neil is to leave Welton and go to military school. Mr Perry asks, "What is it that you feel?" But he does not wait for an answer — or Neil cannot say. His mother does nothing to ease the tension. The scene ends with Neil's half-smile.

Body language is expressive, with Neil sitting while his father stands over him. Low-angle shots are used. Neil's inability to say what he feels is the crucial issue. Notice Neil's body language at that point. He curls himself in the chair; he becomes frail. The high-angle shot accentuates this.

68. Do you think Neil could have been saved if he had been able to answer his father's question?

69. (a) How do you feel about Neil when he curls into himself in the chair?
    (b) How do you feel about Mr Perry at this point? Why?
    (c) What do you feel about Mrs Perry? Why?

92 Perrys' bedroom. Without a word the parents go to bed — Mr Perry placing his slippers with military precision. Mrs Perry cries and is consoled by her husband.

The slippers symbolise rigidity and conformity. Mrs Perry is deliberately stereotyped, as is Mr Perry's response.

70. Describe the stereotyping of Neil's parents.

93 Neil's bedroom. Neil undresses, opens the windows to let in the freezing air and wears Puck's crown. He stands and stares out, then closes his eyes, lowers his head and decides on his future.

Notice how Neil's clothes have been so neatly placed on his bed. The use of Neil's shadow gives a unreal effect. The music is a monotone, eerie and ominous, creating a sense of foreboding. Note that Neil's colouring is pale, the colour of death.

94 Neil moves silently downstairs.

The music links these scenes. The silhouette creates a ghost-like effect.

95 Perrys' bedroom. Mr Perry sleeps, but there is tension in his face.

71. What does the twitching muscle in Mr Perry's face signify?

96 Mr Perry's study. Neil gets out the gun. He is very calm.

The music continues relentlessly. The audience is made to feel powerless, knowing what is about to happen.

72. How is the feeling of powerlessness achieved?

97 Perrys' bedroom. Mr Perry wakes in alarm. "What was that ... that sound?" He goes to see what has happened.

His whisper, his eyes and his body language seem to show that he knows already what has happened but dares not believe it.

98 Neil's bedroom. It is empty. The tension increases. He continues to look.

Mrs Perry's words add to the tension.

73. Why does Mr Perry ignore his wife?

99 The study. At first all appears normal; then the smell, the smoke and the gun reveal what has happened. He screams in anguish: "Oh my son, my poor son!" Mrs Perry, too, screams repeatedly: "He's all right, he's all right." They cling to each other.

This scene is explosive. The use of slow motion and Mr Perry's "Yawp" of pain fills the audience with emotion. The Perrys' body language expresses their shock and devastation. We do not see them again.

74. Describe the emotions this scene creates in you.

75. How do you think the film-makers intend the audience to feel towards the Perrys at this point?

100 Todd's bedroom. Charlie wakes Todd and tells him about Neil's death.

101 Outside the school. A winter landscape. Todd walks alone in the snow, then is followed by others. He is overwhelmed by the beauty of the scene and by the pain of his friend's death. He vomits. He blames Neil's father.

The scene is grey and desolate — a symbol of their pain. This shot is held for a very long time. The boys are dressed in coats with hoods, linking back to the joyful nights of the Dead Poets Society. Todd screams another "Yawp" of pain. Keating's idea has become an expression of tragedy rather than joy. Note how gradually Todd disappears into the snowy landscape.

76. What is the irony of Todd's "Yawp"?

77. What do you think the film-makers intend Todd's gradual disappearance into the snow to represent?

102 Classroom. Keating is devastated. He finds his book *Five Centuries of Verse* in Neil's desk and breaks down.

Music connects this scene. The camera slowly zooms in on the book to highlight the words: "I wanted to live deliberately . . . and not, when I came to die, discover that I had not lived".

78. What do you think is the significance of these words from the book?

103 Assembly Hall. The boys sing a hymn. The headmaster states that there will be an inquiry and that everyone is expected to cooperate.

Everything is in black — the symbol of mourning. The headmaster's tone is threatening.

104 The boys meet in the store-room. Cameron is absent. They believe he is revealing all to the headmaster. Charlie claims the school will have to find a scapegoat.

79. Why is Charlie so sure that Cameron will be disloyal?

80. Why does he believe the school will need a scapegoat for Neil's death?

105 Cameron enters. Charlie accuses him. Cameron claims he had no choice: he was merely obeying orders. He pleads with them to cooperate too. "They're not after us! We're the victims." The others can't believe Keating is to get the blame. Charlie punches Cameron.

This scene is about obeying authority.

81. Is this what we have been expecting from Cameron all along?

82. How have the film-makers given us this impression of him?

83. How do *you* think the boys should have responded in this situation?

106 Todd's bedroom. He looks out as Meeks is led back from the headmaster's office.

Note the effect of the windowpanes like bars in a prison.

107 Corridor. The boys are called for questioning one by one. Todd asks Meeks what happened. "Nuwanda? Expelled!"

Charlie himself, it seems, has become the first scapegoat.

108 Inside the headmaster's office. Todd's parents are there. He is overwhelmed. Keating is blamed for Neil's death. Todd does not agree but cannot say anything. He is asked to sign a document blaming Keating. The other four boys have already signed it.

Powerful negative words are used to describe the attitudes, personality and activities of Keating: "reckless", "self-indulgent", "obsession", "blatant abuse".

84. Do you think Todd signs the document? Support your answer.

109 McAllister is giving a Latin lesson outside. He looks up, sees Keating at the window and waves.

The crane shot makes McAllister look humble. Again the window creates the impression that Keating is behind bars.

110 Keating's room. He smiles sadly; everything is packed.

111 Boys in classroom. The headmaster takes the lesson in place of Keating. Everything is formal, predictable and hushed. "What about the Realists?" he says. Keating timidly collects his belongings. The headmaster asks the boys to read the Pritchard essay which has, of course, been ripped out. As Keating leaves Todd calls out.

The class has returned to conformity. There is no such group as the Realist poets. Todd has finally broken free from his insecurity and spoken out.

85. What is the significance of the reference to the "Realists"?

86. What is the irony in this scene?

87. What is the significance of Todd speaking out?

112 Todd stands on his desk saying, "O Captain! My Captain!" The others follow, except for Cameron. The headmaster is powerless. Keating says, "Thank you, boys". The last shot is of Todd calm and determined.

This scene is the resolution in the storyline of the film. It also reveals the final irony of "O Captain! My Captain!"; in Walt Whitman's poem the ship is sailing home victorious but her captain lies dead.

88. There are many low-angle shots in this scene. What effect do they have?

89. Keating is shown with a high-angle shot? Why?

90. (a) Do you think Cameron was right not to conform here?
   (b) How do you think he would have justified his decision?

91. Why do you think the film ends with a shot of Todd?

92. How does it link to the beginning?

93. What emotions are aroused in the audience in this scene? How?

94. There are many contrasts in *Dead Poets Society*, such as the aggressive narrowness of Mr Perry compared with the creative openness of Neil, the restrictive tension in the school compared with the open peacefulness of the countryside, the humorous freedom of English lessons compared with the boring regimentation of trigonometry lessons. These contrasts help create the conflict, and the conflict in turn creates the dramatic interest for the audience.
    (a) List as many contrasts as you can find in the film.
    (b) Show how one of these contrasts adds conflict to the film.

95. The film deals with many issues, and in most cases each issue is summed up briefly in the dialogue. Explain what the issue is in each of the following.
    (a) "Tradition, honour, discipline, excellence"
    (b) "Travesty, horror, decadence, excrement"
    (c) "Carpe diem"
    (d) "Make your lives extraordinary."
    (e) "The powerful play goes on and you may contribute a verse."
    (f) "Strive to find your own voice."
    (g) "Oh Captain! My Captain!"

96. The film-makers seem to make the audience feel that the tragic end is inevitable. How do they do this?

97. The film-makers have positioned the audience to support Keating rather than the headmaster.
    (a) How has this been done?
    (b) Do you think this is fair? Explain.

98. Who do you think is to blame for Neil's death? In groups, present a case to the School Board showing how one of the following is to blame:
    • Neil himself
    • Mr Perry (Neil's father)
    • Keating
    • the headmaster
    • other.

99. The boys who form the Dead Poets Society develop a strong sense of group identity. Do you think this is a good experience for them to have? Why?

100. Which of the boys do you identify with most? Explain why this is so. Use specific scenes to support your response.

101. Imagine you are a boy in Neil's class but are not part of the Dead Poets Society. Your parents have written to you asking what happened.
    (a) Write a letter in reply explaining what you feel it was all about.
    (b) Now write a letter telling a friend at another school what happened. How does this letter differ from the first? Discuss this with a partner.

102. The film-makers have used many techniques to create the atmosphere in each scene. Choose one scene in the movie.
    (a) List the adjectives that describe the scene.
    (b) Describe the behaviour of the characters.
    (c) Identify some of the camera shots used.
    (d) Describe some of the symbols used.

103. All the characters in the movie seem to have a symbolic meaning; for example, Charlie represents rebelliousness. In one word, say what you feel each of the following characters represents:
    (a) Neil
    (b) Todd
    (c) Meeks
    (d) Cameron
    (e) Knox
    (f) Keating
    (g) Mr Perry
    (h) the headmaster.

Analytical and creative responses

104. Write an essay of approximately 400 words on one of the following topics. Look back at the model of a text response essay on pages 68–70 to help you.
    (a) Explore the idea that romanticism can be dangerous.
    (b) *Dead Poets Society* is really about the power of conformity.
    (c) Adults have all the power. Whether it's the headmaster, Mr Perry or Keating, the boys are merely pawns in the world presented to them by adults.
    (d) In *Dead Poets Society* the audience is not given a choice; we are positioned to side with Keating.
    (e) "*Dead Poets Society* touched audiences and critics alike with its brilliant acting, uplifting story and superb craftsmanship." To what extent do you agree with this statement?

105. Write your own ending to the film.

106. Todd rings up Keating one month later. Describe what they talk about.

107. Do any of the boys remind you of your own friends? In what way?

The film review

Film reviews on TV or radio or in the newspaper tell us, or sometimes warn us, about the quality of a movie. Look at the film review of *Dead Poets Society* on page 196 and at the assessment sheet on page 197.

108. Write a film review of your own on *Dead Poets Society* or on another movie you have recently seen.

109. Show your review to a partner and have them assess your work on the assessment sheet (page 197). Then assess your partner's film review.

- title
- name of film
- cinemas
- rating in stars
- introduction
- director
- star actor
- plot
- setting
- film genre
- comment about main actor
- more about plot
- the main actors, their roles and types of performances
- the writer
- style
- filmcraft
- cinematographer
- method
- tone
- further comment on the plot

Certainly not dead!

Dead Poets Society
Hoyts
★★★★

If you plan to see just one movie this year make sure it is *Dead Poets Society*. Not because it is a Peter Weir film, or because it stars funnyman Robin Williams, or because it won the Academy Award for Best Original Screen play, but simply because by any standards it is superb.

It explores the dynamic lives of a group of boys and their teacher at the prestigious Welton Academy in Vermont, USA, through the autumn and winter months of 1959.

But if you think this is just another charismatic teacher movie, you'll be in for some surprises.

When the new teacher John Keating (Robin Williams — at his best) takes the boys for English lessons a whole new world of mind-blowing experiences opens up for them. The film explores their desires and fears, their hopes and limitations with both wonderful and tragic consequences.

The dynamic energy of Keating is powerfully supported by the crippling shyness of Todd (Ethan Hawke), the sparkling sensitivity of Neil (Robert Sean Leonard), the witty rebelliousness of Charlie (Gale Hansen) and the likeable romanticism of Knox (Josh Charles).

Tom Schulman gives us a script which is humorous, thought-provoking and dramatic. Peter Weir has built the movie around it with sensitive yet powerful brilliance. Scenes and images stay with us long after the film is over. The intense imagery, created by cinematographer John Seale, of the boys cavorting in their cave contrasts strikingly with the seriousness of school. Weir patiently builds up the loyalty between Keating and the boys — their sense of respect and humour for him, their sense of awe at what he opens up for them. This patience is deliberate as it makes the final tragedy and betrayal more poignant, more shocking.

Language features annotations:
- eye-catching title
- Dramatic opening shows a clear opinion.
- Short paragraphs make it easy to follow the main points.
- Strong adjectives give the review power.
- Using second person makes the review more personal.
- Strong adjectives indicate the standard of their performance.
- "Us" includes audience and allows reader to identify with the reviewer.
- Adverbs describe techniques of the film-makers.

Dead Poets Society rams home the awful power of conformity but also the danger of romantic individualism. The film is not so much about school as it is about all of us questioning what we should be doing with our lives. The film in fact could be seen as a threat to any form of authority, governments included.

It is impossible not to be deeply moved by *Dead Poets Society*. Weir, Schulman, Seale and the excellent cast approach the complexity of the themes with sharpness, wit and sensitivity.

It may be a film that rides on the backs of dead poets but it certainly is not dead! See it!

themes

conclusion

Title and "the film" tie the review together.

Clever use of the words of the title creates a strong link.

Text response assessment sheet

Criteria	Level of achievement			
1. Film techniques	**Major problems**		**Highly successful**	
• Are opinions stated clearly and strongly?				
• Is the plot described?				
• Is the theme considered?				
• Are the main characters mentioned?				
• Are comments made on the cinematography?				
• Are comments made on the directing?				
2. Language techniques				
• Has a title been created?				
• Does the review use sentences?				
• Does the review use paragraphs?				
• Are the paragraphs linked?				
• Is correct spelling used?				
• Is correct punctuation used?				

Assessment by: .... of film review by:..

S E L F
ASSESSMENT

Name: ....

1. Can I?

Write "yes" or "no" in the box. If you write "no", go back over your work until you can write "yes".

- Identify the different jobs in making a film .... ☐
- Identify the stages in making a film .... ☐
- Identify the different elements in a film .... ☐
- Understand how an audience is positioned by the film-makers ☐
- Discuss film as text .... ☐
- Write a film review .... ☐

2. Your reaction

(a) Which extract did you like best? Say why.

(b) Which activity did you like best? Say why.

(c) Which skill do you need to work on most? What can you do to improve it?

3. For your folio

From the work you have done in this chapter, choose the pieces you want to include in your folio. Each piece of work in your folio should include a cover sheet which shows the date it was completed, the title, the purpose and the audience.

4. Ongoing skills

Complete the table below by:

- placing a tick at the point at which you feel you usually achieve in each skill
- shading in the range of your achievement in each skill.

When you have completed the table place it in your folio.

Am I improving in these skills?	Level of achievement		
	Same as before	Improving	Much better
Example: Oral work		✓	
Explaining my answers			
Cooperating in groups			
Putting myself in someone else's shoes			
Using powerful adjectives			
Writing an extended essay			

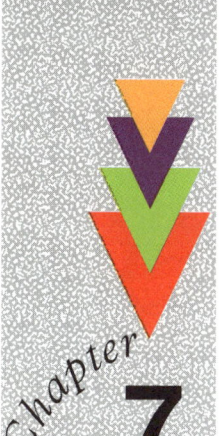

Romeo and Juliet

SHAKESPEAREAN DRAMA

Content

Skills

One day

One day I fell in love
It was just like a butterfly
Emerging from its chrysalis;
So beautiful, I cried.
It was a bite
Out of an apple,
So sweet its juice
Tasted like honey.
It was a tiny
Baby fist,
Clutching a strand of hair;
A golden thread.
It was a rainbow
Of more than seven colours,
Millions and millions.
One day I fell in love
And I grew wings;
I flew. Briefly
I was a bird,
An eagle, flying
Up and up.
One day, one smile
Meant more to me
Than the whole world.
One day, I sang.
All day, I sang.
But then
My butterfly died
And the apple grew old.
The fist let go of the thread,
The golden hair.
My rainbow
Shattered into
A myriad
Coloured pieces.
My wings
Disappeared,
And I fell
Down and down.
I couldn't
Even
Sing.

Then,
One day,

I fell in love.

Rachel Anne-Marie Naylor
(aged 14)

Romeo and Juliet
by William Shakespeare

Romeo and Juliet is one of the most famous love stories of all time. In it we see love and hatred, desire and rejection as Romeo and Juliet struggle to be together. Within this struggle we see teenage rebellion, gang warfare, sexual relationships, family feuds and loyalty between friends.

First enjoyed by Elizabethan audiences 400 years ago, the play is still popular today. The plot and themes of Romeo and Juliet appear again and again in modern movies, musicals, operas, ballets, television shows, plays and stories. The idea of love struggling against the odds has become part of our culture. Shakespeare is able to make us see that there is a little of Romeo and Juliet in all of us.

The Bard's life

Shakespeare is one of the greatest writers of all time. He is so famous that he is often called "The Bard" — the storyteller.

William Shakespeare was born in Stratford-on-Avon, England, in April 1564. While his early life remains largely a mystery, official documents, his plays and what others wrote about him tell us a good deal about his adult life. In 1582, aged 18, he married Anne Hathaway. During the next year their first child, Susanna, was born, and in 1585 Anne gave birth to twins, Hamnet and Judith.

During the next seven or eight years, commonly known as "the missing years", little is known about Shakespeare's life except that he moved to London and began a career as an actor and playwright. In 1592 Robert Greene, another London playwright, wrote a scathing attack on Shakespeare claiming that he was "an upstart crow" who was foolishly attempting to write plays.

In 1594 he became a charter member of the "Chamberlains' Men" which soon became London's leading theatre troupe. The success of the troupe was in part due to Shakespeare's skill as a playwright but also the skills of talented actors such as Richard Burbage and Will Kempe. In 1603, when King James I succeeded Queen Elizabeth I to the throne, the troupe changed its name to the "King's Men". Over the next few years Shakespeare's popularity and wealth grew. He bought property in Stratford-on-Avon and a share of a London theatre, the "Globe".

In 1610 Shakespeare retired and returned to Stratford-on-Avon. He died on 23 April 1616, aged 52. A plaque placed on a wall near his grave marks his passing.

Perhaps these are the last words he ever wrote:

Good friend, for Jesus' sake forbear
To dig the dust enclosed here.
Blessed be the man that spares these stones,
And cursed be he that moves my bones.

The first folio edition of his plays was not published until 1623, seven years after his death.

The Elizabethan playhouse

It is believed that, at first, Elizabethan plays were acted out in animal baiting rings or the courtyard of the local inn. It was not until 1576 that the first playhouse, appropriately known as The Theatre, was built on the outskirts of the city of London.

The most famous of the London theatres of the time was the Globe. Shakespeare owned a one-tenth share of the Globe and it was here that the Kings' Men held most of their performances.

The stage was small and was not protected by a roof. Performances were held only in fine weather and only during the day as there was no artificial lighting.

Playbills were posted up around London to advertise each play and a flag was flown above the theatre to signal that a performance was to be held that day.

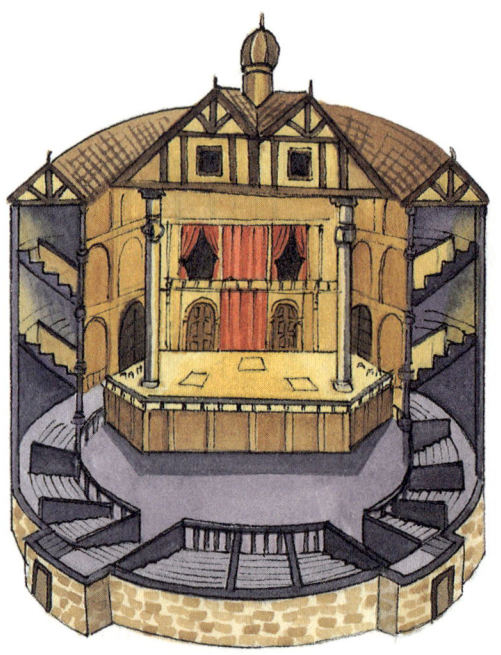

The Globe Theatre

Though elaborate, costumes were usually Elizabethan in style, rather than from the period in which the play was set. There was little or no scenery, as it was considered the playwright's role to use powerful verbal imagery to paint a mental picture of each scene. Sometimes a canopy, painted underneath with stars and planets, was hung above the stage to represent the heavens. Trapdoors were used for ghostly entrances and a raised section of stage acted as castle walls, windows or, in the case of *Romeo and Juliet*, as a balcony.

Because of the nearness of the audience, Elizabethan theatre was very intimate. "Soliloquies" and "asides" were frequently used so that actors could speak directly to the audience.

The plays ran continuously, having no scene breaks or slow points in the action. It was not considered proper for women to become actors, so talented young boys took the female roles. Shakespeare often wrote parts in his plays specifically designed for members of his acting troupe. This allowed them to exhibit their high level of skill as orators, dancers, fencers, acrobats and sometimes as magicians.

Inside an Elizabethan theatre — an artist's impression

# Origins of the story of Romeo and Juliet

The idea of two young lovers struggling to be together can be traced back as far as the Ancient Greek Myth of "Pyramus and Thisbe".

A number of French and Italian writers are known to have used this theme as the basis of their works. The first was Masaccio Salernitana in 1476. It was not until 1530, however, that another Italian, Luigi Da Porto, first used the names Romeo and Giulietta and set the action in Verona.

In 1562 Englishman Arthur Brooke wrote *The Tragical Historye of Romeus and Juliet*, again based upon the work of a number of French and Italian writers. He was also influenced by the works of the great English writer Geoffrey Chaucer. In *Troilus and Creseyde* Chaucer examined the role that fate played in the lives of his characters. Thus the idea of fate controlling our day-to-day lives was introduced to the story of Romeo and Juliet.

William Painter then wrote the first English play version of the story in 1567. Known as *The goodly History of the true and constant love between Rhomeo and Julietta*, it appeared in a collection of work entitled *Palace of Pleasure*. While Shakespeare would most certainly have had a copy of Painter's work to refer to, sadly no copies of it exist today.

Shakespeare's *Romeo and Juliet* was written around 1595 and was first performed at the Theatre in Shoreditch by the Lord Chamberlain's Men.

Modern performances of Shakespeare's *Romeo and Juliet* continue to play to audiences around the world. In 1957 a modern musical adaptation of the play, entitled *West Side Story*, was first performed at the Winter Garden Theatre in New York. In *West Side Story* the feuding families are replaced by two rival gangs, the Sharks and the Jets, and Romeo and Juliet are replaced by Tony and Maria. The plot is essentially the same, except that Maria does not die. As in Shakespeare's work, the death of Tony unites the two gangs and ends the bitterness.

There is some evidence that the story is based upon real life. In thirteenth century Italy a famous feud did arise between the Montecchi family of Verona and the Capelletti family of Cremona. Interestingly, although there is no proof that Romeo and Juliet actually existed, there is a tomb in Verona called Tomba di Guilietta (Juliet's tomb) in the Capuchin cloisters adjoining the little church in which Romeo and Juliet were supposedly married.

 Life in Verona

Shakespeare's *Romeo and Juliet* is set in a period of time known as the Renaissance. It was a time of growth and change throughout Europe. The Renaissance began in Italy and it is here, in the city of Verona, that most of the play takes place. At this time Italy was not a unified nation. Instead, it was a collection of powerful states, each centred around a large city.

City-states of Renaissance Italy

In *Romeo and Juliet*, Verona has its own Prince, Escalus. This implies that Verona was itself a city-state while in reality it was part of the city-state of Venice. Shakespeare's portrayal of the feuding families was, however, very accurate for the time. Powerful individuals and families often struggled against one another in this way for wealth and power. Arranged marriages, such as that intended between Juliet and Paris, were commonplace as parents searched for wealthy and powerful husbands for their daughters. It was also common practice for girls to marry when they were thirteen or fourteen years old.

1. Can you suggest why Shakespeare set *Romeo and Juliet* in Renaissance Italy rather than in Elizabethan England? Discuss your ideas with a partner.

2. (a) Can you suggest why Shakespeare chose Verona and invented the character of Prince Escalus?
   (b) Why do you think he didn't choose an actual city-state and use the name of its prince?

 # Contrasts

Throughout the play, Shakespeare uses contrasting characters and events to emphasise its underlying themes of love and conflict:
- Gentle characters are contrasted with violent and angry ones.
- Success is contrasted with failure.
- True love is contrasted with infatuation and with bitter hatred.

Within each personality, too, are the contrasting characteristics that make Shakespeare's portrayal of human nature so convincing and so enduring.

Who's who in *Romeo and Juliet*

Juliet: At first we see Juliet as a 13-year-old girl, respectful of her parents and their wishes. She shows intelligence in her quick and witty responses. Wary at first of Romeo's passion, she quickly develops a deep love for him.

Romeo: Shakespeare's use of contrast is clearly shown in Romeo's character. To begin with he is infatuated with Lady Rosaline, but soon he falls deeply in love with Juliet. His love-struck speeches contrast strongly with the bawdiness of his good friend Mercutio.

Juliet   **Romeo**

Prince Escalus: As ruler of Verona, Prince Escalus introduces the concept that law and order is vital to society and that it must be maintained at all costs.

Lord Capulet, Juliet's father: A complex character, Capulet is generous as a host but autocratic as head of his household, and despite his declared devotion to his daughter Juliet he fails to see her needs. Yet is it Capulet who first extends the hand of forgiveness once he understands the tragic consequences of the family feud.

Lady Capulet, Juliet's mother: Insensitive to both her husband and her daughter, she is a vengeful character who quickly demands Romeo's death after he kills Tybalt.

Lord Montague, Romeo's father: Sometimes intolerant, yet still full of love and concern for his son, he quickly responds to Capulet's initiative for peace.

Lady Montague, Romeo's mother: A direct contrast to Lady Capulet, she is kind-hearted and caring. She deeply loves both Romeo and her husband.

Benvolio: Cousin and good friend to Romeo, he is sensible and also sensitive to Romeo's ideas of love. It is Benvolio who persuades Romeo to look for another love, thus leading him to Juliet.

Mercutio, Romeo's friend: Clever and witty, he is always looking for a chance to make fun of a situation, especially if it relates to members of the opposite sex. In contrast to Benvolio, he often makes fun of Romeo's feelings.

Paris: Wealthy and of noble birth, he is attractive and well-mannered. Though he wants Juliet for his wife, he shows little true affection for her.

Tybalt, Juliet's cousin: Angry and violent, Tybalt holds his hatred of Romeo in check only because Capulet demands it.

Friar Lawrence, a monk: A sympathetic character, he tries in vain to help Romeo and Juliet. Thoughtful and compassionate, he shows sense and reason when so many others around him are driven by their emotions.

Nurse, Juliet's attendant: Deeply devoted to Juliet, she advises her about love. Like Mercutio, her sense of humour is rather bawdy, acting as a contrast to the romantic ideals of her mistress, Juliet.

These mini-profiles have introduced you to the characters. However, to get a full picture of their complexity you need to consider:
• what they say
• how they act
• how they react to others
• what others say about them.
A vital aspect of Shakespeare's genius was his ability to make his characters live — to give them truly human characteristics.

3. In pairs, choose one or two characters and build up a profile of their characteristics as you explore the play. For each character, use a table like the one below to organise your information.

Character:	
Characteristics	**Evidence from play**

The prologue: let the play begin

Imagine trumpets sounding a fanfare. As the last notes die away a solitary figure appears on stage to set the scene for the events to come.

In ancient Greek times, where modern European drama has its origins, a chorus of voices was used to set the scene and comment on the action and the reasons behind it. Shakespeare used this same device in some of his plays, but usually the chorus is played by a single actor. In *Romeo and Juliet* the chorus speaks the opening words of the play, a prologue written in the form of a sonnet.

Alongside the extract that follows, a "translation" in modern English is provided to make Shakespeare's meaning clearer. You may be surprised, however, to find how clear the words become when they are spoken by professionals. Try listening to tapes or watching videos of the play performed by prominent actors and see how the meaning shines through.

The prologue

ELIZABETHAN LANGUAGE

Enter **Chorus**

Chorus Two households both alike in dignity,
In fair Verona where we lay our scene
From ancient grudge, break to new mutiny,
Where civil blood makes civil hands unclean:
From forth the fatal loins of these two foes,
A pair of star-crossed lovers take their life:
Whose misadventured piteous overthrows,
Doth with death bury their parents' strife.
The fearful passage of their death-marked love,
And the continuance of their parents' rage,
Which but the children's end nought could
   remove,
Is now the two hours' traffic of our stage.
The which if you with patient ears attend,
What here shall miss, our toil shall strive to mend.

MODERN LANGUAGE

Before the play begins, an **Announcer** *addresses the audience.*

Announcer   The play is set in beautiful Verona, in Italy. Two families of equal, noble rank [*the Montagues and Capulets*], have a long-standing vendetta, which has recently flared up: their followers have killed each other in civil strife. The children of these mortal enemies were fated to fall in love; their tragic deaths ended their parents' feud.

The subject of our two-hour play is the harrowing story of their fatal love-affair, the course of their parents' quarrel, and the way in which it could only be ended by their deaths.

If you will give us your patient attention, we'll make up for any shortcomings by performing as well as we can.

The prologue at a glance

The action

The chorus introduces the play, tells of the feud between the two warring households and speaks about the tragic fate awaiting Romeo and Juliet.

The issues

Because the prologue outlines most of what will happen in the play, the focus for the audience now becomes *how* and *why* the tragedy occurs. In this way Shakespeare is able to concentrate on bringing to life the central themes of the play:

- True love often must struggle against forces that oppose it.
- Violence leads to violence.
- Moderation in all things is best.
- Opposition to authority leads to punishment.

The language of Shakespeare

The prologue uses powerful language to convey the violent and tragic events which are to unfold. Words and phrases such as "fatal", "death", "civil blood", and "fearful passage" leave the audience in no doubt as to what will happen in the play. Shakespeare wrote the prologue as a sonnet, a form of poetry popular at the time.

4. What information does the prologue give us about the play?

5. From the prologue, make a list of all words and phrases that hint at the tragic events to come.

6. Identify the lines that mention any of the themes of *Romeo and Juliet*.

7. "Listening to the detailed prologue spoils the play. It is like watching the end of a movie before viewing the rest of it; you know what is going to happen!" Do you agree or disagree with this statement? Explain.

8. The prologue leaves the audience with a number of unanswered questions:
   - Why are the families feuding?
   - How could Romeo and Juliet fall in love when their families are such bitter enemies?
   - In what way do they die?
   - How does their death end the feud?
   (a) Why do you think Shakespeare left so many uncertainties hanging in the minds of his audience? Explain.
   (b) Suggest answers to these four questions. Share your answers with a partner.

9. Being a sonnet, the prologue has a highly stylised structure. The first twelve lines are divided into three groups, each consisting of four lines, known as *quatrains*. The final two lines are known as a *couplet*. Each of these four groups of lines has its own specific message for the audience. Decide what you feel each tells us. Share your answers with the class and compare the range of possible meanings.

10. Imagine that you are directing *Romeo and Juliet* in a modern setting. How would you want your chorus to appear?
    Consider: costume, manner, voice, age, gender . . .
      Present your ideas to the class. You could also draw a sketch to illustrate how you want the character to look.

Having established the plot, Shakespeare then proceeds to introduce the main characters, expands our knowledge of the feud and hints at love.

 # Act one

Scene 1: The city streets of Verona

Servants of the Montagues and Capulets begin a brawl on the street. Verona's Prince, Escalus, threatens death to those who fight in public. Romeo's parents are concerned for his health but his friend Benvolio discovers he is only lovesick.

Scenes 2 and 3: The house of Capulet

Paris, a wealthy nobleman, asks Capulet if he may marry Juliet. Capulet feels that Juliet, not yet fourteen, is too young. That evening Romeo decides to gatecrash Capulet's party to see Rosaline with whom he is infatuated. Lady Capulet tells Juliet that Paris wants to marry her.

Scene 4: A street

Romeo, Mercutio and Benvolio set out in high spirits for the ball at Capulet's house.

Scene 5: The ball — love at first sight

Romeo, Benvolio and Mercutio gatecrash Capulet's ball. Romeo, infatuated with the beautiful Rosaline, hopes that he will meet her there. Instead he meets Juliet.

In this extract from the ball scene, a version in modern English is again provided alongside.

ACT ONE *Scene 5*

ELIZABETHAN LANGUAGE	MODERN LANGUAGE
40 **Romeo** What lady's that which doth enrich the hand Of yonder knight?	**Romeo** [*to a* **Servant**] Who's the lady who's gracing the hand of that gentleman there? [*It is* **Juliet**]
Servant I know not, sir.	**Servant** I don't know, sir.

Romeo O, she doth teach the torches to burn bright.
    It seems she hangs upon the cheek of night
    As a rich jewel in an Ethiop's ear —
45   Beauty too rich for use, for earth too dear.
    So shows a snowy dove trooping with crows
    As yonder lady o'er her fellows shows.
    The measure done, I'll watch her place of stand,
    And touching hers, make blessed my rude hand.
50   Did my heart love till now? Forswear it, sight.
    For I ne'er saw true beauty till this night.
	Romeo [*to himself*] Oh, torches look dim beside her! She embellishes night like a rich jewel in an Ethiopian's ear — too beautiful for everyday use, too valuable for this world. She stands out like a snow-white dove amongst the crows. Once the dance is over, I'll see where she stands, and make my rough hand blessed by touching hers. Did my heart know real love till now? My eyes need look no further: I hadn't seen true beauty till tonight.

ELIZABETHAN LANGUAGE

Tybalt   This by his voice should be a
Montague.

Fetch me my rapier, boy. What, dares the slave

55   Come hither, covered with an antic face

To fleer and scorn at our solemnity?

Now by the stock and honour of my kin,

To strike him dead I hold it not a sin.

Capulet   Why how now, kinsman, wherefore
storm you so?

Tybalt   Uncle, this is a Montague, our foe:

60   A villain that is hither come in spite

To scorn at our solemnity this night.

Capulet   Young Romeo is it?

Tybalt   Tis he, that villain Romeo.

Capulet   Content thee, gentle coz, let him
alone,

A bears him like a portly gentleman;

65   And, to say truth, Verona brags of him

To be a virtuous and well-governed youth.

I would not for the wealth of all this town

Here in my house do him disparagement.

Therefore, be patient, take no note of him.

70   It is my will, the which if thou respect,

Show a fair presence and put off these
frowns,

An ill-beseeming semblance for a feast.

Tybalt   It fits when such a villain is a guest: I'll
not endure him.

Capulet   He shall be endured.

75   What, goodman boy! I say he shall! Go to,

Am I the master here or you? Go to.

You'll not endure him! God shall mend my
soul,

You'll make a mutiny among my guests,

You will set cock-a-hoop, you'll be the man!

Tybalt   Why, uncle, 'tis a shame.

80   **Capulet**   Go to, go to.

You are a saucy boy. Is't so indeed?

This trick may chance to scathe you, I know
what.

You must contrary me. Marry, 'tis time —

Well said, my hearts — You are a princox, go

85   Be quiet, or — More light! More light! —
For shame,

I'll make you quiet. What, cheerly, my hearts!

MODERN LANGUAGE

Tybalt   [*overhearing*] This must be a Montague, judging by his voice. [*To his page*] Fetch me my rapier, boy. [*The page leaves*] How dare the wretch come here wearing a zany face, to jeer and mock at our festivities? By my family's ancestors and honour — I'd regard it no sin to strike him dead!

Capulet   [*passing by and noticing* **Tybalt**'s *anger*] Hello, there, kinsman! What's annoying you so much?

Tybalt   Uncle, this is a Montague, one of our foes: a villain who's come here in hatred, to mock at our celebration tonight!

Capulet   Young Romeo is it?

Tybalt   That's him! That villain, Romeo!

Capulet   Calm yourself, dear boy; leave him alone. He's behaving like a civilised gentleman. Frankly, Verona is justly proud of him as a virtuous and well-behaved youth. Not for all the wealth in the city would I be impolite to him here in my house. So be patient. Take no notice of him. That's my decision: if you respect it, behave in a friendly way, and stop frowning, it's quite inappropriate for a feast.

Tybalt   It's right when such a villain is a guest. I'll not tolerate him!

Capulet   He *is* to be tolerated! What, young Mister Nobody? I say he shall! [*Indignant*] Well, really! Am I the master here, or you? Really! [*Mocking*] You'll not endure him! God bless my soul, you'll start a rumpus amongst my guests? You'll throw your weight about? You'll play the man?

Tybalt   Why, uncle, it's shameful.

Capulet   Really, really! You're a cheeky fellow. So it's shameful is it? This will do you no good, mark my words. You'll go against me? Well, it's time — [*He breaks off to acknowledge the dancers*] Well said, dear friends! [*Back to* **Tybalt**] You're a cocky young pup. Either go, be quiet, or — [*To* **Servants**] More lights! More lights! [*To* **Tybalt**] For shame! I'll quieten you down. [*To the dancers*] Bravo, dear friends!

[*He turns away and circulates amongst the company*]

ELIZABETHAN LANGUAGE

Tybalt Patience perforce with wilful choler meeting
Makes my heart tremble in their different greeting.
I will withdraw; but this intrusion shall
90   Now seeming sweet, convert to bitterest gall.

[Exit]

Romeo If I profane with my unworthiest hand
This holy shrine, the gentle sin is this:
My lips, two blushing pilgrims, ready stand
To smooth that rough touch with a tender kiss.

95 **Juliet** Good pilgrim, you do wrong your hand too much,
Which mannerly devotion shows in this;
For saints have hands that pilgrims' hands do touch,
And palm to palm is holy palmers' kiss.

Romeo Have not saints lips, and holy palmers too?

100 **Juliet** Ay, pilgrim, lips that they must use in prayer.

Romeo O then, dear saint, let lips do what hands do!
They pray. Grant thou, lest faith turn to despair.

Juliet Saints do not move, though grant for prayer's sake.

Romeo Then move not, while my prayer's effect I take.
105   Thus from my lips, by thine, my sin is purged.

Juliet Then have my lips the sin that they have took.

Romeo Sin from my lips? O trespass sweetly urged!
Give me my sin again.

Juliet You kiss by the book.

Nurse Madam, your mother craves a word with you.

Romeo What is her mother?

110 **Nurse** Marry, bachelor,
Her mother is the lady of the house,
And a good lady, and a wise and virtuous.
I nursed her daughter that you talked withal.
I tell you, he that can lay hold of her
Shall have the chinks.

MODERN LANGUAGE

Tybalt Having to control myself when he's so unreasonably angry has got my nerves on edge. I'll go. This Montague intrusion may be welcome now, but later it will turn bitterly sour!

[He goes]

Romeo [*Taking* **Juliet** *by the hand*] If I'm profaning a holy shrine with my most unworthy hand, the lesser sin is this: my lips, like two blushing pilgrims, are ready with a tender kiss to smooth away the roughness of my touch.

Juliet Dear pilgrim, you wrong your hand too much. It is only showing true devotion. Statues of saints are touched by pilgrims' hands, so placing palm-on-palm is a holy pilgrim's kiss.

Romeo Don't saints have lips, and holy pilgrims too?

Juliet Oh yes, pilgrim. Lips that they must use for prayer.

Romeo Well then, dear saint, let lips do what hands do. Their prayer is: 'Grant a kiss, in case I lose my faith.'

Juliet Saints grant prayers, but they don't move.

Romeo Then stay still, while my prayer is granted.
[*He kisses her;* **Juliet** *is statuesque*]
Now the sin of my lips is purged by yours.

Juliet So my lips must have the sin they've taken from you.

Romeo Taken sin from my lips? You've sweetly proved that I've offended! Give me my sin back again! [*He kisses her for the second time*]

Juliet You kiss very formally!

Nurse Madam, your mother would like a word with you. [**Juliet** *leaves*]

Romeo Who is her mother?

Nurse Indeed, young gentleman, her mother is the lady of the house. She's a good, wise and virtuous lady. I nursed her daughter that you've just been talking to. I tell you, the man who gets her will be in the money!

ELIZABETHAN LANGUAGE

115 **Romeo**   Is she a Capulet?
O dear account! My life is my foe's debt.

Benvolio   Away, be gone; the sport is at the
best.

Romeo   Ay, so I fear; the more is my unrest.

Capulet   Nay, gentlemen, prepare not to be
gone,
120 We have a trifling foolish banquet towards.
Is it e'en so? Why then, I thank you all;
I thank you honest gentlemen, good night.
More torches here. Come on then, let's to
bed.
Ah, sirrah, by my fay, It waxes late.
125 I'll to my rest.

[*Exeunt all but* **Juliet** *and* **Nurse**]

Juliet   Come hither Nurse. What is yond
gentleman?

Nurse   The son and heir of old Tiberio.

Juliet   What's he that now is going out of
door?

Nurse   Marry, that I think be young
Petruchio.

130 **Juliet**   What's he that follows here, that would
not dance.

Nurse   I know not.

Juliet   Go ask his name. If he be married,
My grave is like to be my wedding bed.

Nurse   His name is Romeo, and a Montague,
The only son of your great enemy.

135 **Juliet**   My only love sprung from my only hate.
Too early seen unknown, and known too late.
Prodigious birth of love it is to me
That I must love a loathed enemy.

140 **Nurse**   What's this? What's this?

Juliet   A rhyme I learned even now
Of one I danced withal.

[*One calls within 'Juliet!'*]

Nurse   Anon, anon!
Come, let's away. The strangers are all gone.

[*Exeunt*]

MODERN LANGUAGE

Romeo   Is she a Capulet? [*His face falls*]
That's bad news! Now I'm pledged to my
enemy!

Benvolio   [*catching him by the arm*] Let's go.
We've had the best of the party.

Romeo   [*still stunned by the* **Nurse's** *revelation*]
So I fear; much to my distress.

Capulet   [*politely encouraging the* **Maskers** *to stay
longer*] Nay, gentlemen, don't go yet. We'll be
having some simple refreshments shortly. [*The*
Maskers *whisper their excuses to him*] Really?
Well, then, my thanks to you all. Thanks,
gentlemen. Good night! [*To the* **Servants**]
Some more lights here! Come on then: let's
go to bed. [*He yawns*] Upon my word, it's
getting late. I'm off to bed.

[*Everyone goes except* **Juliet** *and the* **Nurse**]

Juliet   Come here, Nurse. [*Nodding towards a
guest*] Who's the gentleman over there?

Nurse   Old Tiberio's son and heir.

Juliet   Who's that just leaving?

Nurse   I think that must be young
Petruchio.

Juliet   [*getting to the real point at last*] Who's the
one following behind the others, who
wouldn't dance?

Nurse   I don't know.

Juliet   Go and ask his name. [*the* **Nurse** *leaves*]
If he's already married, the only wedding-bed
I'll ever have will be my grave!

Nurse   [*returning*] His name's Romeo, and he's
a Montague. He's the only son of your great
enemy.

Juliet   [*to herself*] The one I love the son of the
one I hate! When I first met him,
unrecognized. Now — too late — I know who
he is! How disastrous that first love for me
should be a hated enemy!

Nurse   [*overhearing*] What's this? What's this?

Juliet   [*hastily*] Just a rhyme I learned from
someone I danced with.

[**Juliet's** *mother calls her*]

Nurse   Coming! Coming! Let's be off. The
visitors have all gone.

[*They leave*]

The ball scene at a glance

The action

Soon after arriving at the ball, Romeo sees Juliet and immediately falls in love with her, all thoughts of Rosaline now forgotten.

Juliet's cousin, Tybalt, recognises Romeo as a hated Montague and calls for a sword. However, Lord Capulet demands that Romeo be treated as a guest in his house.

Romeo and Juliet speak briefly of love.

The issues

Capulet's ball is a scene of many contrasts. The fateful meeting of Romeo and Juliet and their love for one another contrasts sharply with the bitterness felt between their two families. This is illustrated by Tybalt's desire to fight with Romeo. Tybalt's brashness and ill-mannered actions contrast with the courtesy shown towards Romeo by Capulet.

Through the use of such stark contrasts Shakespeare focuses our attention on the central theme of the play — that of the young lovers struggling against forces which soon will tear them apart.

The language of Shakespeare

Capulet's joyous greeting to his guests and his easy acceptance of Romeo into his home creates a light-hearted atmosphere at the beginning of the scene. This is further developed when Romeo and Juliet meet. They express their love for each other in the form of a romantic dialogue which begins with Romeo's line, "If I profane with my unworthiest hand". Elizabethan audiences would have immediately recognised this as a symbol of true and lasting love.

The light-hearted language changes abruptly when Romeo and Juliet discover each other's true identity. Both are shocked at having fallen in love with someone who is supposed to be their enemy. Their language is filled with emotion: "My only love sprung from my only hate."

---

11. Read Romeo's description of Juliet when he first sees her. How would you describe his feelings for her?

12. What do we discover of Juliet's feelings for Romeo?

13. At the beginning of the play the Chorus warns us that Romeo and Juliet's love is doomed to failure. How does the action in this scene reinforce this prediction?

14. What would you do if a group of people gatecrashed a party at your place? Share your ideas with a partner.

15. (a) Imagine you are Romeo or Juliet. Write a diary entry describing how you feel, knowing that your family will disapprove of your new love. Write what you think you will do.
    (b) Discuss your plan with a partner.

16. (a) Romeo has claimed he was in love with Rosaline and yet the moment he sees Juliet he states that she is now his only true love. Is it possible that he truly loves Juliet from the moment he sees her? Could he love them both? Was he only infatuated with Rosaline? Does he really love either of them? Using a dictionary and a thesaurus, compile a list of words and phrases that explain the meanings of "love" and "infatuation". Copy the diagram and write the words in the appropriate section. If you feel any words fit in both, write them in the overlap area.

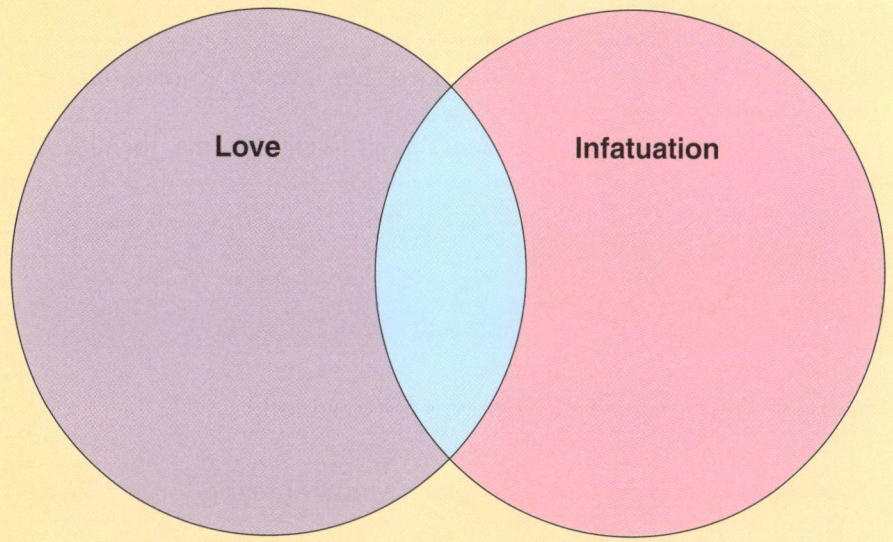

Love   Infatuation

(b) Use the words that you have written into the diagram to describe how you think Romeo and Juliet feel about each other after their first meeting.

17. Read lines 91–104 to yourself. Practise saying the lines until you can deliver them with emotion and sincerity. Perform your lines for the class.

Staging the play

18. Again, imagine that you are directing a modern version of *Romeo and Juliet*. How would you stage this scene? Can you think of somewhere else for them to meet, other than at Juliet's parents' house? Consider the fact that her parents must be present, as well as her cousin Tybalt, also Mercutio and Benvolio together with a crowd of family and friends. Perhaps the scene could take place at a nightclub, a football match, cinema, beach or restaurant. Whatever you decide, write a description of the setting, the action and part of the dialogue between the characters to suit how you would want the scene to be played.

Act two

Prologue

The chorus explains that Romeo and Juliet, now deeply in love, face great peril in order to see each other.

Scene 1: Beside the wall of Capulet's orchard

Romeo climbs the wall and enters Capulet's garden. Mercutio and Benvolio make fun of him.

Scene 2: The balcony

Juliet, looking up at the night sky, speaks of her love for Romeo, unaware that he is standing in the garden below her.

This is one of the most famous scenes in all English drama, the ultimate in romance!

ACT TWO *Scene 2*

Capulet's orchard. Enter **Romeo**

Romeo   He jests at scars that never felt a wound.

[*Enter* **Juliet** *above*]

But soft, what light through yonder window breaks?
It is the east and Juliet is the sun!
Arise fair sun and kill the envious moon
5   Who is already sick and pale with grief
That thou her maid art far more fair than she.
Be not her maid since she is envious,
Her vestal livery is but sick and green
And none but fools do wear it. Cast it off.
10   It is my lady, O it is my love!
O that she knew she were!
She speaks, yet she says nothing. What of that?
Her eye discourses, I will answer it.
I am too bold. 'Tis not to me she speaks.
15   Two of the fairest stars in all the heaven,
Having some business, do entreat her eyes
To twinkle in their spheres till they return.
What if her eyes were there, they in her head?
The brightness of her cheek would shame those stars
20   As daylight doth a lamp. Her eyes in heaven
Would through the airy region stream so bright
That birds would sing and think it were not night.
See how she leans her cheek upon her hand.
O that I were a glove upon that hand,
That I might touch that cheek!

Juliet   Ay me!

25 **Romeo**   She speaks.
　　　O speak again bright angel, for thou art
　　　As glorious to this night, being o'er my head,
　　　As is a winged messenger of heaven
　　　Unto the white-upturned wondering eyes
30　　Of mortals that fall back to gaze on him
　　　When he bestrides the lazy-pacing clouds
　　　And sails upon the bosum of the air.

Juliet   O Romeo, Romeo, wherefore art thou Romeo?
　　　Deny thy father and refuse thy name.
35　　Or if thou wilt not, be but sworn my love,
　　　And I'll no longer be a Capulet.

Romeo   Shall I hear more, or shall I speak at this?

Juliet   'Tis but thy name that is my enemy;
　　　Thou art thyself, though not a Montague.
　　　What's Montague? It is not hand nor foot
40　　Nor arm nor face nor any other part
　　　Belonging to a man. O be some other name.
　　　What's in a name? That which we call a rose
　　　By any other word would smell as sweet.
　　　So Romeo would, were he not Romeo called,
45　　Retain that dear perfection which he owes
　　　Without that title. Romeo, doff thy name,
　　　And for that name, which is no part of thee,
　　　Take all myself.

Romeo   I take thee at thy word.
　　　Call me but love, and I'll be new baptised:
50　　Henceforth I never will be Romeo.

Juliet   What man art thou that thus bescreened in night
　　　So stumblest on my counsel?

Romeo   By a name
　　　I know not how to tell thee who I am:
　　　My name, dear saint, is hateful to myself
55　　Because it is an enemy to thee.
　　　Had I it written, I would tear the word.

Juliet   My ears have not yet drunk a hundred words
　　　Of thy tongue's uttering, yet I know the sound.
　　　Art thou not Romeo, and a Montague?

60 **Romeo**   Neither, fair maid, if either thee dislike.

Juliet   How cam'st thou hither, tell me, and wherefore?
　　　The orchard walls are high and hard to climb,
　　　And the place death, considering who thou art,
　　　If any of my kinsmen find thee here.

65 **Romeo**   With love's light wings did I o'erperch these walls,
    For stony limits cannot hold love out,
    And what love can do, that dares love attempt:
    Therefore thy kinsmen are no stop to me.

Juliet   If they do see thee, they will murder thee.

70 **Romeo**   Alack, there lies more peril in thine eye
    Than twenty of their swords. Look thou but sweet
    And I am proof against their enmity.

Juliet   I would not for the world they saw thee here.

Romeo   I have night's cloak to hide me from their eyes,
75   And but thou love me, let them find me here.
    My life were better ended by their hate
    Than death prolonged, wanting of thy love.

Juliet   By whose direction found'st thou out this place?

Romeo   By love, that first did prompt me to enquire.
80   He lent me counsel, and I lent him eyes.
    I am no pilot, yet wert thou as far
    As that vast shore washed with the farthest sea,
    I should adventure for such merchandise.

Juliet   Thou knowest the mask of night is on my face,
85   Else would a maiden blush bepaint my cheek
    For that which thou hast heard me speak tonight.
    Fain would I dwell on form; fain, fain deny
    What I have spoke. But farewell compliment!
    Dost thou love me? I know thou wilt say 'Ay',
90   And I will take thy word. Yet, if thou swearest,
    Thou mayst prove false. At lovers' perjuries,
    They say, Jove laughs. O gentle Romeo,
    If thou dost love, pronounce it faithfully.
    Or, if thou think'st I am too quickly won,
95   I'll frown and be perverse and say thee nay,
    So thou wilt woo; but else, not for the world.
    In truth, fair Montague, I am too fond,
    And therefore thou mayst think my haviour light,
    But trust me, gentleman, I'll prove more true
100   Than those that have more cunning to be strange.
    I should have been more strange, I must confess,
    But that thou overheard'st, ere I was ware,
    My true love's passion. Therefore pardon me,
    And not impute this yielding to light love,
105   Which the dark night hath so discovered.

Romeo   Lady, by yonder blessed moon I vow,
    That tips with silver all these fruit-tree tops —

Juliet   O swear not by the moon, th' inconstant moon,
    That monthly changes in her circled orb,
110   Lest that thy love prove likewise variable.

Romeo   What shall I swear by?

Juliet   Do not swear at all;
    Of, if thou wilt, swear by thy gracious self,
    Which is the god of my idolatry,
    And I'll believe thee.

Romeo   If my heart's dear love —

115 **Juliet**   Well, do not swear. Although I joy in thee,
    I have no joy of this contract tonight:
    It is too rash, too unadvised, too sudden,
    Too like the lightning, which doth cease to be
    Ere one can say 'It lightens'. Sweet, good night.
120   This bud of love, by summer's ripening breath,
    May prove a beauteous flower when next we meet.
    Good night, and good night! As sweet repose and rest
    Come to thy heart as that within my breast!

Romeo   O wilt thou leave me so unsatisfied?

125 **Juliet**   What satisfaction canst thou have tonight?

Romeo   The exchange of thy love's faithful vow for mine.

Juliet   I gave thee mine before thou didst request it,
    And yet I would it were to give again.

Romeo   Wouldst thou withdraw it? For what purpose, love?

130 **Juliet**   But to be frank and give it thee again;
    And yet I wish but for the thing I have.
    My bounty is as boundless as the sea,
    My love as deep; the more I give to thee
    The more I have, for both are infinite.
135   I hear some noise within. Dear love, adieu.

    [**Nurse** *calls within*]

    Anon, good Nurse! Sweet Montague be true.
    Stay but a little, I will come again.

                                             [*Exit* **Juliet**]

Romeo   O blessed, blessed night. I am afeard,
    Being in night, all this is but a dream,
140   Too flattering sweet to be substantial.

    [*Enter* **Juliet** *above*]

Juliet   Three words, dear Romeo, and good night indeed.
    If that thy bent of love be honourable,
    Thy purpose marriage, send me word tomorrow
    By one that I'll procure to come to thee,
145   Where and what time thou wilt perform the rite,
    And all my fortunes at thy foot I'll lay,
    And follow thee my lord throughout the world.

Nurse   [*within*] Madam!

Juliet   I come, anon — But if thou meanest not well
    I do beseech thee —

Nurse [*within*] Madam!

150 **Juliet** By and by I come —
　　　To cease thy strife and leave me to my grief.
　　　Tomorrow will I send.

Romeo So strive my soul —

Juliet A thousand times good night.

[*Exit* **Juliet**]

The balcony scene at a glance

The action

Standing below her, unseen, Romeo listens as Juliet admits she loves him, even though he is a Montague. She is embarrassed when she realises that Romeo has been listening to her, though they both soon talk openly about their love for one another. Juliet tells Romeo that if he truly loves her she will gladly marry him. Their fateful union is now planned and the play begins to rush towards its tragic climax.

The issues

The issue here is — what is true love? Mercutio speaks of love in purely sexual terms whereas Romeo and Juliet have deeper feelings and they realise that their love is not just infatuation. Their love is so powerful that for them marriage is the only answer. Juliet fears that the bitterness between their families will keep them apart.

The language of Shakespeare

Shakespeare uses a number of references to light and dark to create the atmosphere of the balcony scene. For Romeo the dark of night is replaced by his visions of the shining light that is Juliet.

When he first sees her, Romeo uses emotive, poetic words to describe her beauty. He speaks in much the same way as he did when describing his "feelings" for Rosaline.

> *But soft, what light through yonder window breaks?*
> *It is the east, and Juliet is the sun!*
> *Arise fair sun and kill the envious moon*
> *Who is already sick and pale with grief*
> *That thou her maid art far more fair than she.*

Love was often spoken of in such terms, though again it gives the impression of infatuation rather than true love.

This quickly changes to more direct references to his feelings for Juliet, showing that his love for her is indeed true.

> *It is my lady; O, it is my love!*

Their declaration of love for one another gives powerful emotional impact to the scene.

19. Why was it dangerous for Romeo to enter the orchard?

20. (a) What was Juliet speaking about as she stood alone on her balcony?
    (b) Why do you think she was doing this?

21. These are among the most quoted lines from any of Shakespeare's plays:

    > O Romeo, Romeo! Wherefore art thou Romeo?
    > Deny thy father and refuse thy name ...

    (a) Discuss their meaning with a partner and then rewrite them in your own words.
    (b) Two more often-quoted lines from this scene are:

    > What's in a name? That which we call a rose
    > By any other name would smell as sweet.

    What do you think these lines mean? Share your ideas with the class.

22. How do you think Romeo feels, while he is hidden and gazing up at the beautiful Juliet, as she speaks of her love for him?

23. Describe Juliet's reaction when she discovers Romeo has been listening to her.

24. (a) What do they plan to do the next day?
    (b) Do you think this is wise, considering the feud between their families? Explain.

25. What are some of the possible consequences of such a marriage? Use a table like the one below to help organise your thoughts.

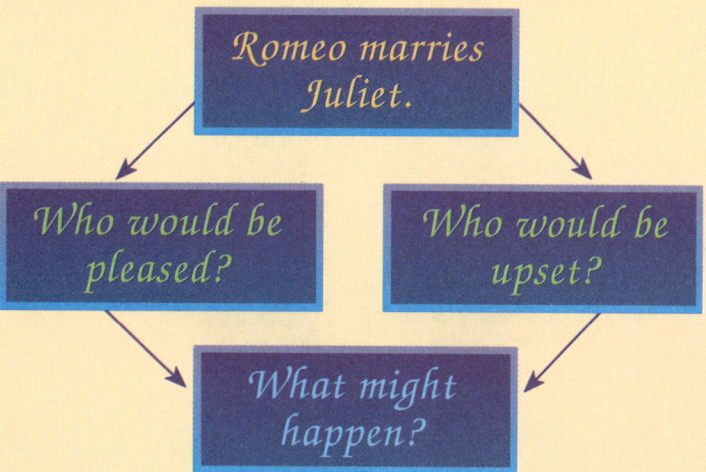

Romeo marries Juliet.

Who would be pleased?   Who would be upset?

What might happen?

26. Romeo and Juliet use poetic images to describe their feelings about love. Look back at the poem on page 200. What is the main difference between the way Rachel sees love and the way Romeo and Juliet see it?

27. (a) Write a poem describing your own feelings about love. Is it eternal, as Romeo and Juliet see it, or does it come and go as Rachel says it does? If you are reluctant to write a personal poem, you could write it in third person.
    (b) Share your poem with the class or perhaps with a person you love.

Staging the play

The balcony scene is played on two levels. Romeo stands on the main stage looking up at Juliet who stands upon her balcony. This use of different levels creates a visual impact for the audience, though more importantly it physically separates the two young lovers. In this way their words, rather than their actions, must convey their love.

In Elizabethan theatres the balcony would have been a small area supported by pillars. Usually centre stage and towards the back, it would have been curtained off to provide for entrances.

The following pictures show how the balcony scene was played in four productions of *Romeo and Juliet* between 1753 and 1980.

Miss Nossiter as Juliet and Spranger Barry as Romeo, Covent Garden 1753

Dorothy Tutin and Brian Murray, Royal Shakespeare Theatre (RST) 1961

Francesca Annis and Ian McKellen, RST 1976

Judy Buxton and Anton Lesser, RST 1980

Look also at Richard Beymer (Tony) and Natalie Wood (Maria) in the "balcony" scene from the 1961 movie of *West Side Story*.

28. (a) What aspects do these different productions have in common?
    (b) How do they differ?
    (c) Which do you like best? Why?

29. Consider how you would stage this scene in a modern version of *Romeo and Juliet*. Aspects to consider include:
    • setting
    • location of actors during the scene
    • costuming.
    You might also like to consider the dialogue and modify it if necessary to suit your ideas for staging the scene. Write down your ideas and discuss them with a partner.

Scene 3: Friar Lawrence's cell

Romeo explains to Friar Lawrence about his love for Juliet and their plans to marry. Friar Lawrence agrees to marry them, believing that such a marriage might end the feud.

Scene 4: In the street

Romeo sends word to Juliet that they are to be married secretly that afternoon. They plan to spend their wedding night, in secret, at her house.

Scene 5: The orchard

The nurse brings Romeo's message, teasing Juliet about her impatience.

Scene 6: Friar Lawrence's cell

Romeo and Juliet are secretly married.

The secret wedding. Niamh Cusack as Juliet, Sean Bean as Romeo and Robert Demeger as Friar Lawrence, RST 1986

Act three

Scene 1: The fight

Soon after his marriage to Juliet, Romeo is drawn into a fight with her cousin Tybalt.

| ACT THREE *Scene 1* |

[*Enter* **Romeo**]

Tybalt Well, peace be with you, sir, here comes my man.

Mercutio But I'll be hanged, sir, if he wear your livery.
Marry, go before to field, he'll be your follower.
55 Your worship in that sense may call him 'man'.

Tybalt Romeo, the love I bear thee can afford
No better term than this: thou art a villain.

Romeo Tybalt, the reason that I have to love thee
Doth much excuse the appertaining rage
60 To such a greeting: villain am I none,
Therefore farewell. I see thou knowest me not.

Tybalt Boy, this shall not excuse the injuries
That thou hast done me, therefore turn and draw.

Romeo I do protest I never injured thee,
65 But love thee better than thou canst devise
Till thou shalt know the reason of my love.
And so, good Capulet, which name I tender
As dearly as mine own, be satisfied.

Mercutio O calm, dishonourable, vile submission:
70 Alla stoccata carries it away! [*He draws*]
Tybalt, you rat-catcher, will you walk?

Tybalt What wouldst thou have with me?

Mercutio Good King of Cats, nothing but one of your nine
lives that I mean to make bold withal, and as you shall use me
75 hereafter, dry-beat the rest of the eight. Will you pluck your
sword out of his pilcher by the ears? Make haste, lest mine be
about your ears ere it be out.

Tybalt I am for you. [*He draws*]

Romeo Gentle Mercutio, put thy rapier up.

80 **Mercutio** Come sir, your passado. [*They fight*]

Romeo   Draw, Benvolio, beat down their weapons.
Gentlemen, for shame, forbear this outrage.
Tybalt! Mercutio! The Prince expressly hath
Forbid this bandying in Verona streets.
85   Hold, Tybalt! Good Mercutio!

[**Tybalt** *under* **Romeo's** *arm thrusts* **Mercutio** *in*]

[*Exit* **Tybalt** *with his followers*]

Mercutio   I am hurt.
A plague o' both your houses. I am sped.
Is he gone, and hath nothing?

Benvolio   What, art thou hurt?

90 **Mercutio**   Ay, ay, a scratch, a scratch. Marry, 'tis enough.
Where's my page? Go villain, fetch a surgeon.

[*Exit* **Page**]

Romeo   Courage man, the hurt cannot be much.

Mercutio   No, 'tis not so deep as a well, nor so wide as a church
door, but 'tis enough, 'twill serve. Ask for me tomorrow and
95   you shall find me a grave man. I am peppered, I warrant, for
this world. A plague o' both your houses. Zounds, a dog, a
rat, a mouse, a cat, to scratch a man to death. A braggart, a
rogue, a villain, that fights by the book of arithmetic — why the
devil came you between us? I was hurt under your arm.

100 **Romeo**   I thought all for the best.

Mercutio   Help me into some house, Benvolio,
Or I shall faint. A plague o' both your houses,
They have made worms' meat of me.
I have it, and soundly too. Your houses!

[*Exit* **Mercutio** *with* **Benvolio**]

105 **Romeo**   This gentleman, the Prince's near ally,
My very friend, hath got this mortal hurt
In my behalf — my reputation stained
With Tybalt's slander — Tybalt that an hour
Hath been my cousin. O sweet Juliet,
110   Thy beauty hath made me effeminate
And in my temper softened valour's steel.

[*Enter* **Benvolio**]

Benvolio   O Romeo, Romeo, brave Mercutio is dead.
That gallant spirit hath aspired the clouds
Which too untimely here did scorn the earth.

115 **Romeo**   This day's black fate on more days doth depend:
This but begins the woe others must end.

[*Enter* **Tybalt**]

Benvolio   Here comes the furious Tybalt back again.

Romeo   Alive, in triumph, and Mercutio slain.
Away to heaven respective lenity,
120   And fire-eyed fury be my conduct now!
Now Tybalt, take the 'villain' back again
That late thou gav'st me, for Mercutio's soul
Is but a little way above our heads.
Staying for thine to keep him company.
125   Either thou, or I, or both must go with him.

Tybalt   Thou wretched boy, that didst consort him here,
Shalt with him hence.

Romeo   This shall determine that.

[*They fight.* **Tybalt** *falls*]

Benvolio   Romeo, away, be gone,
The citizens are up, and Tybalt's slain!
130   Stand not amazed. The Prince will doom thee death
If thou art taken. Hence, be gone, away!

Romeo   O, I am fortune's fool.

Benvolio   Why dost thou stay?

[*Exit* **Romeo**]

The fight scene at a glance

The action

Tybalt is still angry over Romeo's intrusion at last night's ball. He challenges Romeo to a duel but Romeo refuses because Tybalt is Juliet's cousin.

Mercutio mistakenly sees Romeo's refusal to fight as a sign of cowardice and immediately challenges Tybalt to a duel. Romeo tries to prevent the fight, but Mercutio is fatally wounded. In retaliation for his friend's death, Romeo then fights and kills Tybalt. As punishment, Prince Escalus banishes Romeo from Verona.

The issues

Throughout the play so far, Romeo's life has been enriched, scene by scene. He meets Juliet, they fall in love and secretly marry. Now, in an ironic twist of fate, his happiness is destroyed by a fight which he desperately tried to prevent. Fate, as foretold in the prologue, now begins to take control of his life and those around him.

The language of Shakespeare

Mercutio is furious with Romeo for his refusal to fight Tybalt. He describes it as "calm, dishonourable, vile submission". He immediately turns his anger on Tybalt, calling him a "rat-catcher" and describing him as "King of Cats". His words are obviously designed to provoke Tybalt into fighting him, for it is clear that Tybalt's personality is far from "cat-like".

Shakespeare's use of such aggressive words heightens the tension between the two men. Having received a fatal wound, Mercutio speaks out against both Romeo and Tybalt: "A plague o' both your houses!" Notice how he makes this exclamation three times. Shakespeare deliberately uses repetition for effect. His words reflect two of the central themes of the play, which are:

- Violence leads to violence.
- Opposition to authority leads to punishment.

Romeo too recognises that the fight will only end in tragedy: he echoes the warning of the chorus, using words such as "black", "woe" and "end".

---

30. Romeo does not wish to fight with Tybalt because they are now related through his marriage to Juliet. Tybalt, on the other hand, deliberately provokes a fight with Romeo. Why?

31. (a) Mercutio, thinking Romeo's refusal to fight is a sign of cowardice, immediately challenges Tybalt himself. Why do you think he would have done this?

    (b) Imagine you are Mercutio and you are in a similar situation today. What would you do?

32. As Benvolio helps the wounded Mercutio from the stage, Romeo, now left alone, laments what has happened:

> *This gentleman, the Prince's near ally,*
> *My very friend, hath got this mortal hurt*
> *In my behalf — my reputation stained*
> *With Tybalt's slander — Tybalt that an hour*
> *Hath been my cousin. O sweet Juliet,*
> *Thy beauty hath made me effeminate*
> *And in my temper softened valour's steel.*

In this speech he is talking to himself. Shakespeare often uses this technique, known as a "soliloquy", to allow the audience to see directly into the mind of the character. What does Romeo's soliloquy tell us?

33. After Mercutio's death Romeo makes a grim prediction:

> *This day's black fate on more days doth depend:*
> *This but begins the woes others must end.*

What is he suggesting here?

34. Romeo's predictions certainly come true. What further sorrows occur soon after Mercutio's death?

35. Create a "snapshot" of this scene. In groups of six or more show a frozen moment from the fight. You should show how you think each character acted or reacted to the events of the fight.

36. (a) In small groups select a passage of text from the play so far. Transform the Elizabethan text into modern-day language.
    (b) Perform your work to the class.

37. Write a letter from the head of one of the feuding families to the other, offering peace. Explain how the feud has caused enough suffering.

38. Imagine you are a reporter on the local newspaper at that time. Write a news article that would suit the headline and drawing below.

Staging the play

This is a very violent and dramatic scene and gives great scope for actors.

39. In groups decide how you would stage this scene. Include:
   • the setting
   • the props
   • the actions.

40. If this scene were to be part of a film, what type of music and sound effects would you use?

Scene 2: The orchard

When Juliet hears of Tybalt's death she is greatly distressed. However, her love for Romeo outweighs her grief for her cousin.

Scene 3: Friar Lawrence's cell

Romeo seeks advice from Friar Lawrence. He is relieved when the nurse tells him that Juliet still waits for him.

Scenes 4 and 5: Capulets' home

Juliet's parents, unaware of her marriage to Romeo, decide to allow Paris to marry her in an attempt to ease her grief over the death of Tybalt. However, Juliet secretly spends the night with Romeo. In the morning, after he has gone, Juliet learns of her parents' plan for her to wed Paris.

Act four

Scene 1: Friar Lawrence's cell

Juliet frantically seeks advice from Friar Lawrence. If he cannot help her she plans to commit suicide.

ACT FOUR *Scene 1*

[*Enter* **Juliet**]

Paris   Happily met, my lady and my wife.

Juliet   That may be, sir, when I may be a wife.

20 **Paris**   That may be, must be, love, on Thursday next.

Juliet   What must be, shall be.

Friar Lawrence   That's a certain text.

Paris   Come you to make confession to this father?

Juliet   To answer that, I should confess to you.

Paris   Do not deny to him that you love me.

25 **Juliet**   I will confess to you that I love him.

Paris   So will ye, I am sure, that you love me.

Juliet   If I do so, it will be of more price
Being spoke behind your back than to your face.

Paris   Poor soul, thy face is much abused with tears.

30 **Juliet**   The tears have got small victory by that,
For it was bad enough before their spite.

Paris   Thou wrong'st it more than tears with that report.

Juliet   That is no slander, sir, which is a truth,
And what I spake, I spake it to my face.

35 **Paris**   Thy face is mine, and thou hast slandered it.

Juliet   It may be so, for it is not mine own.
Are you at leisure, holy father, now,
Or shall I come to you at evening mass?

Friar Lawrence   My leisure serves me, pensive daughter, now.
40   My lord, we must entreat the time alone.

Paris   God shield I should disturb devotion.
Juliet, on Thursday early will I rouse ye.
Till then, adieu and keep this holy kiss.

[*Exit*]

Barry Warren as Paris, Dorothy Tutin as Juliet and Max Adrian as Friar Lawrence, Royal Shakespeare Theatre 1961

45 **Juliet**   O shut the door, and when thou hast done so,
   Come weep with me, past hope, past cure, past help!

   Friar Lawrence   O Juliet, I already know thy grief;
   It strains me past the compass of my wits.
   I hear thou must — and nothing may prorogue it —
50   On Thursday next be married to this County.

   Juliet   Tell me not, Friar, that thou hearest of this,
   Unless thou tell me how I may prevent it.
   If in thy wisdom thou canst give no help,
   Do thou but call my resolution wise,
55   And with this knife I'll help it presently.
   God joined my heart and Romeo's, thou our hands;
   And ere this hand, by thee to Romeo's sealed,
   Shall be the label to another deed,
   Or my true heart with treacherous revolt
60   Turn to another, this shall slay them both.
   Therefore, out of thy long-experienced time
   Give me some present counsel, or behold:
   'Twixt my extremes and me this bloody knife
   Shall play the umpire, arbitrating that
65   Which the commission of thy years and art
   Could to no issue of true honour bring.
   Be not so long to speak. I long to die
   If what thou speak'st speak not of remedy.

Friar Lawrence   Hold, daughter. I do spy a kind of hope

70   Which craves as desperate an execution
      As that is desperate which we would prevent.
      If, rather than to marry County Paris,
      Thou hast the strength of will to slay thyself,
      Then it is likely thou wilt undertake

75   A thing like death to chide away this shame,
      That cop'st with death himself to scare from it.
      And if thou dar'st, I'll give thee remedy.

Juliet   O, bid me leap, rather than marry Paris,

80   From off the battlements of any tower,
      Or walk in thievish ways, or bid me lurk
      Where serpents are. Chain me with roaring bears,
      Or hide me nightly in a charnel-house
      O'ercovered quite with dead men's rattling bones,
      With reeky shanks and yellow chapless skulls.

85   Or bid me go into a new-made grave,
      And hide me with a dead man in his shroud —
      Things that, to hear them told, have made me tremble —
      And I will do it without fear or doubt.
      To live an unstained wife to my sweet love.

90   **Friar Lawrence**   Hold then. Go home, be merry, give consent
      To marry Paris. Wednesday is tomorrow;
      Tomorrow night look that thou lie alone.
      Let not the Nurse lie with thee in thy chamber.
      Take thou this vial, being then in bed,

95   And this distilling liquor drink thou off;
      When presently through all thy veins shall run
      A cold and drowsy humour, for no pulse
      Shall keep his native progress, but surcease;
      No warmth, no breath shall testify thou livest,

100   The roses in thy lips and cheeks shall fade
      To wanny ashes, thy eyes' windows fall
      Like death when he shuts up for the day of life.
      Each part deprived of supple government
      Shall stiff and stark and cold appear, like death,

105   And in this borrowed likeness of shrunk death
      Thou shall continue two and forty hours
      And then awake as from a pleasant sleep.
      Now when the bridegroom in the morning comes
      To rouse thee from thy bed, there art thou, dead.

110   Then as the manner of our country is,
      In thy best robes, uncovered on the bier
      Thou shall be borne to the same ancient vault
      Where all the kindred of the Capulets lie.
      In the meantime, against thou shalt awake,

115 Shall Romeo by my letters know our drift
And hither shall he come, and he and I
Will watch thy waking, and that very night
Shall Romeo bear thee hence to Mantua,
And this shall free thee from this present shame,
120 If no inconstant toy nor womanish fear
Abate thy valour in the acting it.

Juliet   Give me, give me! O tell me not of fear.

Friar Lawrence   Hold. Get you gone. Be strong and prosperous.
125 In this resolve. I'll send a friar with speed
To Mantua with my letters to thy lord.

Juliet   Love, give me strength, and strength shall help afford.
Farewell, dear father.

[Exeunt]

Friar Lawrence's plan at a glance

The action

When Juliet arrives at Friar Lawrence's cell, Paris is there. He speaks of their intended marriage, while she answers only in riddles and double meanings. When they are alone Juliet asks the Friar for help. He, understanding her anguish, says he has a plan to reunite her with her beloved Romeo, though he warns her that it is extremely dangerous.

She is to take a herbal potion which will make her appear as if dead for 42 hours. Romeo will be told of the plan by letter and, together with Friar Lawrence, will rescue her from the family tomb after her "funeral". Juliet agrees to this dangerous plan.

The issues

Was this elaborate plan to keep the truth from Juliet's parents justified? Should Friar Lawrence have become involved in such a conspiracy? Should Juliet simply have told her parents she was already married?

The language of Shakespeare

The conversation between Juliet, Paris and Friar Lawrence is sharp and tense: argument and counter-argument. Shakespeare achieves this through a series of short one-line sentences. Later in the scene Juliet uses powerful images when she describes the horror of having to marry Paris:

> *Or bid me go into a new-made grave,*
> *And hide me with a dead man in his shroud*

Shakespeare uses similes to create power in his imagery in this scene such as when he describes what Juliet will look like when she takes the potion:

> *Shall stiff and stark and cold appear, like death*

It is Juliet's emotional language that moves Friar Lawrence to help her:

Give me some present counsel, or behold:
'Twixt my extremes and me this bloody knife
Shall play the umpire . . .

41. What does Paris speak about when he meets Juliet at Friar Lawrence's cell?

42. Each of Juliet's remarks to Paris is in fact a clever play on words, concealing a hidden meaning. Working with a partner, identify the true meaning behind her words in lines 19–38. Share your answers with the class.

43. What does Juliet plan to do if Friar Lawrence can offer no solution to her problem?

44. Draw up a table like the one below. In the second column describe how, at the point where Paris leaves, you think Juliet feels about Paris, Friar Lawrence and Romeo. In the third column describe how you feel about them yourself.

Character	How Juliet feels about him	How I feel about him
Paris		
Friar Lawrence		
Romeo		

45. Friar Lawrence has a plan to reunite the young lovers but tells her that it is very dangerous.
    (a) Why is it dangerous? What could go wrong?
    (b) How does Juliet respond?
    (c) Do you think Friar Lawrence should have become involved in such a conspiracy? Explain your opinion.

46. Each step of Friar Lawrence's plan is listed below. Place the steps in the correct order.
    (a) The next morning, she will be found, apparently dead.
    (b) Romeo and Friar Lawrence will rescue her from the tomb.
    (c) Juliet is to go home and agree to marry Paris.
    (d) Romeo and Juliet will go to live in Mantua.
    (e) The night before the planned wedding she must take a potion which will take her into a death-like coma for 42 hours.
    (f) She will be buried in an open coffin inside the family tomb.
    (g) Romeo will be told of the plan by letter.

47. Like Juliet's decision to proceed with the plan, much of the action in the play is affected by the characters' attitudes towards love. The following graphic organiser illustrates how some of the characters in *Romeo and Juliet* feel about love.

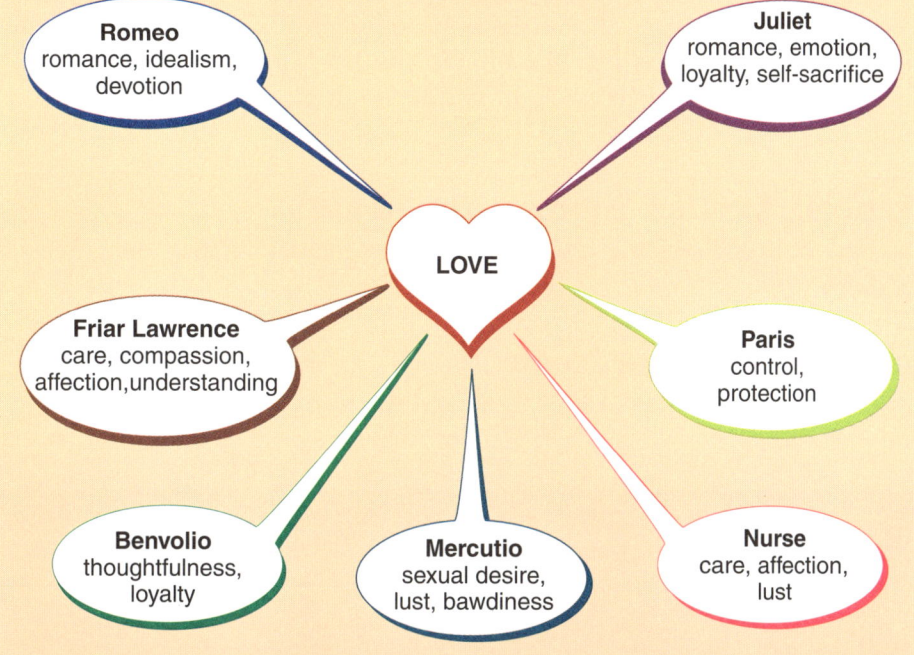

Romeo
romance, idealism, devotion

Juliet
romance, emotion, loyalty, self-sacrifice

LOVE

Friar Lawrence
care, compassion, affection,understanding

Paris
control, protection

Benvolio
thoughtfulness, loyalty

Mercutio
sexual desire, lust, bawdiness

Nurse
care, affection, lust

(a) Use quotes from the play to support these.
(b) Add further words to your character table (page 207) to describe how they feel about love. Share your answers with a partner.
(c) Which of these definitions do you relate to most? Explain.

Staging the play

This scene opens with an unemotional first meeting between Paris and Juliet. Though he wishes to marry Juliet, Paris shows no real affection for her. Juliet in return treats Paris with little more than contempt.

This lack of emotional response gives way to Juliet's passionate plea that Friar Lawrence help her find a solution to her dilemma.

Friar Lawrence also shows great compassion and affection for Juliet as he plans his desperate bid to help her.

48. In groups of three decide how you would act out this scene using modern language and setting. You might also like to change Friar Lawrence's character or even his plan. After all, thirteenth century sleeping potions are a little outdated by today's medical standards. However, try to retain the changing level of emotional involvement: show Paris' lack of sensitivity, Juliet's passionate appeal for help and Friar Lawrence's care and compassion.

Scene 2: Capulets' home

Juliet's pretence that she will marry Paris greatly pleases her parents.

Scene 3: Juliet's bedroom

The feeling of impending disaster is heightened by the vivid pictures Juliet paints in her imagination of the terrors which might await her in the family tomb. It is only her great love for Romeo and her burning desire to be reunited with him that eventually brings her to drink Friar Lawrence's potion.

Scene 4: Another room in the house

The next morning sees the Capulets happy on the day of their daughter's wedding.

Scene 5: Juliet's bedroom

Her nurse finds Juliet apparently dead and the household is plunged into grief.

Francesca Annis as Juliet and Marie Kean as the Nurse, Royal Shakespeare Theatre 1976

# Act five

Scene 1: The town of Mantua

Balthazar tells Romeo of Juliet's death. Romeo is overcome with grief and buys poison to end his own life. He sets off to return to Verona.

Scene 2: Friar Lawrence's cell

Friar John has been unable to deliver the letter explaining Friar Lawrence's plan to Romeo. As soon as he hears this, Friar Lawrence sets out for the tomb.

Scene 3: The Capulet family tomb

Romeo visits the tomb to see Juliet once more before he takes his own life. He finds that Paris has arrived at the tomb before him.

ACT FIVE *Scene 3*

[*Enter* **Romeo** *and* **Balthazar** *with a torch, a mattock and a crow of iron*]

Romeo   Give me that mattock and the wrenching iron.
Hold, take this letter. Early in the morning
See thou deliver it to my lord and father.
25 Give me the light. Upon thy life I charge thee,
Whate'er thou hear'st or seest, stand all aloof
And do not interrupt me in my course.
Why I descend into this bed of death
Is partly to behold my lady's face
30 But chiefly to take thence from her dead finger
A precious ring, a ring that I must use
In dear employment. Therefore hence, be gone.
But if thou jealous dost return to pry
In what I farther shall intend to do,
35 By heaven I will tear thee joint by joint,
And strew this hungry churchyard with thy limbs.
The time and my intents are savage-wild,
More fierce and more inexorable far
Than empty tigers or the roaring sea.

40 **Balthazar**   I will be gone, sir, and not trouble ye.

Romeo   So shalt thou show me friendship. Take thou that.
Live and be prosperous, and farewell, good fellow.

Balthazar   For all this same, I'll hide me hereabout.
His looks I fear, and his intents I doubt.

45 **Romeo** Thou detestable maw, thou womb of death
Gorged with the dearest morsel of the earth,
Thus I enforce thy rotten jaws to open,
And in despite I'll cram thee with more food.

[**Romeo** *opens the tomb*]

Paris This is that banished haughty Montague
50 That murdered my love's cousin — with which grief
It is supposed the fair creature died —
And here is come to do some villainous shame
To the dead bodies. I will apprehend him.
Stop thy unhallowed toil, vile Montague.
55 Can vengeance be pursued further than death?
Condemned villain, I do apprehend thee.
Obey, and go with me, for thou must die.

Romeo I must indeed, and therefore came I hither.
Good gentle youth, tempt not a desperate man.
60 Fly hence and leave me. Think upon these gone.
Let them affright thee. I beseech thee, youth,
Put not another sin upon my head
By urging me to fury. O be gone.
By heaven I love thee better than myself,
65 For I come hither armed against myself.
Stay not, be gone, live, and hereafter say
A mad man's mercy bid thee run away.

Paris I do defy thy conjuration
And apprehend thee for a felon here.

70 **Romeo** Wilt thou provoke me? Then have at thee, boy!

[*They fight*]

Page O Lord, they fight! I will go call the Watch.

[*Exit* **Page**]

Paris O, I am slain! If thou be merciful,
Open the tomb, lay me with Juliet.

[**Paris** *dies*]

Romeo In faith I will. Let me peruse this face.
75 Mercutio's kinsman, noble County Paris!
What said my man, when my betossed soul
Did not attend him, as we rode? I think
He told me Paris should have married Juliet.
Said he not so? Or did I dream it so?
80 Or am I mad, hearing him talk of Juliet,
To think it was so? O, give me thy hand,
One writ with me in sour misfortune's book.
I'll bury thee in a triumphant grave.
A grave? O no, a lantern, slaughtered youth.

85	For here lies Juliet, and her beauty makes
	This vault a feasting presence, full of light.
	Death, lie thou there, by a dead man interred.
	How oft when men are at the point of death
	Have they been merry! Which their keepers call
90	A lightning before death. O how may I
	Call this a lightning? O my love, my wife,
	Death that hath sucked the honey of thy breath
	Hath had no power yet upon thy beauty.
	Thou art not conquered.
	Beauty's ensign yet
95	Is crimson in thy lips and in thy cheeks,
	And Death's pale flag is not advanced there.
	Tybalt, liest thou there in thy bloody sheet?
	O, what more favour can I do to thee
	Than with that hand that cut thy youth in twain
100	To sunder his that was thine enemy?
	Forgive me, cousin. Ah, dear Juliet,
	Why art thou yet so fair? Shall I believe
	That unsubstantial Death is amorous,
	And that the lean abhorred monster keeps
105	Thee here in dark to be his paramour?
	For fear of that I still will stay with thee,
	And never from this place of dim night
	Depart again. Here, here, will I remain
	With worms that are thy chambermaids. O here
110	Will I set up my everlasting rest
	And shake the yoke of inauspicious stars
	From this world-wearied flesh. Eyes, look your last.
	Arms, take your last embrace! And lips, O you
	The doors of breath, seal with a righteous kiss
115	A dateless bargain to engrossing Death.
	Come, bitter conduct, come unsavoury guide,
	Thou desperate pilot now at once run on
	The dashing rocks thy seasick weary bark.
	Here's to my love! [*He drinks*] O true apothecary,
120	Thy drugs are quick. Thus with a kiss I die.

[*He falls*]

[*Enter* **Friar Lawrence** *with lantern, crow and spade*]

Friar Lawrence   Saint Francis be my speed. How oft tonight
Have my old feet stumbled at graves. Who's there?

Balthazar   Here's one, a friend, and one that knows you well.

Friar Lawrence   Bliss be upon you. Tell me, good friend,
125   What torch is yond that vainly lends his light
To grubs and eyeless skulls? As I discern,
It burneth in the Capels' monument.

Balthazar It doth so, holy sir, and there's my master,
One that you love

Friar Lawrence Who is it?

130 **Balthazar** Romeo.

Friar Lawrence How long hath he been there?

Balthazar Full half an hour.

Friar Lawrence Go with me to the vault.

Balthazar I dare not, sir.
My master knows not but I am gone hence,
And fearfully did menace me with death
If I did stay to look on his intents.

135 **Friar Lawrence** Stay then, I'll go alone. Fear comes upon me.
O, much I fear some ill unthrifty thing.

Balthazar As I did sleep under this yew tree here
I dreamt my master and another fought,
And that my master slew him.

Friar Lawrence Romeo!

[**Friar Lawrence** *stoops and looks on the blood and weapons*]

140 Alack, alack, what blood is this which stains
The stony entrance of this sepulchre?
What means these masterless and gory swords
To lie discoloured by this place of peace?
Romeo! O, pale! Who else? What, Paris too?
145 And steeped in blood? Ah what an unkind hour
Is guilty of this lamentable chance?
The lady stirs.

[**Juliet** *rises*]

Juliet O comfortable Friar, where is my lord?
I do remember well where I should be,
150 And there I am. Where is my Romeo?

Friar Lawrence I hear some noise. Lady, come from that nest
Of death, contagion, and unnatural sleep.
A greater power than we can contradict
Hath thwarted our intents. Come, come away.
155 Thy husband in thy bosom there lies dead,
And Paris too. Come, I'll dispose of thee
Among a sisterhood of holy nuns.
Stay not to question, for the Watch is coming.
Come, go, good Juliet. I dare no longer stay.

¹⁶⁰ **Juliet**   Go get thee hence, for I will not away.

[*Exit* **Friar Lawrence**]

What's here? A cup closed in my true love's hand?
Poison, I see, hath been his timeless end.
O churl. Drunk all, and left no friendly drop
To help me after? I will kiss thy lips.
¹⁶⁵ Haply some poison yet doth hang on them.
To make me die with a restorative. [*She kisses him*]
Thy lips are warm!

Watchman   [*Outside*] Lead, boy. Which way?

Juliet   Yea, noise? Then I'll be brief. O happy dagger.
This is thy sheath. There rust, and let me die.

[*She stabs herself and falls*]

Olivia Hussey and Leonard Whiting in Franco Zeffirelli's movie of
Romeo and Juliet

The death scene at a glance

The action

Romeo meets Paris at Juliet's tomb. They begin to fight and Paris is killed.
Romeo enters the tomb and upon seeing Juliet he drinks the poison and dies.

Friar Lawrence arrives at the tomb just as Juliet awakes. Hearing voices he
urges her to flee but she refuses. Instead she takes Romeo's dagger and kills
herself.

Prince Escalus, the Montagues and the Capulets arrive at the tomb and Friar Lawrence explains all that has happened. Both families agree to end the terrible feud, realising the tragedy it has caused.

The issues

The tragedy of Romeo and Juliet reaches everyone. Mercutio, Tybalt, Lady Montague and Paris all fall victim to the feud. The Montagues and Capulets suffer the loss of their only children. In the ultimate tragedy of the play, Romeo and Juliet lose their lives because of the love they have for each other. Why is it that so often in life people don't realise the consequences of their actions until it is too late? In our world hate and love so often seem to go hand-in-hand. How much of what happened to Romeo and Juliet depended on fate?

The language of Shakespeare

The depth of emotion presented in the final scene acts as a summary for what has come before it. It is the language of desperate grief and anger.

Romeo and Juliet's final words for each other prove the strength and eternal nature of their love. And in the closing lines of the play, Prince Escalus echoes the words spoken by the chorus in the prologue, recounting the tragic nature of the loss suffered by all.

49. Describe what happens when Paris and Romeo meet at the tomb.

50. "... with a kiss I die." Are these fitting last words for Romeo? Explain.

51. Friar Lawrence urges Juliet to flee when they hear the constables coming. Why does she refuse to leave?

52. It is not clear whether Shakespeare wrote "rust" or "rest" in line 169. Which word do you think Juliet would have spoken? Explain your choice.

53. Explain how the tragic deaths of Romeo and Juliet brought about an end to the feud.

54. Throughout the play we see great changes in the character of both Romeo and Juliet. How do they change? Find passages from the play to support your answer.

55. (a) Romeo describes the tomb as if it were human. Why do you think Shakespeare uses this technique?
    (b) Known as "personification" this technique is used a number of times throughout the play. What words does he use to make the tomb human?

56. How far were Mercutio, the nurse and Friar Lawrence responsible for the death of Romeo and Juliet? Hold a class discussion to decide on their degree of guilt, ranging from "0" for innocent to "5" for guilty.

The essay below is a student's response to question 56, together with a teacher's comments.

How far were Mercutio, the nurse and Friar Lawrence responsible for the deaths of Romeo and Juliet?

The combined actions of Mercutio, the Nurse and Friar Lawrence contribute to the final tragedy, the death of Romeo and Juliet. All three people play a part in altering the young lovers' ultimate fate. Without their involvement, be it consciously or otherwise, circumstances may have differed with many young lives saved.

Your opinion is clearly stated.

Mercutio, a good friend of Romeo and relative of the Prince, indirectly contributes to the final tragedy in two ways. Firstly, through his well meaning intentions, the couple meet and fall in love at first sight. Genuinely concerned when Romeo becomes despondent over his unreturned love for his beautiful Rosaline, Mercutio is responsible for persuading him to attend a masque at Capulets house, where the ill fated couple meet, "Nay gentle Romeo, we must have you dance."[1] Secondly, Mercutio fighting in defence of Romeo is killed. Through his secret marriage to Juliet, Romeo is now a cousin to Tybalt and when the latter attempts to goad him into a fight, Romeo controls his personal emotions and resists. However, Mercutio, witnessing this scene, becomes so incensed that he fights Tybalt and is subsequently fatally injured. Seeing his friend die, Romeo avenges the death of Mercutio by slaying Tybalt, this leading to his banishment from Verona. In this way Mercutio was partly responsible for the final tragedy.

Good topic sentence

Use of quotes supports your opinion well.

Good link back to the topic

In contrast to Mercutio, Juliet's nurse acts as a "go-between" in the clandestine love of Romeo and Juliet. With Juliet being closer to the nurse than her own mother, she feels she can tell her anything, including the forbidden love of herself and Romeo. Prior to the masque at which Romeo and Juliet meet, the nurse supports Lady Capulet when she

Clear link to previous paragraph

---

[1] Act 1, Scene 4, Line 13

encourages Juliet to marry Paris. However, Juliet, impressed when she first meets Romeo, requests her nurse find out who he is. "... Go ask his name. If he be married, My grave is like to be my wedding bed."[2] In doing so, the nurse is supporting Juliet and thus unknowingly becoming part of the conspiracy. The nurse represents Juliet at a meeting with Romeo to arrange the young lovers' secret wedding. By conveying the messages between the two, she is condoning the drastic actions they are taking, especially after knowing each other for only one night. As the nurse adores Juliet and thinks of her as her own child, she will do anything to make her happy. This includes allowing Romeo to stay secretly overnight in Juliet's chamber, after his banishment for killing Tybalt. With the nurse protecting Romeo in this way, she is going against the Capulets, endangering her position in the family. This act shows the nurse's acceptance of Romeo and Juliet's love, which was similar to the attitude taken by Friar Lawrence.

[margin note: You need to link back to the topic. How responsible is she?]

Friar Lawrence, a Franciscan Monk and herbalist who concocts remedies and drugs out of medicinal and poisonous plants, gives Romeo and Juliet advice when they seek it from him. Firstly giving Romeo advice on his "love" of Rosaline, Friar Lawrence is suprised at how quickly Romeo's affections change, when he comes to him for advice about his love of Juliet. He is concerned for the welfare of the two lovers and so warns Romeo about moving too hastily. However, he agrees to marry them as he hopes it will restore peace in Verona by bringing the two feuding families together:

[margin note: Your topic sentence should include a more direct statement about Friar Lawrence's involvement.]

[margin note: spelling]

> "For this alliance may so happy prove
> To turn your household's rancour to pure love."[3]

When Capulet insists that his daughter marry Paris, the nurse urges Juliet to forget the banished Romeo and do as she is bid by her father. Juliet rejects the

---

[2] Act 1, Scene 5, Line 141–142

[3] Act 2, Scene 4, Line 91–92

nurse, leaving her with no other option except to seek the help of Friar Lawrence or "If all else fails, myself have power to die."[4] Friar Lawrence offers his assistance by giving Juliet a herbal potion, which will give her a lifeless appearance. She is to drink this the night before her wedding to Paris, so as she will be presumed dead, put in her tomb and then rescued by Romeo. He also writes to Romeo telling him of the plan and gives the letter to some monks to deliver. However the letter never reaches Romeo and when Balthazar comes with the news that Juliet is dead and buried Romeo acts with great haste. Before returning to Verona, he seeks out a poor Apothecary from whom he purchases poison. He enters Juliet's tomb and finding his love, who appears to be dead, drinks the poison so as to be with her for eternity.

wonderful use of quote

Be careful— you are lapsing into story-telling here.

Friar Lawrence enters to find his plan has failed. As Juliet regains her consciousness, she sees Romeo's body, and despite the urges of Friar Lawrence, refuses to leave the tomb. Finding no help in the empty poison bottle that lies by Romeo's side, she grabs his dagger and quickly takes her own life.

Very strong topic sentence

Despite the fatal outcome of this story, Mercutio, the nurse and the Friar Lawrence all had good intentions towards Romeo and Juliet. They were not all equally responsible for the tragic ending, with each having a different degree of involvement. Mercutio, responsible for their meeting and Romeo's banishment, the nurse for her encouragement of the affair by her support in acting as an intermediary, and finally the Friar Lawrence who condoned and performed the marriage and who was the author of the ill-fated scheme to bring the couple together. The Friar Lawrence had the most impact, unintentionally being a catalyst for the deaths of Romeo and Juliet. But without the deeds of Mercutio and the nurse, the Friar Lawrence's actions may not have lead to what they did. Fate was lent a helping hand in the death of Romeo and Juliet — the actions of everyone involved lead to the story being a "tragedy of mistakes."

Solid evaluation

Melanie Cameron

You show an excellent knowledge of the play, and have answered the question well.

[4] Act 3, Scene 5, Line 254

Text response assessment sheet

Criteria	Level of achievement — tick the appropriate point on the line.
1. Knowledge of the text • Does the essay show understanding of the various elements of the play? • Have relevant quotations been used?	Major problems Highly successful
2. Structure of the essay • Is the structure appropriate for the audience? • Is it logical? • Are the different aspects connected effectively? • Does the introduction clearly outline the intent? • Does the conclusion tie together the main ideas? • Is the whole essay relevant to the topic?	
3. Language and presentation • Is the language level and presentation appropriate for the audience? • Is it fluent and clear? • Are spelling and punctuation correct? • Are the sentences constructed correctly? • Are the paragraphs linked? • Has the correct format been used for quoting from the text?	

Assessment by: .... **of essay by:** ....

Your turn

58. Write an analytical essay on one of the following topics. Before you begin, look at the criteria included in the assessment sheet on page 246. When you have completed your essay, have a partner assess your work using those criteria.
    (a) *Romeo and Juliet* is more about love than it is about death.
    (b) The real tragedy in *Romeo and Juliet* is that everyone loses.
    (c) In *Romeo and Juliet* Shakespeare shows us that love is a most powerful, complex and dangerous emotion.
    (d) Considering their ages, Romeo and Juliet were really let down by the adults in their lives.

Relationships: family, friend or foe?

The relationships between characters in *Romeo and Juliet* range from deep love to the most bitter enmity. Look at the relationship web below.

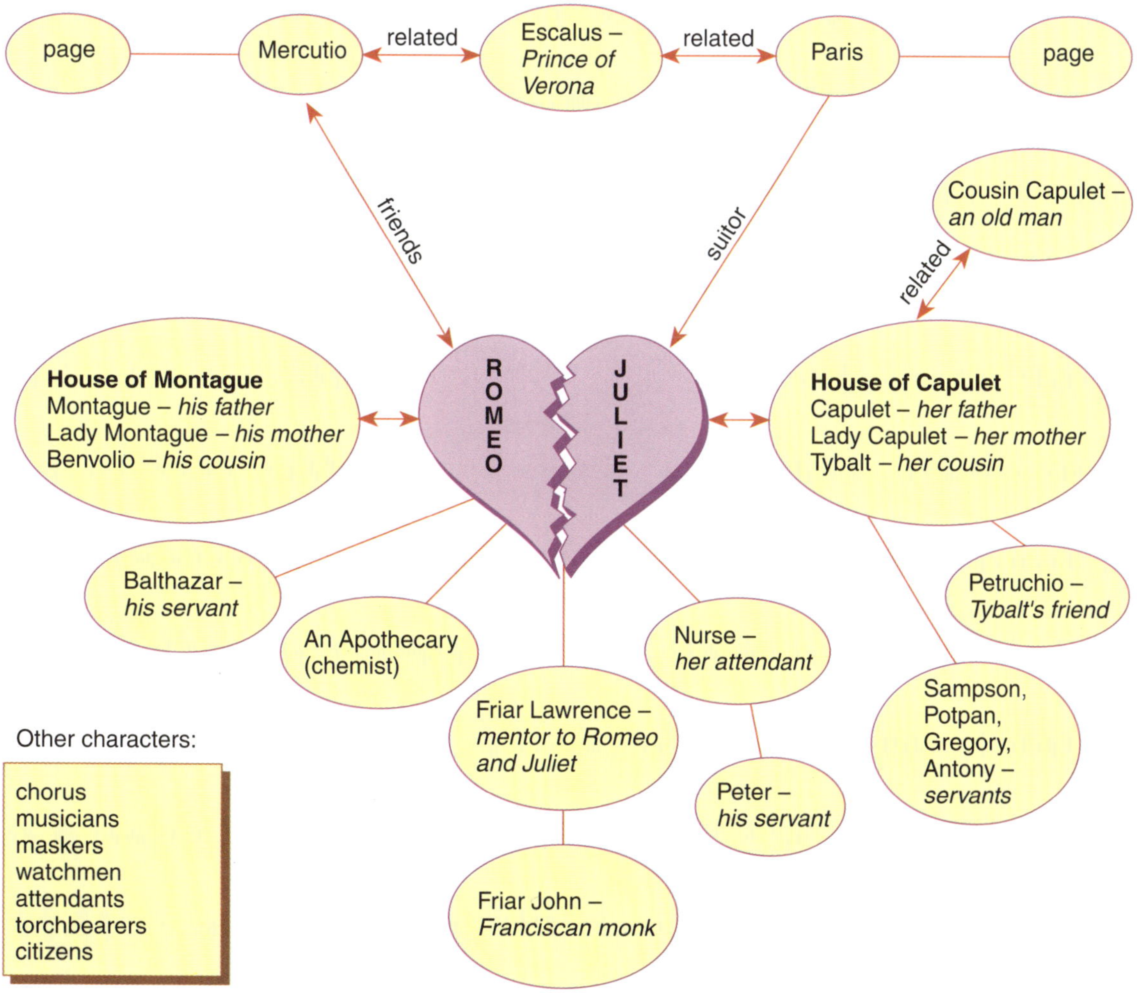

```
page — Mercutio —related→ Escalus –
                           Prince of   ←related— Paris — page
                           Verona

                    friends                    suitor              related → Cousin Capulet –
                                                                             an old man

House of Montague          ROMEO | JULIET        House of Capulet
Montague – his father      (broken heart)        Capulet – her father
Lady Montague – his mother                       Lady Capulet – her mother
Benvolio – his cousin                            Tybalt – her cousin

Balthazar –                                      Petruchio –
his servant                                      Tybalt's friend

        An Apothecary        Nurse –             Sampson,
        (chemist)            her attendant       Potpan,
                                                 Gregory,
            Friar Lawrence –                     Antony –
            mentor to Romeo    Peter –           servants
            and Juliet         his servant

                 Friar John –
                 Franciscan monk
```

Other characters:

chorus
musicians
maskers
watchmen
attendants
torchbearers
citizens

59. Apart from the names of the characters, what information does the relationship web give us?

60. While there are two main groups of characters in *Romeo and Juliet*, each quite separate from the other, there are a number of ways in which various characters are linked together. Copy and complete the table below. One line is done for you as an example.

Character	Someone with whom he/she is linked	How they are linked
Romeo	*Juliet*	*They are in love.*
Mercutio		
Paris		
Tybalt		
Lawrence		

61. Choose a TV serial and draw up a relationship web similar to the one on page 247, showing the major characters and their relationships. Use a Venn diagram like the one below to illustrate the similarities and differences between *Romeo and Juliet* and the serial you chose.

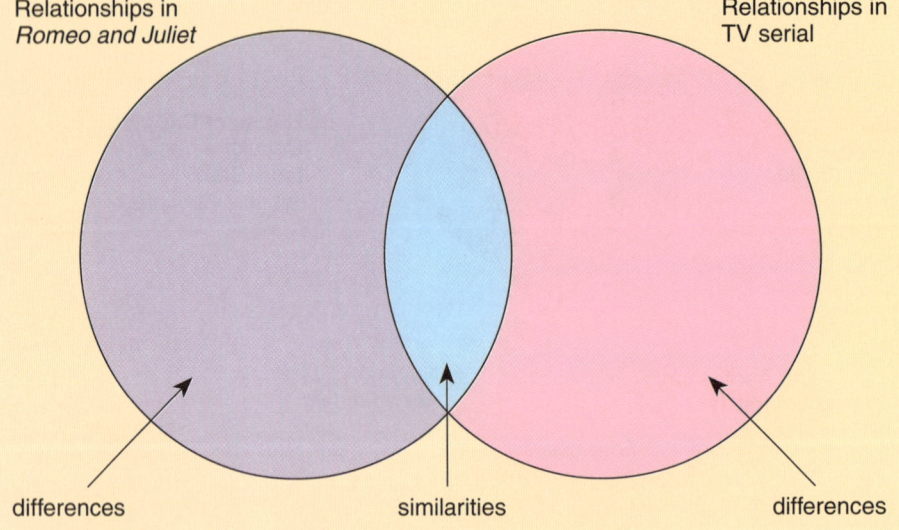

Relationships in
Romeo and Juliet

Relationships in
TV serial

differences   similarities   differences

62. In the play, Romeo falls in love with Juliet the moment he sees her. Do you believe in "love at first sight"? Explain.

63. Romeo and Juliet meet, are married and tragically die, all within a few days. What effect does this short time-span have on the play?

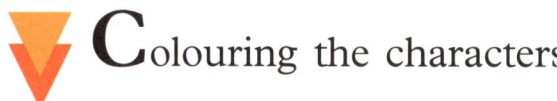

64. Draw upon what you have already learned about the characters and, using the words from the box below, fill in the blank spaces.

loves	Mercutio	Tybalt	reason
Benvolio	nurse	hatred	aggressive

(a) The love Romeo and Juliet have for each other contrasts with the _____ between the Montagues and the Capulets.

(b) Paris desires Juliet for his wife, whereas Romeo truly _____ her.

(c) Benvolio is peaceful while Tybalt is _____ .

(d) Juliet's relationship with her nurse is equivalent to that between Romeo and _____ .

(e) Escalus tries to stop the fighting by using the law; Friar Lawrence uses _____ to find a solution.

(f) The name of Romeo's cousin is _____ .

(g) Mercutio's bawdy personality is matched by that of the _____ .

65. Shakespeare often gave his characters names that were clues to their personalities. Mercutio comes from the name Mercury and means quick, fast-moving and lively, just as we see him in the play. Match the following characters with a word from the box.

(a) Romeo

(b) Juliet

(c) Tybalt

(d) Benvolio

sweet
romantic
kind
tyrannical

66. Use adjectives from the list below, or any of your own, to describe the following characters from the play. Many of the adjectives will apply to more than one character.

(a) Romeo

(b) Juliet

(c) Mercutio

(d) Benvolio

(e) Tybalt

(f) Montague

(g) Capulet

(h) Lady Montague

(i) Lady Capulet

(j) Nurse

(k) Prince Escalus

(l) Friar Lawrence

loving	uncaring
caring	hospitable
lovesick	selfish
thoughtful	rich
beautiful	quiet
aggressive	knowledgeable
bawdy	naive
handsome	kind
intelligent	driven
peaceloving	regal
sensible	loyal
just	calculating
unforgiving	vengeful

67. Look at these photos from the 1988 Australian production of *Romeo and Juliet* by the NIDA Company, Sydney. Identify each of the characters. Discuss your reasoning with a partner.

A

B

Fate plays its part

Much of the tragedy in *Romeo and Juliet* is based upon "fate". In the prologue, the chorus speaks of "The fearful passage of their death-mark'd love", clearly a symbol that Romeo and Juliet are fated to die. The Elizabethans firmly believed in destiny: that a person's future was decided by fate. In the play, fate creates a string of coincidences:

- The Montagues and Capulets are bitter enemies, yet Romeo and Juliet fall in love.
- At the same time Paris also asks for Juliet's hand in marriage.
- Friar Lawrence's letter to Romeo fails to be delivered.
- Romeo drinks the poison and dies just before Juliet awakes.
- Juliet kills herself only moments before the Montagues and Capulets, together with Prince Escalus, arrive at the tomb.

68. (a) If you could change just one of these tragic coincidences which one would it be?
    (b) Explain how this change could have affected the outcome of the play.

69. The play makes a number of actual references to fate. The extracts below from Acts One and Two emphasise that tragedy for the two lovers cannot be avoided.
    (a) In pairs identify the speaker for each one.
    (b) Write in your own words what the person is saying about fate.
    (c) What effect does the theme of fate have on the play?
        (i) *The fearful passage of their death-marked love*
        (ii) *From forth the fatal loins of these two foes*
             A pair of star-crossed lovers take their life
        (iii) *This day's black fate on more days doth depend;*
              This but begins the woes others must end.
        (iv) *I fear too early; for my mind misgives*
             Some consequence, yet hanging in the stars,
             Shall bitterly begin this fearful date
             With this night's revels and expire the term
             Of a despised life closed in my breast,
             By some vile forfeit of untimely death.
             But he that hath the steerage of my course,
             Direct my sail! On, lusty gentlemen.

Staging the play

Juliet uses Romeo's dagger to end her life, thus ending their tragic love affair. But how else could the play have ended? Could it in fact have ended happily? What if Romeo had received Friar Lawrence's letter and all had gone to plan? What if Juliet had awakened before Romeo entered the tomb? If Paris had killed Romeo would Juliet still have taken her own life?

70. In small groups brainstorm ideas for your own ending to the play.

Four hundred years later

As popular today as it was during Shakespeare's time, *Romeo and Juliet* continues to play to appreciative audiences around the world.

The following review looks at a recent production of the play.

Structure

Language features

- headline
- play title
- director and set designer
- theatre season, reviewer's name
- information about director
- setting, stage design, lighting
- information about cast
- positive comments on staging
- details of lead roles
- plot
- supporting roles
- details on staging
- comments on pace of play
- audience reaction

- words from the play
- words describing the emotional impact of the play
- powerful descriptive words
- words showing depth of emotion
- Short paragraphs keep the review moving.

Romeo a superb finale for Mellor

ROMEO & JULIET, by William Shakespeare. QTC, directed by Aubrey Mellor. Designer Dale Ferguson. Suncorp Theatre. Until Sept 4. Reviewed by DES PARTRIDGE.

THE tragedy of Shakespeare's star-crossed lovers is achingly felt in this arresting production which marks director Aubrey Mellor's finale with the state theatre company.

There's a contemporary relevance to the tragedy in Verona in the hints of the continuing Muslim-Christian war in Bosnia suggested by the broken concrete and twisted metal elements of the starkly-lit set.

Mellor hasn't challenged with a radical production. This is still Shakespeare, and there is the eternal difficulty at times of making the excess of Elizabethan language flow naturally in the long play.

Yet, overall, it has to be said the all-local cast makes this a vital, thrilling and "romantic" production that is brimming with emotion.

The verbal sparring among Romeo and his teenage friends, and the joy of the Capulet ball where Romeo first sees the lovely Juliet (an artfully staged scene), captures the spirit of the principals' youth.

Paul Bishop as Romeo and Veronica Neave, a graceful and lovely Juliet, bring dignity, depth and youthful zest to these classic roles. These are young adults driven to desperate measures by the power of their obsession for each other, determined to break free of the hate around them by the supreme sacrifice.

But this is not just about Romeo and Juliet. The seasoned cast is intent on making subsidiary roles vital, and there's much joy to be had from the contributions by Eugene Gilfedder, providing wit and intensity as Mercutio, and an over-costumed Jennifer Flowers as the nurse.

Jonathan Hardy is assured (and speaks beautifully) as the Friar and Sally McKenzie and Leo Wockner as Juliet's parents undergo a powerful conversion from arrogance to grief at the death of their beloved daughter.

Michael Futcher's Tybalt is notably aggressive, and his "fatal brawl" scenes with Mercutio and Romeo are among the most exciting and breathtakingly staged among all of this notable company's work.

The emotion layering the theatre at the end of the first act takes a while to build up again in the second (what a pity Shakespeare kills Mercutio off *before* interval), but there's an eerie stillness from a rapt audience as the tomb tragedy unfolds.

Mellor has paid minute attention to every facet of the production, which has mood-enhancing music and lighting.

The controversial nude scene, with the young (married) lovers entwined in passion beneath apricot coloured sheets, is tantalisingly brief and beautiful.

With this *Romeo and Juliet* Aubrey Mellor should leave the QTC not with a whimper — but a resounding roar of approval.

An ecstatic moment for Romeo (Paul Bishop) and Juliet (Veronica Neave) in the QTC's new production

71. (a) What was the reviewer's overall impression of this production of *Romeo and Juliet*?
    (b) Which lines or paragraphs best describe his feelings for the play?

72. How did he describe the following aspects of the production?
    (a) the direction of Aubrey Mellor
    (b) the lead roles
    (c) the supporting cast
    (d) the staging, lighting and sound effects
    (e) the nude scene

73. If possible attend a live performance or watch one of the many movie versions of *Romeo and Juliet*. Keeping the features of a review in mind, write your own review of the play.

SELF ASSESSMENT

Name: ....

1. Can I?

Write "yes" or "no" in the box. If you write "no", go back over your work until you can write "yes".

- Understand Shakespearean text .... ☐
- Understand characterisation .... ☐
- Write a text response essay .... ☐
- Write a play review .... ☐

2. Your reaction

(a) Which part of the play did you like best? Say why.
(b) Which activity did you like best? Say why.
(c) Which skill do you need to work on most? What can you do to improve it?

3. For your folio

From the work you have done in this chapter, choose the pieces you want to include in your folio. Each piece of work in your folio should include a cover sheet which shows the date it was completed, the title, the purpose and the audience.

4. Ongoing skills

Complete the table below by:
- placing a tick at the point at which you feel you usually achieve in each skill
- shading in the range of your achievement in each skill.

When you have completed the table place it in your folio.

Am I improving in these skills?	Level of achievement		
	Same as before	Improving	Much better
Example: Oral work		✓	
Interpreting issues			
Analysing language			
Cooperating in group work			
Oral work			
Explaining ideas			
Writing dialogue			
Analysing character webs			
Using graphic organisers			
Using evidence to support an answer			
Discussing emotions			

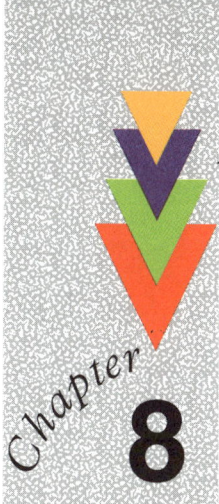

Striving for harmony

8 THE CHALLENGE

Content

- Conflict and peace
- Features of a short story
- Propaganda
- The United Nations
- Human rights
- Medical ethics
- Presenting an issue
- Human relationships
- Writing a short story

Skills

- Identifying biased language
- Making a political news report
- Writing an official protest letter
- Using the dictionary
- Notemaking
- Writing an argumentative essay
- Writing a short story

 our world in the year 2020.

 Where will we be?

 What will we be doing?

 How will we relate to others?

 How will we be treating our planet?

 How will we feed ourselves?

These are some of the challenges of our future.

Conflict and peace

One of the greatest challenges we face is to overcome war and create a peaceful world for all. It is an enormous challenge which seems at times impossible to achieve. Despite the efforts of many, wars still break out, resulting in untold suffering, death and hardship for innocent people.

Perhaps the most devastating of all is the civil war in which people in one country fight against each other.

The theme of Liam O'Flaherty's short story *The Sniper* is the tragedy of a war that seems to have become a way of life for many.

Structure

Language features

title

author

introduction

setting

main character

The Sniper

a short story by Liam O'Flaherty

The long June twilight faded into night. Dublin lay enveloped in darkness, but for the dim light of the moon, that shone through fleecy clouds, casting a pale light as of approaching dawn over the streets and the dark waters of the Liffey. Around the beleaguered Four Courts the heavy guns roared. Here and there through the city machine guns and rifles broke the silence of the night, spasmodically, like dogs barking on lone farms. Republicans and Free Staters were waging civil war.

On a roof-top near O'Connel Bridge, a Republican sniper lay watching. Beside him lay his rifle and over his shoulders was slung a pair of field-glasses. His face was the face of a student — thin and ascetic, but his eyes had the cold gleam of a fanatic. They were deep and thoughtful, the eyes of a man who is used to looking at death.

Proper nouns indicate exactly where story takes place and who is involved.

Adjectives describe main character's appearance.

He was eating a sandwich hungrily. He had eaten nothing since morning. He had been too excited to eat. He finished the sandwich, and taking a flask of whisky from his pocket, he took a short draught. Then he returned the flask to his pocket. He paused for a moment, considering whether he should risk a smoke. It was dangerous. The flash might be seen in the darkness, and there were enemies watching. He decided to take the risk. Placing a cigarette between his lips, he struck a match, inhaled the smoke hurriedly and put out the light. Almost immediately a bullet flattened itself against the parapet of the roof. The sniper took another whiff and put out the cigarette. Then he swore softly and crawled away to the left.

Cautiously he raised himself and peered over the parapet. There was a flash and a bullet whizzed over his head. He dropped immediately. He had seen the flash. It came from the opposite side of the street.

He rolled over the roof to a chimney stack in the rear, and slowly drew himself up behind it, until his eyes were level with the top of the parapet. There was nothing to be seen — just the dim outline of the opposite house-top against the blue sky. His enemy was under cover.

Short sentences create the tense mood.

complication

Strong verbs describe the action.

further complication

Just then an armoured car came across the bridge and advanced slowly up the street. It stopped on the opposite side of the street fifty metres ahead. The sniper could hear the dull panting of the motor. His heart beat faster. It was an enemy car. He wanted to fire, but he knew it was useless. His bullets would never pierce the steel that covered the grey monster.

Then round the corner of a side street came an old woman, her head covered by a tattered shawl. She began to talk to the man in the turret of the car. She was pointing to the roof where the sniper lay. An informer.

The turret opened. A man's head and shoulders appeared, looking towards the sniper. The sniper raised his rifle and fired. The head fell heavily on the turret wall. The woman darted toward the side street. The sniper fired again. The woman whirled round and fell with a shriek into the gutter.

Suddenly from the opposite roof a shot rang out and the sniper dropped his rifle with a curse. The rifle cluttered to the roof. The sniper thought the noise would wake the dead. He stopped to pick the rifle up. He couldn't lift it. His forearm was dead. 'Christ,' he muttered, 'I'm hit.'

Dropping flat on to the roof, he crawled back to the parapet. With his left hand he felt the injured right forearm. The blood was oozing through the sleeve of his coat. There was no pain — just a deadened sensation, as if the arm had been cut off.

Quickly he drew his knife from his pocket, opened it on the breastwork of the parapet and ripped open the sleeve. There was a small hole where the bullet had entered. On the other side there was no hole. The bullet had lodged in the bone. It must have fractured it. He bent the arm below the wound. The arm bent back easily. He ground his teeth to overcome the pain.

Then, taking out his field-dressing, he ripped open the packet with his knife. He broke the neck of the iodine bottle and let the bitter fluid drip into the wound. A paroxysm of pain swept through him. He placed the cotton wadding over the wound and wrapped the dressing over it. He tied the end with his teeth. Then he lay still against the parapet and, closing his eyes, he made an effort of will to overcome the pain.

Annotations:

Adjectives describe type of vehicle and who it belongs to.

Metaphor presents visual image of the car.

Adverbs of time to start paragraphs pinpoint the sequence of events.

further complication

Speech creates sense of drama.

Alliteration creates a powerful image.

In the street beneath all was still. The armoured car had retired speedily over the bridge, with the machine gunner's head hanging lifeless over the turret. The woman's corpse lay still in the gutter.

The sniper lay for a long time nursing his wounded arm and planning escape. Morning must not find him wounded on the roof. The enemy on the opposite roof covered his escape. He must kill that enemy and he could not use his rifle. He had only a revolver to do it. Then he thought of a plan.

Taking off his cap, he placed it over the muzzle of his rifle. Then he pushed the rifle slowly upwards over the parapet, until the cap was visible from the opposite side of the street. Almost immediately there was a report, and a bullet pierced the centre of the cap. The sniper slanted the rifle forward. The cap slipped down into the street. Then, catching the rifle in the middle, the sniper dropped his left hand over the roof and let it hang, lifelessly. After a few moments he let his rifle drop to the street. Then he sank to the roof, dragging his hand with him.

Crawling quickly to the left, he peered up at the corner of the roof. His ruse had succeeded. The other sniper, seeing the cap and rifle fall, thought that he had killed his man. He was now standing before a row of chimney pots, looking across, with his head clearly silhouetted against the western sky.

The Republican sniper smiled and lifted his revolver above the edge of the parapet. The distance was about fifty metres — a hard shot in the dim light, and his right arm was paining him like a thousand devils. He took a steady aim. His hand trembled with eagerness. Pressing his lips together, he took a deep breath through his nostrils and fired. He was almost deafened with the report and his arm shook with the recoil.

Then, when the smoke cleared, he peered across and uttered a cry of joy. His enemy had been hit. He was reeling over the parapet in his death agony. He struggled to keep his feet, but he was slowly falling forward, as if in a dream. The rifle fell from his grasp, hit the parapet, fell over, pounded off the pole of a barber's shop beneath and then clattered on to the pavement.

Then the dying man on the roof crumpled up and fell forward. The body turned over and over in space and hit the ground with a dull thud. Then it lay still.

Repetition of noun links the story.

Simile creates strong image.

climax

resolution

The sniper looked at his enemy falling and he shuddered. The lust of battle died in him. He became bitten by remorse. The sweat stood out in beads on his forehead. Weakened by his wound and the long summer day of fasting and watching on the roof, he revolted from the sight of the shattered mass of his dead enemy. His teeth chattered. He began to gibber to himself, cursing the war, cursing himself, cursing everybody.

He looked at the smoking revolver in his hand and with an oath he hurled it to the roof at his feet. The revolver went off with the concussion, and the bullet whizzed past the sniper's head. He was frightened back to his senses by the shock. His nerves steadied. The cloud of fear scattered from his mind and he laughed.

Repetition creates emphasis.

Onomatopoeia creates the image of sound.

Taking the whisky flask from his pocket, he emptied it at a draught. He felt reckless under the influence of the spirits. He decided to leave the roof and look for his company commander to report. Everywhere around was quiet. There was not much danger in going through the streets. He picked up his revolver and put it in his pocket. Then he crawled down through the sky-light to the house underneath.

When the sniper reached the laneway on the street level, he felt a sudden curiosity as to the identity of the enemy sniper whom he had killed. He decided that he was a good shot whoever he was. He wondered if he knew him. Perhaps he had been in his own company before the split in the army. He decided to risk going over to have a look at him. He peered around the corner into O'Connel Street. In the upper part of the street there was heavy firing, but around here all was quiet.

The sniper darted across the street. A machine gun tore up the ground around him with a hail of bullets, but he escaped. He threw himself downwards beside the corpse. The machine gun stopped.

Then the sniper turned over the dead body and looked into his brother's face.

Very short sentences create suspense.

Simple sentence gives impact to the final tragedy.

1. (a) What is a sniper?
   (b) In which "hotspot" in the world is the story set?
   (c) What type of war is being fought?
   (d) Who did the sniper shoot in the first part of the story? Why did he do this?
   (e) Did he kill them? How do you know?

2. What could have affected the sniper's actions while he was on the roof?

3.   *The lust of battle died in him. He became bitten by remorse.*

   What do these words mean to you? Do you have any sympathy for him? Explain.

4. The sniper kills at long range, removed from the horror of his action by the power of his rifle. How do you think this affects his attitude towards killing?

5. How has the author created the tense mood in the story?

6. What words does the author use to describe the sniper? How do these words make you feel towards him?

7. What is the most powerful image for you in this story? What words create this picture?

8.   *Then the sniper turned over the dead body and looked into his brother's face.*

   Try to imagine what the sniper's thoughts and actions would have been following his tragic discovery. Write your thoughts in the form of a final paragraph for the story.

9. What message do you get from this story?

A DIARY FROM SARAJEVO

A young Bosnian girl's diary turns into a journal of war when fighting breaks out in her home city of Sarajevo.

Excerpts from Zlata Filipovic's Diary

12-year-old Zlata Filipovic

May 27, 1992: A slaughter! A massacre! A horror! This is a description of Vaso Miskin Street today. Two shells fell on the street and one fell on the market. And my mummy was so near it. She ran to grandmother's home. Dad and I went mad because she was not coming back. Dad decided to go to the hospital to look for mummy, but a moment later we saw her running over the bridge. She was shaking when she entered the door. 'I saw massacred people,' she said.

June 16, 1992: Our weekend house in Dobrosevici, about 200 years old, was burned (we spent last summer there). All burned. To the foundation stone. Our neighbors Ziga, Meho and Becier were killed. A lot of people were killed.

April 6, 1992: Nothing and nobody is sane here. ... Now they shoot at people from the roof from the Holiday Inn. ... I don't hear any shooting around the house anymore. KNOCK KNOCK. I am knocking on the wood for good luck.

September 15, 1992: A boy from my literary group was killed. A shell fell in front of his building and a horrible fragment of it killed him. His name was Edin and he was a refugee from Grbavica. Oh God, what is happening here?

Zlata Filipovic was twelve years old when she wrote these entries in her diary. Her life has been changed by a war she doesn't understand.

10. As you read the entries in Zlata's diary, write down some of the emotions you think she was feeling. Use words you have chosen as the base for a short poem.

11. *Nothing and nobody is sane here ...*
Compare these words from Zlata's diary with the following extract from *The Sniper*:
He began to gibber to himself, cursing the war, cursing himself, cursing everybody.
Do you think they express a similar idea? Explain your answer.

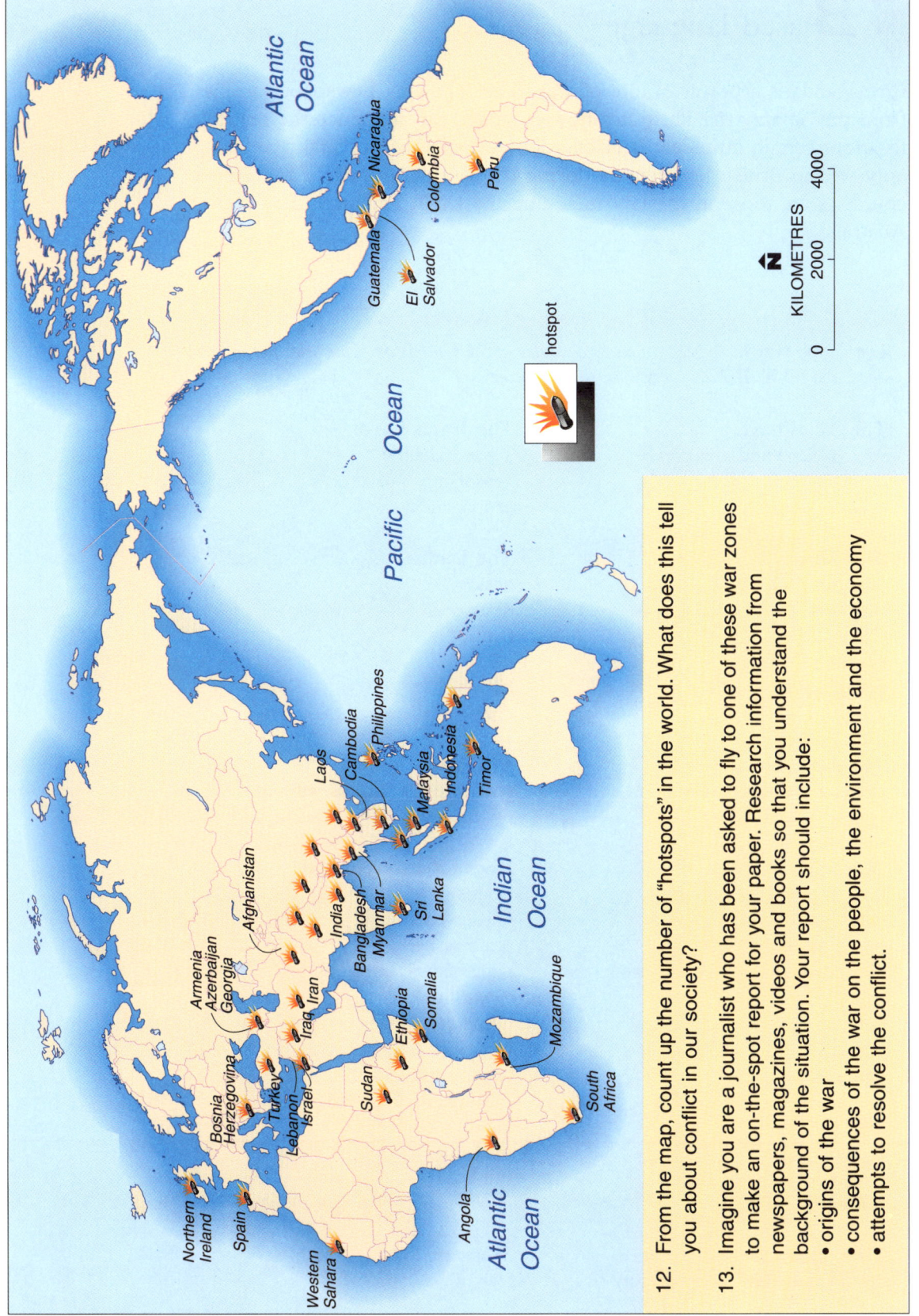

hotspot

KILOMETRES

0   2000   4000

Atlantic Ocean

Pacific Ocean

Pacific Ocean

Indian Ocean

Atlantic Ocean

Nicaragua
Guatemala
El Salvador
Colombia
Peru

Northern Ireland
Spain
Western Sahara
Bosnia Herzegovina
Turkey
Lebanon
Israel
Armenia
Azerbaijan
Georgia
Afghanistan
Iran
Iraq
Sudan
Ethiopia
Somalia
Angola
Mozambique
South Africa
India
Bangladesh
Myanmar
Sri Lanka
Laos
Cambodia
Philippines
Malaysia
Indonesia
Timor

12. From the map, count up the number of "hotspots" in the world. What does this tell you about conflict in our society?

13. Imagine you are a journalist who has been asked to fly to one of these war zones to make an on-the-spot report for your paper. Research information from newspapers, magazines, videos and books so that you understand the background of the situation. Your report should include:
   • origins of the war
   • consequences of the war on the people, the environment and the economy
   • attempts to resolve the conflict.

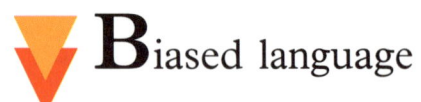

Biased language

Propaganda is a powerful tool of war. The following newspaper article from the *Sunday Age* illustrates how language can influence the reader to adopt certain attitudes. It takes a look at some of the language that appeared in British newspapers during the 1991 Gulf War. (The Allied countries are those in the UN including the USA, Britain and Australia.)

The war of words

Objectivity may have been an early casualty of the Gulf War. This selection of terms appeared in the British press over the past week.

The Allies have:	The Iraqis have:
Army, Navy and Air Force	a war machine
reporting guidelines	censorship
press briefings	propaganda

The Allies:	The Iraqis:
take out	destroy
suppress	destroy
eliminate	kill
neutralise	kill
decapitate	kill
dig in	cower in their foxholes

The Allies launch:	The Iraqis launch:
pre-emptive first strikes	sneak missile attacks without provocation

Allied troops are:	Iraqi forces are:
boys	troops
lads	hordes
professional	brainwashed
lion-hearts	paper tigers
cautious	cowardly
confident	desperate
heroes	cornered
dare-devils	cannon fodder
young knights of the skies	Bastards of Baghdad
loyal	blindly obedient
Desert Rats	mad dogs
resolute	ruthless
brave	fanatical

Motivated by:	Motivated by:
an old fashioned sense of duty	fear of Saddam

Allied pilots:	**Iraqi forces:**
fly into the jaws of hell	cower in concrete bunkers

Allied ships are:	**Iraqi ships are:**
an armada	a navy

Israeli non-retaliation is:	**Iraqi non-retaliation is:**
an act of great statesmanship	blundering/cowardly

Allied missiles are:	**Iraqi missiles are:**
like Luke Skywalker zapping Darth Vader	ageing duds (rhymes with Scuds)

Allied missiles cause:	**Iraqi missiles cause:**
collateral damage	civilian casualties

The Allies:	**The Iraqis:**
precision bomb	fire wildly at anything in the sky

Allied POWs are:	**Iraqi POWs are:**
gallant boys	overgrown schoolchildren

George Bush (US President) is:	**Saddam Hussein (Iraqi President) is:**
at peace with himself	demented
resolute	defiant
statesmanlike	an evil tyrant
assured	a crackpot monster

Allied planes:	**Iraqi planes:**
suffer a high rate of attrition	are shot out of the sky
fail to return from missions	are zapped

(*Sunday Age*, from an original article in the *Guardian*)

14. Read through the list of words. Overall, how are the Iraqis portrayed? How are the Western Allies portrayed?

15. It is important when reading or listening to news reports to be aware of how we can be influenced by the journalist's use of words. What different feelings do you get from the following words?
    (a) "dig in" compared to "cower in their foxholes"
    (b) "cautious" compared to "cowardly"
    (c) "gallant boys" compared to "overgrown schoolchildren"
    (d) "resolute" compared to "defiant"

16. Choose three examples where the actions of the Allies and the Iraqis would have been the same but are presented differently.

17. Why do you think news reporters use biased language?

After a war

The outcome? Conflicting rumours
As to what faction murdered
The one who, had he survived,
Might have ruled us without corruption.
Not that it matters now:
We're busy collecting the dead,
Counting them, hard though it is
To be sure what side they were on.
What's left of their bodies and faces
Tells of no need but for burial,
And mutilation was practised
By Right, Left and Centre alike.
As for the children and women
Who knows what they wanted
Apart from the usual things?
Food is scarce now, and men are scarce,
Whole villages burnt to the ground,
New cities in disrepair.

The war is over. Somebody must have won.
Somebody will have won, when peace is declared.

Michael Hamburger

18. What do you think Michael Hamburger is saying about war?

19. The challenge for the world is to resolve such conflicts without war. What do you think is the answer? Discuss your ideas with a partner. Present your answer to the class.

20. Design a poster and symbol that conveys a message of peace.

Peace is the challenge

Many people believe there is an alternative to violence as a means of resolving conflict. Perhaps the United Nations is the answer.

The three main aims of the United Nations are to:

- maintain international peace
- develop friendly relations amongst nations
- cooperate internationally in solving economic, social and cultural problems and to protect human rights.

A Weight of Thistledown

a short story by H. M. Tolcher

Every year, thousands of people are jailed without trial, beaten, tortured and sometimes even killed by governments trying to crush any opposition to their will. This story is about one man's struggle to survive his world of deprivation.

This was his world: thirty square feet of stained cement floor, four walls of rough-cast concrete, a dull-finished steel door with a closed peephole, a tiny window high in the opposite wall with two heavy steel bars, a steel bed, with a thin pallet, a grey pillow, two darker grey blankets; a covered bucket and a tin dish under a brass tap.

The window opened onto a covered cloister surrounding a cement-paved yard, enclosed by a wall. The cloister roof cut off the sky, so that the view outside merely repeated the composition of the cell. Concrete — steel — silence.

He woke at dawn each day. He tidied his bed, washed, and stood in the middle of the floor to repeat aloud his litany of survival.

'My name is Edward Davis Crawford, and I am fifty-four years old. Today is Wednesday, June 25th, 1969. I have been here for five years and three months. I will be released in fourteen years and nine months.'

It was important to him that he remember these things, otherwise he would sink into the ultimate limbo of forgotten men — forgotten even in his own mind. To strengthen him for the long day that lay ahead, he would solemnly recount his blessings:

'I am in good health. My cell is clean and dry, the air is fresh. I have enough food. My body is sound, and I am in full possession of all my senses. It is possible that some people might even envy me.'

In the silence that followed he would listen to the bump of his heart and the creak of his breathing — the only living sounds he ever heard.

Then he would pull himself up to the window and look out at the cement yard. Sometimes there was a hot glow of sunshine on the baking surface; at others the slick shine of water with an occasional pockmarking of raindrops in the tiny puddles.

After he had done this he would rest on his bed until with a click the peephole would open and an anonymous leather-gloved hand would present him with a stainless steel dish containing his first meal — one compartment filled with thick porridge, the other with black sweetened coffee. He ate the porridge slowly; there were always twenty spoonfuls. There were always twenty sips of coffee.

After a time an unknown finger would press an unseen button and with a subdued internal clunking of disengaging locks the door would swing inwards. Edward Crawford would step out into a long corridor running between other blind steel doors.

He walked the length of the corridor, the brushing of his trouser legs and the slither of his rope-soled shoes making a swishing whisper echo in front and behind him. Another steel door at the far end of the corridor opened into a walled exercise yard.

Sometimes he ran a little, or hopped, or skipped, or walked backwards, but his favorite progression was a smart military march, arms swinging, head high. It made him feel more of a man. He had discovered that if he started at once and walked briskly and purposefully around the circumference of the yard, he could make exactly thirty-seven circuits before a buzzer summoned him back into the cell block.

As soon as the cell door closed on him, he would hear the faint echo of some other door unlocking, from which he deduced that some other prisoner was about to take his exercise. But he never saw prisoners or guards — only a gloved hand bearing food; the only sounds he heard were the locking and unlocking of door or peephole, and those of his own making. He was confined in steel, concrete — and silence.

The prisoner was reconciled to his solitude. It was the penalty for 'non-co-operation'. If he had chosen to answer their questions into the whirling silvery plastic reels with their brown tape, write the things they wanted with the smooth, blue pen on their smooth white paper, the trial might have had a very different ending. Prison, yes — but among other men, with the privilege of communication, perhaps even to work outdoors with the smell, the sounds, the colours of living things. But at that stage he still allowed himself emotions — pride in his country, loyalty to his comrades, self-respect.

He still had his self-respect; he had smothered his emotions. He had chosen silence — he had been condemned into silence. So be it. This too he could overcome. There had been a beginning, and there would be an end.

He was intensely proud of his sanity, his health, his reasonableness. He had been a professional soldier most of his life, and had lived in foul dugouts with death underfoot until the sight and sound and smell of his fellow men was an abomination; had lived alone on mountain tops and in caves for months on end with only his field glasses, his notebook and radio for company. He was convinced that he would emerge from this incarceration sound in mind and body.

It was difficult — he had to admit that. In the beginning the smallest things had the power to torture; to be able to see the sunshine but not the blue sky — the rain but not the boil and tumble of thick cloud from which it fell. The rough wall above his bed bore in one place the imprint of the boards between which the concrete had been poured, and the manifold implications of the swirling wood-grain pattern — the silky texture of fine furniture, the sweet tang of new-cut timber, the sigh of leaves in the wind, the ripple of treetops against a clear sky, bare boughs making black lace against the moon, the infinite gradations of green in a forest seen from the air — brought for a while a sickness almost physical.

After a time he learned to discipline his thoughts so that he saw only the concrete, the furnishings of his cell, the light that fell on the outside compound, and could progress from that to a self-induced trance which disposed of most of his day. Edward Crawford was a very strong man.

During his absence in the exercise yard, the bucket would be replaced with a clean one. Once a week he would find a change of clothes placed on clean blankets on his bed, and a clean towel and a small block of yellow soap. In comparison with prisons he had read about, the inmates here could be said to be very well treated.

Late in the day another meal would be presented. One compartment of chunky pieces of meat and vegetables, the other of cereal pudding with a piece of fruit. Three times a week, a slice of greyish, crustless bread.

Just before dark, his door would open again. He would take his towel and soap, step into the corridor and walk to the other end, where a door opened into a shower block. One minute later the water would run warm for just three minutes, then be cut off. Two minutes later, the buzzer sent him back to his cell.

He was very well off. It was only the concrete, the steel, the silence.

Today there was a high wind blowing; he could hear it whistle outside the wall of the yard. He walked the yard very slowly, and somewhere near the middle he found the thistledown.

It was a perfect ball of silvery-white. It lay on the clean pavement of the yard, quite still. He stared in disbelief; in five years and three months he had not seen a flower, or a leaf, or a blade of grass, or a grain of soil, and here was a piece of thistledown, complete even to the tiny brown seed it had carried into this man-made sterility.

He lifted it in his fingers, hardly daring to breathe lest he crush its delicacy. The light put a sheen on each white thread, on the fragile fur of little filaments that covered each fine spike. He held it in his cupped hands, and his breath stirred it so that it appeared about to escape, to dart away again.

Unbidden, images from the past flew into his mind.

'Father Christmas! Here's a Father Christmas, Daddy!' The brown earth curving away from the plough-share, the thistles crushed and bleeding white into the shining surface of the turned clod. Finches hanging on a blur of wings under a downy purple thistle-head. A young thistle making a prickly green star between the rose bushes. Yellow thistles beside a white gravelled road. A thistle-head exploding at the flick of a finger into a downy cloud like a puff of smoke from an exploding shell over the enemy lines. The light casting into relief the thistles on the cap badge of one of the dead after a Highland regiment had passed by. Thistles spikily silhouetted against the sky in the wasteland along the border, the sweetish smell of crushed thistle stems close under his chin, and the prickle of them through his sleeve. A darkly glistening gun barrel poking through the thistle flowers, and shining black military boots stamping them flat.

He stared at the frail thing with horror. It was weightless on his palm, a thing of light and air, and yet it had brought the world rushing back to crush him.

Concrete and sky swam before his eyes. He clenched his fingers on it, feeling the spikes crush into a tangle of fibre on his palm. He opened his hand and spilled it onto the pavement, ground it under his heel until it was only a pale dust, scattered the dust with his foot. His clenched fists rose seemingly of themselves towards the empty sky, while the tears trickled in two hot streams down his upturned face, and a cry of agony echoed and re-echoed around the walls. He bellowed and howled, salt on his writhing lips, trying to drown the echoes of that world be had schooled himself to forget. The discipline of one thousand nine hundred and fifteen days was undone; he knew he could never regain it.

He did not see or hear the guards when they came to get him; he obeyed the pressure of their hands blindly, deaf to all but the raging torrent of returning memory.

A hand reached for a pen, ink gleamed wetly on a yellow card.

'Send the recorder to Crawford's cell. I think he's ready to talk now.'

The swivel chair squeaked, swung to face the window, with its view across the shining river between its swaying willow trees, where kingfishers darted from diamond-bright riffle of miniature rapids to eddying brown pool, and the creaking country carts went slowly by the hayfields towards the distant town.

'He was a tough one, that Crawford. The tough ones always do crack wide open when they do go. I wonder what finally broke him down?'

24. (a) What is the setting of the story?
    (b) What was the prisoner's occupation before he was jailed?

25. Why do you think it was an important daily routine for the prisoner to repeat his name and age, the date and how long he had been in prison?

26. Do you think the prisoner was treated humanely? Explain your answer.

27. Why was Crawford sentenced to solitary confinement instead of an ordinary prison?

28. (a) How long was Crawford's sentence?
    (b) Do you think it was fair to imprison him for so long when it appears that his only "crime" was withholding information? Explain your answer.

29. The thistledown was small and fragile, but its effect on Edward Crawford was powerful. It triggered a memory of his freedom and brought back images of the life he had disciplined himself to forget. Do you think he would have remained strong without this reminder of his past? Explain your answer.

30. In this story the thistledown is a symbol. Think of something which symbolises a powerful memory in your life. It could be a song, a smell ... Use your symbol as a title for a short poem which describes your feeling of these memories. Present your poem attractively. Perhaps you could use calligraphy and illustrate it, or use a computer to present your work. Keep this work in your writing folio.

The United Nations proclaimed the *Universal Declaration of Human Rights* in 1948. Four of these articles are given below.

Article 1
All human beings are born free and equal in dignity and rights. They are endowed with reason and conscience and should act towards one another in a spirit of brotherhood.

Article 3
Everyone has the right to life, liberty and the security of person.

Article 5
No one shall be subjected to torture or to cruel, inhuman or degrading treatment or punishment.

Article 9
No one shall be subjected to arbitrary arrest, detention or exile.

31. Do you think any of these rights or freedoms were abused in this story? Explain your answer.

If we don't do something, then we are participants in a vast human crime.

Bob Geldof

This candle is the symbol for **Amnesty International**, one of the world's largest human rights organisations. It works for the release of prisoners of conscience and for fair trials for political prisoners.

Many of the governments involved in human rights abuses like to believe they are acting in secret and that the world does not know or care about what is happening under their regime. This illusion can be broken simply by letting them know that *you* know what they are doing. The main way of doing this is by letter. Amnesty International believes: "The letter is remarkable for its power and simplicity. Sometimes a single letter may be enough to improve a prisoner's situation."

Your class may wish to investigate the possibility of joining Amnesty International. However, you may also write letters on your own behalf.

Below is a table showing the sorts of abuses that occur in some countries.

Human right	Abuses in some countries
Freedom to:	
1. Travel in own country	Women forbidden to drive cars and to travel alone.
2. Travel outside own country	Exit visas required and difficult to obtain. Women over 40 years and men over 45 given preference.
Freedom from:	
3. Serfdom, slavery, forced or child labour	Traditional customs permit child labour. Domestic servants have few legal rights.
4. Extrajudicial killings or "disappearances"	The many deaths in prison from torture and starvation, and killings by police when controlling crowds, indicate little regard for life.
5. Torture or coercion by the state	Widespread torture by the warring sides of a bitterly divided country. Beatings, burnings, electric shocks, food deprivation etc.
6. Capital punishment by the state	Beheading. Sometimes in public. Stoning for sexual crimes.
7. Court sentences of corporal punishment	Floggings common. Guidelines state: "The stripes should be spread over the whole body."
8. Indefinite detention without charge	Many prisoners kept in leg irons. Many deaths from starvation. Others held without charge and unlikely to be brought to trial.
9. Political censorship of press	Total censorship.
10. Censorship of mail or telephone tapping	Wide interception of correspondence. All forms of communication under surveillance.

(continued)

Human right	Abuses in some countries
Freedom to have:	
11. A peaceful political opposition	Not permitted.
12. Political and legal equality for women	Tradition and religion prevent equality in politics and professions.
13. Social and economic equality for women	Women at disadvantage in most areas. The word of two women equals that of one man. May not drive vehicles; must enter public transport by special entrances, etc.
14. Social and economic equality for ethnic minorities	Ethnic and religious conflict caused by civil war.
15. Independent book publishing	All publishing houses state controlled. Also imports of foreign books carefully checked.
Legal rights:	
16. To be considered innocent until proved guilty	Many people imprisoned without trial.
Personal rights:	
17. Inter-racial, inter-religious or civil marriage	Forbidden to marry foreigners.
18. Equality of sexes during marriage and for divorce proceedings	Husband may divorce "at will". Women are subordinate, including their inheritance rights.
19. To practise any religion	Minor religious groups discriminated against.
20. To use contraceptive pills and devices	Little public support. Availability limited.

32. Which five freedoms or rights do you think are the most important? Explain your choice.

33. Which abuse do you find the most frightening? Why?

34. Why do you think governments deprive their citizens of certain freedoms and rights?

35. Do you think Australia is free of any human rights abuse? Explain your answer.

36. Write a letter to Amnesty International requesting information on human rights abuses throughout the world.

Controlling our future

Advances in scientific knowledge may involve difficult moral decisions for scientists. This short story explores some of the hazards of making decisions that will affect future generations.

The Chimera

a short story by Roger Vaughan Carr

Debbie and her parents are faced with a whole new world: is she their daughter or is she a child of the future?

'Brassy ... !' she sobbed. 'Brassy!'

'Hey! Come on. Brassy's not so bad.'

'It's *horrible*! Look at my skin, it *is* brassy!'

'It's just ... yellowish. When you've been in the sun. It's beautiful skin. It's unblemished.'

'Oh, you're so stupid! I wish it *was* blemished. *Feel it*!' She thrust out her arm towards him.

He swallowed his sudden rush of anger. 'I know what your skin feels like,' he said gently, but he reached out a hand anyway and felt it. So smooth, so perfect, so ... so ... 'It's really beautiful.'

'For a car,' she said bitterly, jerking her arm back. 'I've just been to the pool — for the first time in my *life*! The other kids said I was reflective!'

'You never sunburn,' he said, avoiding a direct response. 'Wow! You don't know how good that is. I go red and crisp. You've seen me.'

'I'd like to sunburn,' she said. 'I'd like to *cry* with sunburn — I'd give anything to be as normal as that!'

'Who needs a pool, anyway? Look at the great time we have down along the Ninety Mile.'

'Oh, yes,' she said bitterly. 'On an ocean beach where there isn't anyone else at all. I want to be with the other kids!' Her eyes flashed suddenly. 'I think even you're ashamed of me!'

'No! Don't you ever say that. Never!'

'Then if you aren't ashamed of me, you're embarrassed by me. That's why Mum always buys me clothes that cover just about everything except my face.'

'You get cold,' he protested. 'You need lots of clothing.'

'To hide my skin!'

'To keep you warm.' He put his arms round her and hugged her, held her there a moment when she struggled, then let her free, reluctantly, because it was not helping. Not taking the hurt away.

'I am adopted aren't I,' she stated more than questioned. 'I'm not even an Australian, am I?'

He sighed and turned away, smacking his right fist into the open palm of his other hand.

'You're not adopted.'

'Mum doesn't go brassy! You don't!'

'You're our daughter. Our natural daughter.'

'I'm an IVF!' she flared as if she had caught him in a lie. 'I was a *test-tube* baby!'

'Yeah. Yeah. Okay. But we've never hidden that, have we?' He wished they had now. Being open from the start had seemed right at the time, but now they both regretted it. 'IVF but special. You don't know how special.'

'Different,' she sneered.

'Everybody is ...'

'Not *this* different,' she completed for him. 'I want you to take me to a doctor.'

'You're not ill.'

'I'm *different*! I was always at doctors when I was younger. We just about *lived* in Uncle Simon's surgery; his and a whole heap of others! And I wasn't even sick then, mostly.'

'You don't need a doctor. Mum and I will know when you need a doctor.'

'Thanks,' she said bitterly. 'Will you know when I need a psychiatrist?'

'Cut that out,' he said sharply. 'People don't go to shrinks because they get a nickname they don't like.'

'But I *am* brassy ... !' she cried, and ran.

'Ah, *hell*!' He smacked his fist into his palm again, watching through the window as she ran down the path. She was so pretty. She had been sort of gawky when she was a little kid, but now she was a teenager all that had gone.

He remembered acne suddenly and ran his fingertips over the side of his face. There were still pits. It had been like hell when he was about fifteen — he could remember telling his parents he would rather have cancer, and Debbie would do anything to *have* acne.

He swore. Maybe it had not been such a smart idea to move out here to a small town. Somehow they had thought a local high school where she knew everybody would make it easier.

But it had made her more of an oddity, a one-off. At least in the city there had been Japanese, Chinese, Africans, Vietnamese, maybe even some Red Indians for all he knew. Maybe she would have been better off where she was just different, not unique.

He pressed a recall button. 'It's Pete Walker,' he said. 'Is Dr Graham free?'

He listened, watching down past the mulberry tree to the stables as Debbie led her horse back from the paddock, starting a little in surprise as the voice returned. 'Yeah, I'll hold for him, thanks.'

Debbie looped the reins round the hitching-rail and disappeared through the doorway of the tack room. The horse stood, its back skewed sideways, as it eased its weight off a hind leg to rest it.

Maybe they should have stayed in the city for Debbie, but for him this was just right. There was plenty of time to dabble with his mathematics between cooking and washing dishes, and Jenny was like a kid in the veterinary practice she had bought into. City cats and goldfish had just been a frustration to her, and she'd carried a guilt complex for using her years of study on medicating only pets.

'Pete ...?'

'Simon! How's the technopolis?'

'Listen,' Simon Graham snarled. 'I don't need hints about meadow breezes or non-plastic flowers or I might chuck myself out of a high window.'

'I didn't think you could open them in the big smoke?'

'Okay, *through* a high window. Did you ring to gloat?'

Debbie came from the tack room with a saddle-blanket, and her father sighed.

'Listen,' he said into the phone. 'They call her "Brassy" now, but not as in "bold as".'

'Yeah. I'm not stupid. I told you and Jenny where there were Asians ...'

'Okay. So maybe we'll have to come back before ... before the time. It's not going to do Jenny any good, leaving all this. But, maybe we just have to.'

Debbie was putting on the saddle now, cinching up the girth. Competent. Like her mother.

'You know,' the voice repeated through the phone, 'right now you're all thinking that maybe you've made a big mistake.'

'Well, maybe every one of us is right.'

'Nope. Listen, some of them think it's time to start talking enclave ...'

'*No!* We're going to get at least a few more years as a family. You'll need a government decree and force ...'

'Okay! Okay. Don't steam. But maybe it's time to tell her? Puberty seems to be accelerating the effect, and she's very mature for her age.'

Pete sighed and dug a fingernail into the soft wood of the old kitchen bench, watching Debbie through the window as she mounted Hayburn, the big roan gelding. She was a princess there in the saddle, sitting lightly as Hayburn did his usual spins and head tosses.

Then Debbie bent and looked down past the mulberry towards the kitchen, and he lifted a hand in acknowledgement.

She wanted him to know she wasn't angry with him. Just with the rest of the world. She lifted a hand in response and spun the big gelding away down the drive.

'It's ... sort of like losing her,' he continued into the phone, 'but, yeah. I guess it is time to talk.'

'Right. I'll be down. Friday night through ...?'

'Thanks.'

'Ciao.'

Along the open ground by the fenceline on the Three Chain Road, Hayburn rolled out a gallop which would not have shamed him when he was racing.

Debbie lay out along his neck with the reins so short her hands were catching the wetness of his breath. She closed her eyes and just let the feeling of speed and power become a part of her body, not caring if the horse needed guidance to avoid some mistake; perhaps, she acknowledged, even hoping for one ... running too close to a tree, to a low branch ...

He galloped for half a kilometre or so before the urgent hooting of a car horn made her open her eyes and glance sideways, then sit back as a signal to him to slow as she confirmed that it was the Range Rover.

'Thanks,' she whispered, patting his neck as she pulled him back to a walk. She turned him through the undergrowth between the trees to where the Range Rover had jolted to a halt against a low bank.

'It's all right!' she called, but that didn't stop her mother running towards her.

'Don't you ever! Not ever again!'

'I'm all right,' she said, a little ashamed, a little sorry, as the two hands gripped her thigh, the fingers biting in.

'Don't you *ever*!'

'I wasn't really trying to hurt myself,' she whispered.

Hayburn tossed his head and snorted, stretching his neck against the reins.

'I'll drive you back.'

'No. I promise I won't even get out of a trot. I promise.' She was crying now. They both were.

'Come home Deb, and we'll talk.'

'What can we talk about?' she demanded. 'I've just come from talking to Dad. He just says ... all the same old things.'

'Then it's time we talked more.'

'About why my skin goes brassy?' she asked bitterly. 'Like metal?'

'It might be that time,' her mother said softly. 'Come home.'

'Time ...?' she whispered, almost fearful.

'Come home. You can let him canter — gallop. But where it's safe.'

Debbie nodded, a sudden excitement, a sudden feeling of dread mixing inside her. There *was* something.

She turned Hayburn away as her mother went back towards the road.

Time? Time for what? To learn she had some hideous skin disease? Something that would snatch her life away? She shook her head impatiently. No. It couldn't be that. They would not have brought her out here to the country if it were that. They'd have been taking her from doctor to doctor, around the world if they had to, until they found a cure. Or until the disease won.

No. Somehow she knew it wasn't that. Not that kind of disease, anyway. Not one that was killing her. And not one that was infectious, or she wouldn't be allowed at school.

Something that went wrong when they did the IVF?

Debbie's Uncle Simon arrives from the city. He shows her a photo album of children who all have the same "brassy" skin as Debbie. As the family sit around the fireplace, Simon begins to explain.

'I guess I'm talking pre-history here to you, Deb,' the doctor said, 'but about twenty years ago the first Ameri-Euro lander to return successfully to Earth from Venus brought enough samples for all the disciplines to have a nibble. The biologists found living bacteria; maybe the dawn of life on the planet, or maybe the last vestige of a life that hadn't been able to adapt to a loss of atmosphere and a rising heat.'

'It was pretty exciting stuff,' Pete said softly. 'Even for students.'

'Remember the religious despair?' Jenny said. 'The contortions they went through to explain it?'

Simon shuddered. 'But it gave biotechnology the tools to shape the future.' He picked up the poker and stabbed around in the fire.

'You're ruining a perfectly good blaze there, pal,' Pete said.

'I'm a guest,' Simon told him. 'And an outdoor man at heart.' He half turned. 'How would you like to go to Venus, Deb?'

She shrugged, still turning back and forth amongst the pages, beginning to identify the kids in different shots. All of them — *us* her mind said — with the same suggestion of brassy metallic skin.

'I've never thought,' she answered.

'Someone has to go, but the heat ...' He leapt to his feet. 'Hell! I forgot the chestnuts!'

He thundered out to the kitchen. Jenny and Pete exchanged a quick grin, then sobered suddenly as they saw Deb crying silently, her tears falling onto the photographs.

'Kiddo ...'

'Lovey!' Jenny leaned and hugged her.

'I'm not your daughter, am I? You've been lying.'

'No!' her father snapped. 'You're *our* daughter!'

'I'm one of these!' she shouted at him, stabbing at the album with a finger. 'I'm an alien!'

'*No!*' Pete roared.

'Lovey, you're our natural daughter with ...'

'Ashpan?' Simon demanded, a bag of nuts clutched in one hand, choosing to ignore what was happening. 'Come on, Debs. You're the one who takes heat best.'

He thrust the bag at her, and clanged the ashpan out from amongst the tongs and poker. 'Spill 'em.'

Debbie sucked air in through her nose to try and stop the tears. She poured a dozen of the chestnuts onto the ashpan and took the handle, moving closer to the fire.

She did take heat best: the flames were just warmth to her. Where other people had to move back, uncomfortable, she was pleasantly warm. It had worried her parents when she was younger, worried them that she might burn herself with matches or hot water without knowing it. Fire or water that was too hot for other people, hot enough to scald or blister them ...

'It's okay, but primitive, running the technology from Earth. And it's really not much more than mining and atmosphere regeneration that we can do without somebody actually *there*,' Simon said. 'And the whole point is population, anyway.'

'What ...?' she asked.

'People living on Venus. A new world for humans. We're running out of space here.'

The chestnuts rattled on the ashpan. She was shaking.

' "One day someone has to go" was the consensus about the time we three were graduating. "One day somebody has to go and we have to be ready with the people".'

A chestnut rattled over the edge and into the coals, and her hand darted forward and picked it out and put it back.

Simon whistled. 'That would have been third-degree burns for me. Let's see your fingers.'

She showed him. There was an ash stain, but it was on the skin, not in it.

'It was a hell of a decision for parents to make,' Pete said, slipping off his chair and sitting with her on the hearth rug, one hand going round her waist. 'A decision that could only be made in the ignorance of youth.'

'That's what broke up my marriage,' Simon almost whispered. 'Cassie said no. I thought we all had an obligation and I was angry ... then. I'm selfishly glad now.'

There was a sudden explosion.

'Forgot to prick 'em!' Simon exclaimed, as another chestnut spread itself across the hearth.

Debbie jerked the ashpan and tipped them onto the bricks.

'Ouch!' Jenny exclaimed, dropping the one she had reached for.

Debbie picked it up and broke the shell off for her, then one each for her father and Simon.

'And you?' Pete said.

She shook her head.

'Tell me,' she whispered.

Simon jiggled the hot nut round inside his mouth. 'They isolated the DNA coding for the bacterium's ability to withstand heat.' He bit and chewed, and smiled blissfully. 'Wonderful! Husk me another, Deb. They injected the fertilised egg that was you with the DNA from the Venusian bacterium, then ... gave you back to your mother to finish off.' He pulled out a pocket-knife and opened a spike and stabbed at the uncooked chestnuts.

'What do I have to do now?' Debbie repeated tonelessly, holding the fresh panful of chestnuts over the fire.

'In about ten years,' Simon said softly, 'you're scheduled to go to Venus.'

They said other things then, but she didn't hear.

Her mind followed her line of sight into the fire, into the glowing coals, into that jewel-like luminosity where there was something so beautiful, some feeling so warm, yet so distant, stirring deep within the recesses of some ... some genetic memory?

Of home?

'Hey!' her father snapped shakily. 'Cut it out, Deb. You're spooking me!'

She turned her face to look at him, blank.

'You don't *have* to go!' her mother whispered.

A warm peace permeated her body, her mind.

'I *want* to go home,' she said.

37. What is biotechnology?

38. Why do you think Debbie rode her horse so recklessly?

39. A journalist has heard about Debbie and arranged an interview with her father. From your knowledge of the story, how do you think he would answer the following questions?

(a) **Interviewer:** What happened during the IVF procedure?

Father: _____

(b) **Interviewer:** Did Debbie have a normal childhood?

Father: _____

(c) **Interviewer:** What sort of traumas has your daughter experienced?

Father: _____

(d) **Interviewer:** How does she feel now?

Father: _____

(e) **Interviewer:** Your wife mentioned religious despair — what did she mean by this?

Father: _____

(f) **Interviewer:** You were very young at the time — do you think you would be a part of such an experiment again?

Father: _____

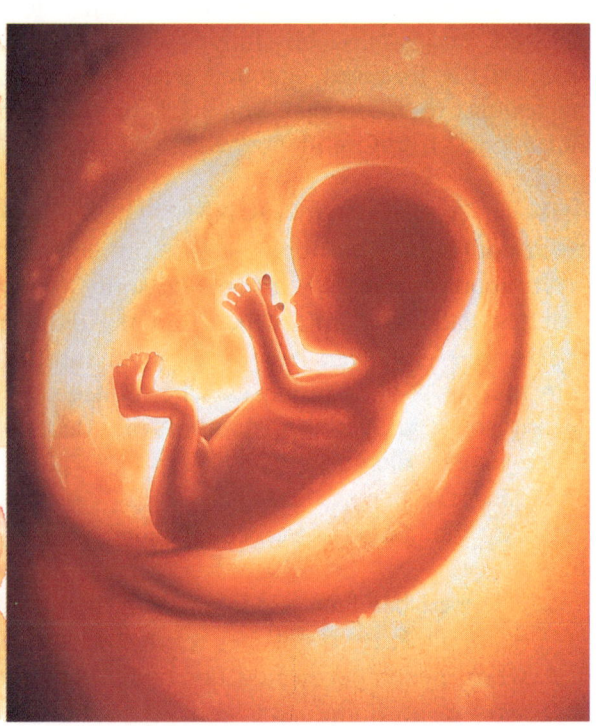

40. Below are the dictionary meanings of the word *chimera*. Which one do you think applies to the title of this story? Explain.

phonetic pronunciation

part of speech (noun)

headword

chimera /kɪ'mɪərə, kə-/, *n.*, *pl.* **-ras. 1.** (*oft. cap.*) a mythological fire-breathing monster, commonly represented with a lion's head, a goat's body, and a serpent's tail. **2.** a grotesque monster, as in decorative art. **3.** a horrible or unreal creature of the imagination; a vain or idle fancy. **4.** *Genetics.* an organism composed of two or more genetically distinct tissues, as **a.** an organism which is partly male and partly female. **b.** an artificially produced creature having tissues of several species. Also, **chimaera.** [L *chimaera*, from Gk *chímaira* lit., she-goat; replacing ME *chimere*, from F]

definitions numbered/lettered — most common meaning first

origins of word

41. Your dictionary will contain a guide to pronunciation. Look at the pronunciation guide below. Then write your full name, using the appropriate symbols, so that your name can be pronounced correctly by anyone who reads it.

Pronunciation guide

i = peat   ɪ = pit   ɛ = pet   æ = pat   a = part   ɒ = pot   ʌ = putt
ɔ = port   ʊ = put   u = pool   ɜ = pert   ə = apart   aɪ = buy
eɪ = bay   ɔɪ = boy   aʊ = how   oʊ = hoe   ɪə = here   ɛə = hair
ʊə = tour   g = give   θ = thin   ð = then   ʃ = show   ʒ = measure
tʃ = choke   dʒ = joke   ŋ = sing   j = you   ṽ = Fr. bon

42. Look up the word *metropolis* in your dictionary and write down the following information in your workbook:
    (a) headword
    (b) pronunciation
    (c) part of speech
    (d) definition
    (e) origin.

43. The author has used the word *technopolis* in the story. Although this word is not in the dictionary, we can tell from the meaning of the Greek words *technikos* (a skill) and *polis* (a city) that *technopolis* could be "a city where skilled people live".

Working in pairs, find three more words that have been derived from the Greek words *technikos* or *polis*.

44. Use the table of Latin and Greek roots below to make up five new words of your own. For example, *cadastron* could mean "falling star".

Latin roots	Meanings
ago, actus	act, do
cado, casus	fall
capio, captus	take captive
cedo, cessus	go, yield
cito, citatus	rouse
colo, cultus	till (the soil)
curro, cursus	run
decem	ten
dico, dictus	say
duco, ductus	lead
facio, factus	make
fortis	strong
jacio, jactus	throw
lego, lectus	choose
magnus	great
memor	mindful
minor	small
multis	many
rego, rectus	rule
rumpo, ruptus	break
sentio, sensus	feel
tendo	stretch
teneo	hold
traho, tractus	draw
verto, versus	turn
video, visus	see

Greek roots	Meanings
astron	a star
baros	weight
bios	life
demos	people, common people
graphos	something drawn or written
metron	a measure
phono	sound
therme	heat
zoion	animal

Presenting an issue

An issue usually involves controversy, as people take opposing views. When presenting an issue in an argumentative essay, you should consider all sides of the argument before forming your own opinion.

FACT OR OPINION?

When presenting an issue, it is important to know the difference between a fact and an opinion.

A fact is something that:
- actually happened
- most people would agree with
- often involves numbers or measurements.

An opinion is:
- a personal judgement or view
- something people may disagree with
- based on someone's beliefs, feelings or guesses.

FACT   OPINION

The story *The Chimera* challenges us to think about several issues:
- medical ethics
- IVF ("test tube" babies)
- DNA experimentation
- population control.

If you feel strongly about one of these issues you may try to persuade people to adopt your point of view. The art of persuasion involves adding your opinion to the facts.

45. (a) Choose one of the issues listed above. Then think about a particular aspect of that topic which interests you. For example, if you chose "medical ethics", you might decide to focus on euthanasia.
    (b) Research your topic. Gather as much information as you can from a range of sources.

Your next task will be to write an argumentative essay on your topic. The following steps will help you.

Step 1: Notemaking

(a) When taking information from a book always make note of the author, title, date of publication, publisher and place of publication. You will need this information if you are doing a bibliography and it will be helpful if you need to refer to the book again later.
(b) Look at the photographs and captions.
(c) Look at the headings and subheadings.
(d) Skim read each paragraph.
(e) Now read more thoroughly, making note of **key words** and **main ideas**. Write in point form, using abbreviations.

Step 2: Forming an opinion

To help you form an opinion about your topic, brainstorm with other students who have chosen the same topic as you. Discuss the issue with anyone who is willing to listen. Jot down any ideas or opinions that are put forward.

Graphic organisers will help you to organise your notes, so that you can form an opinion. For example, research into medical ethics might lead you to explore the question of euthanasia. The graphic organiser below shows how one student organised his notes to help him form an opinion.

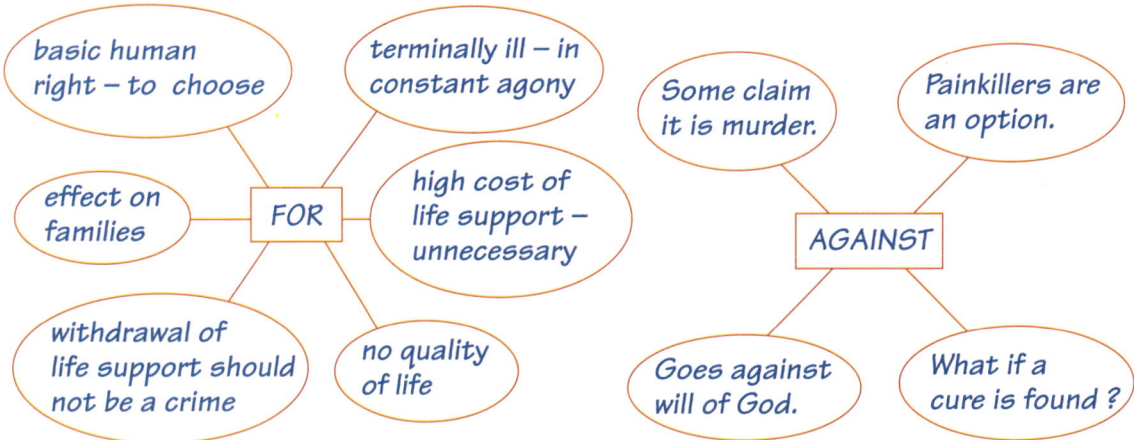

The student decided to argue that *euthanasia should be legalised*.

Step 3: Planning

The student's essay plan was something like this.

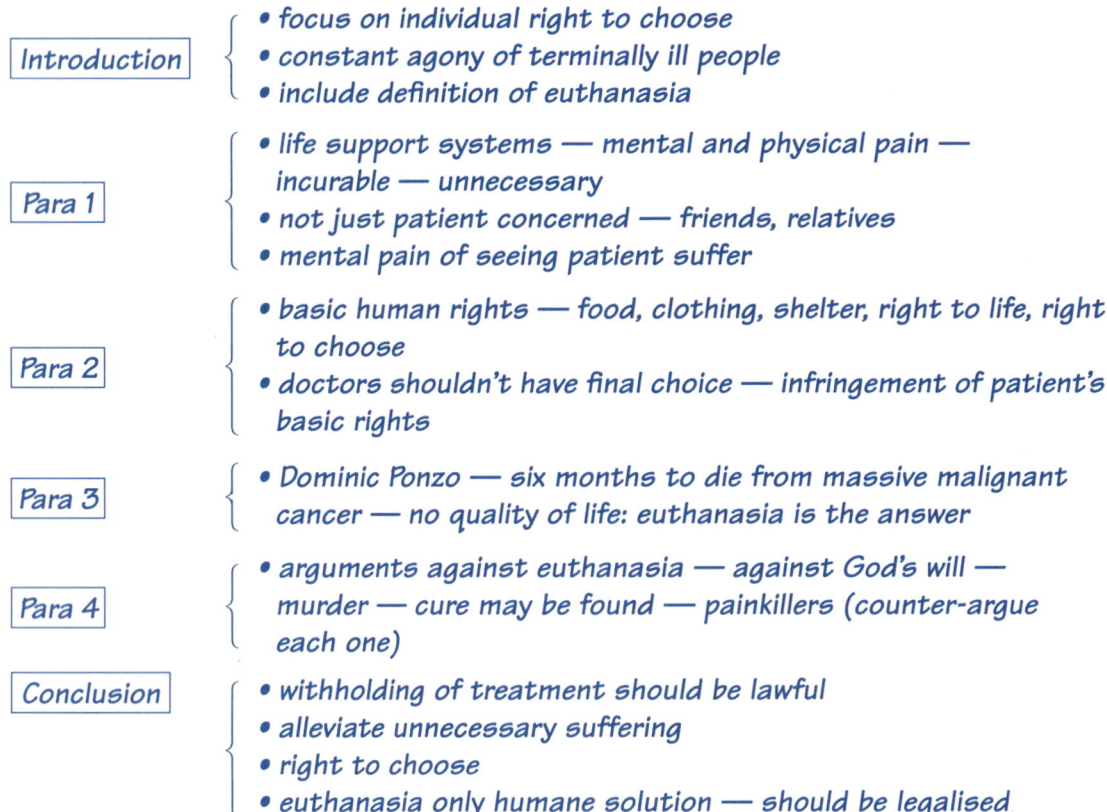

Step 4: Drafting

The student then wrote a first draft, making sure that there were wide margins and double spacing to allow for corrections.

Next, he checked the spelling and punctuation, and tried to make the language suit the audience and the purpose. Then, after discussion with his teacher, he wrote his argumentative essay.

The essay he wrote relies more heavily on opinion than on fact — the student obviously feels strongly about his topic, but does not always have facts to support his arguments. You may prefer to collect more facts and present a more balanced argument in your own essay.

The essay — the final product

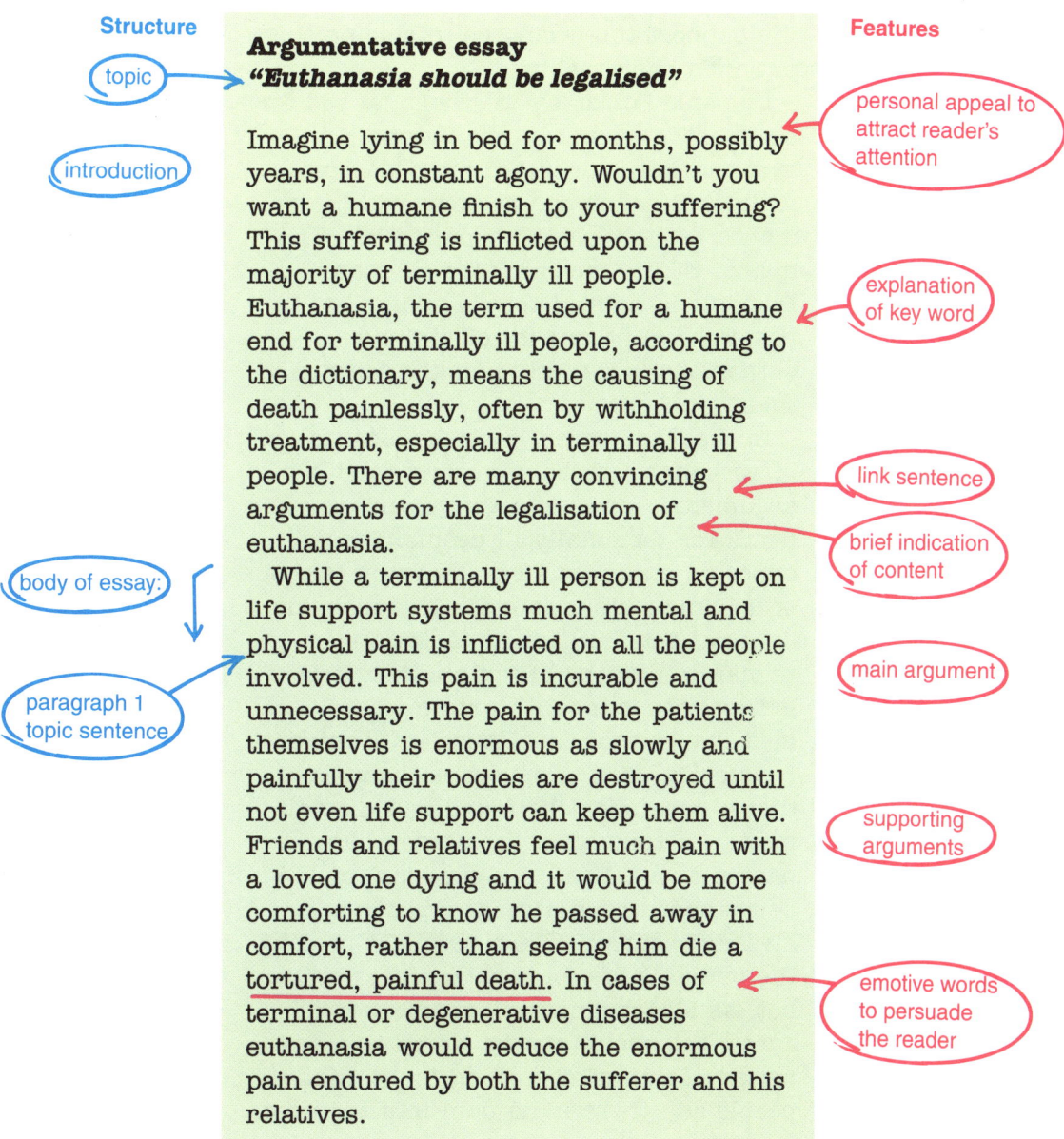

Structure

topic

introduction

body of essay:

paragraph 1
topic sentence

Argumentative essay
"Euthanasia should be legalised"

Imagine lying in bed for months, possibly years, in constant agony. Wouldn't you want a humane finish to your suffering? This suffering is inflicted upon the majority of terminally ill people. Euthanasia, the term used for a humane end for terminally ill people, according to the dictionary, means the causing of death painlessly, often by withholding treatment, especially in terminally ill people. There are many convincing arguments for the legalisation of euthanasia.

While a terminally ill person is kept on life support systems much mental and physical pain is inflicted on all the people involved. This pain is incurable and unnecessary. The pain for the patients themselves is enormous as slowly and painfully their bodies are destroyed until not even life support can keep them alive. Friends and relatives feel much pain with a loved one dying and it would be more comforting to know he passed away in comfort, rather than seeing him die a tortured, painful death. In cases of terminal or degenerative diseases euthanasia would reduce the enormous pain endured by both the sufferer and his relatives.

Features

personal appeal to attract reader's attention

explanation of key word

link sentence

brief indication of content

main argument

supporting arguments

emotive words to persuade the reader

paragraph 2
topic sentence

As humans we have basic rights, such as the right to basic food, clothing and shelter, the right to live and the right to choose what is best for ourselves. We are making choices every day. If we get a cold we choose whether we see a doctor or not. If we do see a doctor we choose whether to follow the doctor's advice or not. This should be the same when choosing whether we wish life support or not, a choice which is presently the doctors'. If a person wishes not to have their life supported artificially and the doctor connects them to life support this would be infringing the patient's basic rights.

explanation
of supporting
arguments

paragraph 3

Domenic Ponzo lay in a hospital bed for six months as slowly one by one his systems were consumed by a massive malignant cancerous growth. Within one month he had lost all hope for life. The quality of life for sufferers such as Domenic is non-existent. Terminally ill people have no quality of life and euthanasia is the only humane solution to their problem.

real-life example
to add strength
to the argument

paragraph 4
topic sentence

In the controversy over the legalisation of euthanasia there are many fallible arguments opposing a gentle and easy death for terminally ill people. People opposing euthanasia say that any taking of a human life is murder, a punishable, criminal act. Euthanasia is not one human taking the life of another, it is letting nature take its course where medicine cannot cure. Another argument frequently used to oppose euthanasia is that a cure might be found just a small matter of time after the person has passed away. Even if a cure is found, permanent tissue damage will have already occurred. The cure might prolong the person's life for maybe a year or two but, as all terminally ill people would agree, this would not be worth the long period of suffering waiting for it. Many people say there is no pain inflicted upon

statement of
other points of
view, with
counter-arguments

the sufferers as painkillers can be used. But the fact of the matter is that the bodies of these people are often too weak to stand drugs. The people who argue about painkillers obviously don't realise the heartbreak of seeing a loved one lying helpless and in agony; no drugs can suppress this pain. Though there are many arguments opposing euthanasia they all contain many flaws and fallacies.

appeal to reader's emotions

conclusion

The causing of death painlessly by withholding treatment should be made lawful as it would save many people enormous amounts of suffering, allow people to fully exercise their rights and save terminally ill people from having to endure a subhuman life. There are many arguments against euthanasia but all of these are based on misconceptions of the real situations. The supporting evidence and lack of rational opposition can only lead to one conclusion: that euthanasia is the only humane solution to the incurable problems of the terminally ill and should therefore be legalised.

personal opinion

summary of arguments

opinion restated

student's name

Noel Straker (15 years)

---

46. Write your own argumentative essay of about 500 words based on the research you have done. Your purpose is to *persuade* your audience to *believe your argument*.

Remember the steps

1. Notemaking

2. Forming opinion

3. Planning

4. Writing the draft

5. The essay

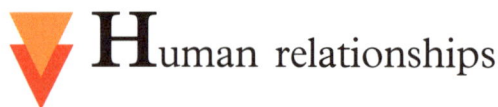

Human relationships

Human relationships face many challenges, particularly when threatened with impending tragedy.

a short story by Sophie Masson

This short story is about relationships within a family, and the way the various members of it deal with something no-one wants to talk about.

Far away down the beach, a few specks seemed to be moving. Closer and closer they came, until they became distinct figures. Two young men and two young women, all four on horseback. They reined in their horses on the edge of the sea and stood very still against the dying light and the first whisper of night.

'Damn it!' Freya said aloud, chewing her pen and staring angrily at the sea. 'That just doesn't sound right! I'll never get it right!' She scrubbed furiously at what she had written, and closed her exercise book. The afternoon was fading gently, the waves touched with the first grey cool of evening. Freya got up and began trudging home, her feet squeaking in the sand.

Around her, other people were also leaving the beach. Freya walked slowly, thinking of her novel, her dress ballooning around her in the strengthening sea wind. She smoothed it down at each step; she loved the feel of the material, the glossy depth of its blue. Dad *had* remembered then. Remembered that when she was a child, she'd loved that old fairytale where the princess asked for three dresses — one made of the sky, one of the moon, one of the sun. The blue dress had come in a parcel, from Iceland, with a note attached: 'The first dress — for my princess'. Freya's face had burned when she read the note — how dare he call her that after what he'd done! But she hadn't been able to resist the blue dress, not even when she'd seen Mum's sad smile, or heard Daniel's gentle comment, 'Well, that's nice of him, isn't it, love?' Unconsciously, Freya quickened her steps. The sand was cool underfoot. She could feel the grains rubbing into her skin, and she looked back at the sea, wanting to hold that familiar sweeping sight of it, just for a moment longer, before the walk along the promenade and then up the steep hill towards the house where she lived with her mother and Daniel and Thor.

As always, the sea roared unceasingly, but today Freya felt a pang at its uncaringness. It was magnificent, the sea, it could give her a kind of peace, but even here, at her spot, it didn't exist just for her. She remembered asking Thor, years ago, 'Does the sea keep going, even when we're not here to look at it?' and he'd laughed. 'Of course, you nincompoop! Why on earth wouldn't it?'

Thor was in tonight. She could see his motorbike parked outside the house. Most evenings, he was out either playing, or rehearsing, or plain fooling about with his band, *Thor's Hammer*. Freya thought it was a stupid name, but her brother had said, 'If we're saddled with names like ours, we may as well use them!'

Sometimes, Freya thought of changing her name. Years ago, when Mum had first met Daniel, Freya had even wondered about Danielle. But she'd been too shy to broach the subject. She didn't want Daniel to think she was crawling. And he'd said often enough in his quiet voice, 'Freya-Thor. Aren't you two lucky, having such names?'

Thinking of Daniel, now, made Freya's footsteps heavier. She knew why Thor was here tonight, too, just as she knew the reason she'd left the beach early. *It's not fair, it's just not fair.* She tugged at her dress. There was Dad, on the other side of the world, in Iceland, doing exactly what he'd always wanted to do, happy, healthy, sure of himself. While Daniel, gentle, loving Daniel . . . A lump formed in her throat. She blinked back tears.

~

She could hear their voices in the kitchen, talking, laughing, as they drank their coffee. She wondered how they could . . . but caught hold of herself and called out, 'Hey, I'm back! Are we going out, like you said?'

Daniel turned to her first. His smile was real, his thin face glowing with it.

'Freya! You're back early! How's your novel going?' Daniel was the only one who ever asked about her writing. Mum was uncertain about it, Thor bemused.

'OK,' Freya mumbled. 'I get a bit stuck, sometimes.' Dear God — was it her imagination, or did Daniel look thinner this afternoon? Freya took her eyes off him, quickly.

'Hungry again?' Freya knew Mum was relieved when she went to the fridge. Her mother dreaded the thought that someone would come out with it, would mention the terrifying word, and then she'd have to cope, she'd have to face the truth. Freya grabbed a piece of cheese and stood there, eating without tasting.

'We're going out,' Thor said. 'Treat. We're going for a meal at the *Retreat*, then you're coming to hear the band!' He grinned, and flipped back his long blond hair. He was really living up to his name, Freya thought, sourly. Big and blond and unaware. Like their father.

Mum had told them, once, about how she'd met Olaf Larsen. 'I'd never seen anyone like him,' she said. 'Your father was so beautiful — thick blond hair, eyes like ice, tall, broad — he looked exactly like a Viking.' And he'd acted like one, thought Freya. Came, saw, conquered. Then when he was tired of it, sailed off back home. Back to his midnight sun, his book-lined study at the university, his research into old, long-gone, fierce people and sagas. That was why the children had been named Thor and Freya, after the gods that their father so relished.

Thor reckoned it made a good story, but Freya had, over the years since he'd left them so abruptly, built up a picture of a fierce man with the eyes and the heart of an eagle. Someone as uncaring, as unending, as the sea. Mum smiled a little nervously. 'I'm sure it will be great fun to hear your band, Thor.' Mum was small and light, and gave the impression of great fragility. If you didn't know her, that is. If you did, you knew she was tough, stubborn, and sometimes only heard what she wanted to hear. Occasionally Freya had caught herself wondering whether perhaps Mum hadn't been entirely the victim in the breakup of her marriage to Olaf Larsen. But the treacherous thought was always quickly pushed aside. Of course it was all that man's fault! Leaving her alone, with two young children.

Daniel said, 'We're looking forward to it, Thor. You two are so artistic. I'm humbled by such talent.'

Well, you shouldn't be, thought Freya. You have what really counts. In fairy tales, wasn't it always the step-parents who were mean and wicked and unloving? But here it was different. Oh, quite different! Of course she didn't say anything like that. Instead, she said in a voice that must have sounded grudging, 'Do you want to take a look at what I've written so far? It's pretty hopeless, but …'

'Of course I want to,' Daniel said, while Thor raised an eyebrow. 'Freya's undying prose,' he said.

'Shut up!' Freya snapped. She and Thor had a sort of unspoken policy of not letting each other get 'big headed', but sometimes it was annoying. Couldn't Thor take anything seriously? Especially since … Then she remembered that he was here, when normally he'd be out, and she knew that his flippancy was a cover.

Daniel was looking at her shrewdly, his spiky-boned face alert, and she felt herself blushing. Damn it, she was sick of pretending and lying and making out that everything would be all right, when she knew it wouldn't be. And it wasn't as if it was for Daniel's sake. If it had been, she'd have borne it more easily. But it was for Mum, who after all was not the one who was going to ...

See? She couldn't even say it to herself, in her own mind. The word poisoned her, tormented her, but she couldn't even frame it. She turned abruptly from them all, skidding the exercise book across the table to Daniel. 'Here it is. For what it's worth.' She wanted to touch him, to hug him, but she was fifteen now, not five, she couldn't just fling herself at him and be hugged and have everything set right, just like that. She was fifteen and she knew things wouldn't be all right. Her body already ached with an emptiness.

'We'll be going soon,' Mum said. 'Get ready, won't you, love?' Typical of Mum. She thought that if you just said ordinary words, that somehow the evil would stay outside. Still, Freya knew that sometimes she thought like that, too. If you made beautiful words, words of love and healing and magic, they'd make you safe, and happy, for ever and ever.

After her shower, she chose to wear the same dress. It smelt salty and even a bit sweaty, but it was cool, and swirling, this dress cut out of sky. You could imagine the scissors, gleaming, sharp, cutting carefully into the improbable blue, the deep, full, living blue.

Her father certainly knew how to pick a dress. But then, Freya thought, he is a ladies' man, isn't he? She'd heard her mother say that once, years ago, and it had stuck in her mind. A ladies' man. It had sounded funny to her then, but now, she loaded the term with contempt. It simply meant he was a Viking. A pirate. Someone who used, and abused. Who came in from the sea, and went away on the sea. She hadn't been fooled.

When she went into the kitchen again, Daniel was sitting alone at the table. The exercise book was open in front of him, but he seemed elsewhere, perhaps inside himself where the thing crouched, devouring. It was almost as if he'd left his body there, sitting in the chair. Freya's heart thudded. She coughed loudly and walked across to him. He started, then smiled, a little tiredly, she thought.

'You've read it?' she said. She wanted to say, Daniel, Daniel, please don't leave us, please don't! But the words were dust in her mouth. He must think she was so selfish, that she only cared about her miserable small words, that he must face the fear all alone.

'I have,' he said. 'It's good. Or parts of it are. I think you're going to be a writer, Freya.'

Tears stung her eyes. She picked up her exercise book. 'Parts of it are real rubbish, I know,' she gabbled. 'But I want to make it real, make it exciting, make it say something. It's hard, though.'

'Of course,' he said. 'Worthwhile things are.'

'Daniel,' Freya spoke quickly, trying to say it before anything stopped her. She could already hear her mother coming down the corridor.

'That is, I ... Do you think this blue dress is OK to go out in?'

Daniel looked at her. Only his mouth smiled when he said, 'Yes, it looks lovely, Freya. It's a very nice dress, and suits you well.'

Mum came in, then, her eyes a little beady and suspicious, as if she thought they'd been talking seriously. No fear of that, Mum, Freya thought bitterly. I'm too much of a chicken.

'Do I look OK, Dan?' Freya's mother asked. Of course she did. She always did.

'You look gorgeous, Amy,' Daniel said. He took her hand. 'You'll always look gorgeous.'

'No lovey-doveying,' Thor said, coming in at that moment. 'No time for that.'

Daniel smiled, a real smile this time. 'I'm not sure if we'll obey, Thor of the hammer,' he said jauntily. Thor always seemed to make him smile, Freya thought. Despite the fact that Thor's jokes were always weak. Maybe because they are weak.

The *Retreat* was a plush restaurant, the kind where waiters swished past in tuxedos, and where fine wine was decanted into tall thin glasses at the table. Freya felt a little intimidated by it all; her thick dark hair pulled back into a ponytail, was still damp from the shower; her Chinese cotton happi shoes felt embarrassingly inadequate. Only her blue dress hung satisfyingly around her, the material gleaming richly under the dim restaurant lights.

The main character in her novel, the Dragon Princess, Chalias, would have a dress just like this, she thought. She could see Chalias standing there by her horse, in her dress as blue as sky, waiting for the others to dismount from their own horses into the tiny lapping waves at the edge of the sea. They would climb down, and they would look into the distance to the twinkling lights of the city of Haldon, and then Chalias would say . . .

'What would you like to eat?' a voice was asking, and Freya started. For a moment, she had forgotten about being here, and even about Daniel. The thought made her feel ashamed.

~

Dinner was over quickly, thanks to Thor, who kept reminding them that he had to get over to the pavilion to set up things for his band. Freya was glad of this. It meant that they didn't have to stay in that uncomfortable place. It meant, too, that everyone had concentrated on the food. Even Daniel had eaten well, tonight. Inside Freya a thin hope wavered. Perhaps nothing bad had really happened. Perhaps anyway, it was all a horrible mistake.

The pavilion was only a short distance away, and they walked there. It was right on the promenade, and they could hear the sea, smacking at the sand in a relentless kind of frustration. It looked deep and black and shining, black as the night, without beginning or end. In darkness, lit only by a few street lamps, Freya's dress, too, looked black.

'The sea looks beautiful, doesn't it, at night?' Daniel said.

'It looks like something we don't even know,' Freya's mother said quietly. It surprised Freya, recognising the appeal in her mother's voice, and she wanted to respond to it, to break the evil spell of fear cast on them all. But then they were at the pavilion, and the lights were blazing, and Thor was inside, banging around and moving things. The moment had passed.

Quite a few people came to see *Thor's Hammer*. Thor himself, in his horned helmet, leather jerkin and plaited hair, didn't look like her brother under the lights, but like a stranger — a character from a Viking saga, fierce and unknowable. Freya realised with a shock that there were girls in the audience who seemed to think Thor was glamorous, or something. His plaits bounced at his shoulders as he pounded the drums, the terrifying roll of them thundering down Freya's back. He was good, she thought in surprise. Somehow Thor always seemed so careless that she thought he could never be serious about anything. But there was a real power, a real danger, a real passion in his drumming, and the songs he'd written were good, very good.

She looked across at Daniel and her mother. They were sitting near the front, holding hands. Mum's eyes were closed; Daniel was looking hard at Thor, his stepson, hammering away at the drums as if he were truly one of the gods. Then Mum looked up at Daniel, and Freya saw that her eyes were bright with tears. Daniel smiled at her, then put his head on her shoulder. They stayed like that for some time, not moving. Freya felt the tears rising again. The music, more frenzied now, more powerful, seemed to have reached into her body, coursing through her very veins and filling her with the throb of an unexpected excitement, even a kind of understanding. She knew she wanted to jump, to dance, to send the world spinning, to send the blue dress, the piece-of-the sky dress, whirling until it became a sail, a wing that would send her reeling beyond the known universe.

She joined the other dancers who had leapt to their feet, cramming the aisles. She caught sight of her brother, his face golden with sweat, drumming as if his life, her life, Daniel's life, everyone's life, depended on it. Tonight, he was truly Thor of the hammer, mighty god whose power could stop death.

Someone caught her, spun her around. The dress flew all around, the material snapping and swishing, like the small waves at the edge of the sand. Through the open door of the pavilion, she caught sight of the sea; but turned from it, back to the roar of life. Freya danced throwing out her arms, her heart filling and filling until she felt it would burst. We are stronger than death, she thought, for we love. We are stronger!

The music stopped suddenly, like a summer story. Someone said, 'Wow'. Freya looked up. A boy was standing there, his face red from exertion, his hair a bit wet.

'You're a good dancer.' He smiled, and Freya smiled back.

'Yes,' she said. 'Because it's good music. My brother's band.'

'Your brother?' the boy stared at her. 'Up there?'

'Thor,' Freya nodded. 'He's great.'

When Freya returned to her seat, thoughts and feelings assailed her. About Thor, and how he'd played; about the boy, Jesse, and how she hoped she might see him again; about her dad and how she would write a good long letter to him; about her novel, and how she'd have lots to put in it; about Daniel, and Mum, and how, maybe ... They were still sitting close together, their bodies touching, but Daniel's head no longer on Mum's shoulder. They were talking in low tones, and Freya saw that her mother had been crying, and Daniel, too, and yet both faces bore an expression of calm. She came to sit next to them.

'Wasn't Thor good?'

'Wonderful,' her mother said. 'I had no idea, really.'

'Neither did I,' Freya said. 'You sort of . . . don't, do you?'

Her mother squeezed her hand. 'The two of you,' she said, her voice a little hoarse. 'You and Thor . . .' her voice trailed off, 'we've been so lucky,' she finished, her eyes full of tears.

'We're still lucky,' Daniel said, looking across at Freya. Then Freya found the words at last, the words that had lodged in her throat and her heart for so long.

'Oh, but Daniel,' she said. 'We've been the lucky ones, lucky that Mum found you. And I can't bear to think that you're going to die!'

The last word came out in a kind of croak. Freya looked at Daniel, seeing more clearly than before the bones under his fine skin, the hollowness under his eyes. Yes — yes — he is going to die, she thought, terrified. He is.

Daniel let go of Mum's hand. He leaned over to Freya. Under the slow, quiet drumming of Thor's final song, his words were muted, but Freya caught them, understood them as she felt she understood the constant whispering voice of the sea.

'I may die sooner than I want to,' he said. 'But nothing is certain. Except for one thing — and that is something you mustn't forget. Nobody lives in vain, nobody wastes their time here, while ever they are given life, and love. You and your mother and your brother have given me something eternal, something so precious that I can almost die before my time. Almost. Because of course I'm scared, Freya. Of course sometimes I'm ready to give up, to give in to the fear. But always something pulls me back.'

'I'm scared, too,' Freya whispered. Her fingers plucked at her dress, the material wrinkling like sorrow in her hand.

'I know,' Daniel said. 'And it hurts me, to see you like this. But some things we just can't do for others. Do you understand me, Freya?'

'I think so,' said Freya. 'I'm trying.'

~

The afternoon light was fading, the waves touched with the first grey hint of evening. Freya got up, her feet squeaking in the sand, and took a last look at the sea before turning for home. She thought over the words she had just written in her exercise book.

'Chalias,' said the man on the black horse to the woman in the blue dress. 'We have arrived in the lands of the West.' Chalias looked out towards the horizon. 'Yes,' she said softly. 'We have come to the isles of the Blessed, where all are free and death holds no fear.'

The sea hissed behind the travellers, secretive now, as they made their way towards the distant roofs of the eternal city of Haldon.

47. From whose viewpoint is the story being told?

48. Why were the children given the names *Freya* and *Thor*?

49. Is the blue dress important to Freya? Why/why not?

50. What is the challenge that is facing Freya and her family?

51. Create a short biography of Freya using what you know from the story and your own imagination.

52. What do you think made Daniel and Amy face the reality of his impending death and also helped Freya finally speak about her fears?

53. Music can have a powerful influence on our lives. Our favourite music can help:
    • create the right atmosphere
    • entertain
    • tell stories or carry powerful messages.
    (a) How important do you think Thor's music was in the story? Why?
    (b) What type of music helps you to overcome stress? Perhaps you could bring this music to school to share with your class.

54. While the family can be a source of comfort and support for individual members, there are times when whole families need support. There are many factors that can stress the family unit: for example, financial pressures, emotional problems, family breakdown, death of a family member, health problems and abuse. Many community-based support schemes provide support for families in crisis.

    Compile a list of family support groups in your community and the types of problems they deal with. Your local telephone directory and your nearest library will be useful sources of information.

Something extra

55. Arrange to interview an elderly member of your family or community. Ask them to talk about what challenges they have faced as young people and how they were supported during those times. You will need to make notes or, if the person agrees, you may like to use a tape recorder.
    Remember the following points.
    • Organise a time for the interview.
    • Have your questions prepared — but be flexible. The person you are interviewing may talk about something you hadn't thought of.
    • Check that you have a fresh tape and batteries for your tape recorder.
    • Be polite and pleasant.
    • Don't dwell on a question if the person seems uncomfortable with it.
    • Thank the person for sharing their memories with you.

56. Write a report on the interview. Compare the information with the challenges you face today. Perhaps you could include this in your folio or school magazine.

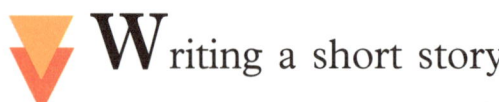

Writing a short story

Daniel encouraged Freya to continue with her writing:

> 'It's good. Or parts of it are. I think you're going to be a writer, Freya.'
>
> Tears stung her eyes. She picked up her exercise book. 'Parts of it are real rubbish, I know,' she gabbled. 'But I want to make it real, make it exciting, **make it say something**. It's hard, though.'
>
> 'Of course, he said. 'Worthwhile things are'.

Theme

Writers are able to make their work "say something" through the theme, which is the underlying message of a story. Short stories are an ideal form of writing to get your message across.

Themes can be as simple as the relationship between two people or as complex as unknown futures. Choosing a theme can be a good starting point for a story of your own.

From the following stimulus material, choose a theme about the challenge of managing our environment which could form the underlying message of your own short story.

Treat the earth well.
It was not given to us by our parents:
it was loaned to us by our children
                          Kenyan Proverb

Never doubt that a small group of thoughtful, committed citizens can change the world. Indeed it is the only thing that ever has.

Margaret Mead

Setting

It is important to establish the time and place as early as possible in the story. Re-read the first paragraph of *The Sniper* to see how clearly Liam O'Flaherty creates the setting. In *A Weight of Thistledown*, also, H. M. Tolcher describes the setting early in the story.

Decide on the setting (time and place) for your story.

Plot

The plot is the basic framework of the story and is usually structured in a certain way. There is an introduction, a series of complications which lead to a climax (the high point of the story), followed by the resolution. Some writers prefer to plan the plot or storyline before actually starting to write.

The plot for *The Chimera* could be summarised in the following way:

Debbie knows that she was an IVF baby, but suspects that there is something wrong with her because her skin is "brassy". Her parents eventually decide to tell her that, as part of an experiment, DNA from Venusian bacteria was injected into the fertilised egg which became Debbie. The plan was to produce humans who would be able to tolerate the temperatures on Venus and settle there. Debbie accepts that her fate is to eventually live on Venus, and even welcomes the prospect.

Write a plot using the theme and setting you have chosen.

Characters

The characters in a story are closely linked with the plot. Any change in the storyline will usually affect the characters. There is not a lot of room to develop characters in a short story. Often, there is one main character and the reader may not know every detail about that person — just what is necessary for the story. However, a writer can imply certain things about a character through dialogue. In *The Chimera* we read:

> He swallowed his sudden rush of anger. 'I know what your skin feels like,' he said gently, but he reached out a hand anyway and felt it. So smooth, so perfect, so ... so ... 'It's really beautiful.'
>
> 'For a car,' she said bitterly, jerking her arm back. 'I've just been to the pool — for the first time in my life! The other kids said I was reflective!'

From this conversation between Debbie and her father, we can tell that he is probably a kind, understanding man and that Debbie is confused, upset and bitter about her skin being different.

In *The Sniper* we are unaware of the main character's name and know only what is essential to the story.

Blue is unusual as there are five characters all of whom are named. Because this story is about relationships, the characters have been developed more fully.

Some authors write a short biography of the main character before starting to write. This can be useful even if it is not necessary to use all the details. It can help your story to be more believable.

> From the plot you have written, write a short biography of the main character and details of any other characters you think are necessary to your story. Perhaps you could base your character on the photograph below.

Style

Style is the way an author presents the story:
- use of dialogue — slang, friendly or aggressive language
- use of imagery — metaphors, similes, alliteration, personification
- use of short or long sentences.

In *The Sniper*, the author uses only three words of dialogue in the whole story. Short, sharp sentences add to the tension in this story. In *The Chimera*, on the other hand, the author uses a great deal of dialogue and varying sentence lengths.

Style also depends on who is telling the story. This is called "point of view". *The Chimera*, for example, has been told in the third person. In other words, the author has told the story as an "all-knowing" observer. The style of the story would have been quite different if it had been told through the eyes of the main character, Debbie. If it had been written in first person, Debbie's personality would have dominated the story.

Think about the different elements of style which could enhance your story.

When the five elements of a short story are combined they come together like a jigsaw.

Your turn

57. Create your own short story of about 500 words for an article in a teenage magazine of your choice. Perhaps you could submit it to the magazine for publication.
    (a) Choose a theme relating to the environment — *The challenge of the future*.
    (b) Decide on the setting.
    (c) Write a summary of the plot.
    (d) Write a short biography of the main character and minor characters if necessary.
    (e) Experiment with style.

S E L F
ASSESSMENT

Name: ....

1. Can I?

Write "yes" or "no" in the box. If you write "no", go back over your work until you can write "yes".

- Identify biased language .... ☐
- Write a political news report .... ☐
- Write an official letter of protest .... ☐
- Use all features of a dictionary .... ☐
- Make notes from sources .... ☐
- Write an argumentative essay .... ☐
- Write a short story .... ☐

2. Your reaction

(a) Which short story did you like best? Say why.
(b) Which activity did you like best? Say why.
(c) Which skill do you need to work on most? What can you do to improve it?

3. For your folio

From the work you have done in this chapter, choose the pieces you want to include in your folio. Each piece of work in your folio should include a cover sheet which shows the date it was completed, the title, the purpose and the audience.

4. Ongoing skills

Complete the table below by:
- placing a tick at the point at which you feel you usually achieve in each skill
- shading in the range of your achievement in each skill.

When you have completed the table place it in your folio.

Am I improving in these skills?	Level of achievement		
	Same as before	Improving	Much better
Example: Oral work		✓	
Being imaginative			
Using imagery			
Explaining my reasons			
Research			
Cooperating in groups			
Oral work			

AUTHOR INDEX

SUBJECT INDEX